MALE MASOCHISM

MALE MASOCHISM

Modern Revisions of the Story of Love

Carol Siegel

Indiana University Press

Bloomington and Indianapolis

The paper used in this publication meets the minimum
requirements of American National Standard for Information
Sciences—Permanence of Paper for Printed Library Materials,
ANSI Z39.48-1984.

Manufactured in the United States of America

Library of Congress Cataloging-in-Publication Data

Siegel, Carol, date
    Male masochism : modern revisions of the story of love / Carol
Siegel.
        p.   cm.
    Includes bibliographical references (p.) and index.
    ISBN 0-253-35228-2 (cloth : alk. paper)
    1. Love stories, English—History and criticism. 2. English
fiction—20th century—History and criticism.   3. Postmodernism
(Literature)—Great Britain. 4. Masculinity (Psychology) in
literature. 5. Man-woman relationships in literature. 6. Modernism
(Literature)—Great Britain. 7. Psychoanalysis and literature.
8. Love in motion pictures. 9. Masochism in literature. 10. Sex role in
literature. I. Title.
    PR888.L69S5   1995
    823'.08509—dc20   94-15404

1 2 3 4 5 00 99 98 97 96 95

To Gerhard

CONTENTS

ACKNOWLEDGMENTS

THIS PROJECT BEGAN while I was a graduate student. My preoccupation with my dissertation kept me from realizing then that response to a seminar paper on Joyce was later going to lead to my researching a very different sort of book. When John Bishop told me that I could not ignore Freud but instead should explain why I believed that Freud's theories did not provide a useful approach to literary representation of masochism, this project was born. I will always be grateful for John's interest in my perverse and rebellious readings.

The willingness of scholars in a variety of fields to read and comment on sections of this book has been wonderful for me. My colleagues in English—Dale Bauer, David Brande, Casey Charles, Bruce Henricksen, Virginia Hyde, Lindsay Kaplan, Thaïs Morgan, and Louise Schleiner—have all contributed greatly to my understanding through their responses to my writing. I want to thank John Biguenet for sharing with me his knowledge of issues involved in translation. I am also indebted to my psychologist friends—Barbara Hammond, Howard (Sandy) Shore, and Mary Stewart both for their advice and for their patience with my diatribes against major ideas in psychoanalytic theory. My dear friend, the historian Lillian Taiz, also offered numerous useful suggestions.

The discussions with my graduate students in feminist theory at Washington State University were invaluable to me. I thank them all. I'm especially grateful to Bryce Campbell, T.A. extraordinaire, and Theresa Thompson, first for reading and commenting on sections of the manuscript and second for volunteering on several occasions to act as research assistants and to do clerical work in support of my teaching, leaving me time to write.

Because of the intense feelings many people have about so-called deviant sexualities and many literary critics' profound allegiance to Freud and Lacan, it has not always been a pleasure for me to present my work at conferences or to discuss it with colleagues. I would,

therefore, particularly like to thank Tom Campbell, Elizabeth Langland, Leland Monk, Mary Ann O'Farrell, and Robin Sheets not only
for the helpful suggestions they gave me for the development of this
material, but also for their moral support generously given when I
needed it most. No one deserves my thanks more than Sherwood
Williams, who has been a remarkably supportive friend and col-
league, as he discussed this project with me at every stage since 1986.
Any virtues the book has are due in large part to his conversations
with me.

The suggestions for revision that I received from Robert Sloan,
my editor at Indiana University Press, and Robert Caserio, the
reader of my manuscript, made the present form of this book possible. Their encouragement was especially welcome.

A version of chapter 5 was first published as an article, "Post-
modern Women Novelists Review Victorian Male Masochism," in
Genders 11 (Fall 1991). And thereby hangs a tale of some of the most
encouraging help I have received while working on this project. I
want to thank Eve Kosofsky Sedgwick for her positive response to
that article and all her detailed suggestions for changes. I am also
deeply indebted to Ann Kibbey for her support of the article and
her continuing helpful interest in my work. I thank *Genders* and the
University of Texas Press, which then published it, for permission to
reprint material from the article.

A version of chapter 1 appeared as "Male Masochism and the Colonialist Impulse: Mary Webb's Return of the Native Tess," in *Novel*
24 (Winter 1991). And a version of chapter 2 appeared as " 'Venus
Metempsychosis' and *Venus in Furs:* Masochism and Fertility in
Ulysses," in *Twentieth Century Literature* 33 (Summer 1987). I thank
the publishers of these journals for permitting me to reprint material from the articles in this book.

Material included in chapter 4 also appears in my essay "From
Pact with the Devil to Masochist's Contract: *Dangerous Liaisons'*s
Translation of the Erotics of Evil," included in *Narrative and Cul-
ture*, edited by Janice Carlisle and Daniel R. Schwarz (University of
Georgia Press, 1994). I want to thank the editors for their help, and
the press for permission to reprint. I am thankful, also, for permis-
sion to reprint some sections of "When No Means No and Yes
Means Power: Locating Masochistic Pleasure in Film Narratives,"

published in *After Poststructuralism: Interdisciplinarity and Literary Theory*, edited by Nancy L. Easterlin and Barbara Riebling (Northwestern University Press), and for these editors' suggestions and friendship.

This investigation was supported in part by funds provided by Washington State University, for which I am very grateful. My gratitude is due, as well, to Loyola University of New Orleans for providing financial support for this work in its early stages.

Friends outside the academic world also helped make this book possible. I think this book is better for the reality-checks provided through conversation with Isadora Alman and with the dozens of anonymous but appreciated volunteers who told me about their experiences in S/M. And I especially want to thank Jamie O'Toole for his unfailing hospitality and Chris Toomey for his enthusiastic help in tracking down texts. Their assistance and their charming presence made my research trips a delight.

INTRODUCTION

And watching their shadows lashed by wind, I cried,
"Master, what souls are these the very air
lashes with its black whips from side to side?"

Dante Alighieri, *The Inferno*, trans. John Ciardi

IN THE WAKE of Michel Foucault's discussions of the construction of sexualities, much important work has been done in recent
literary theory to historicize theory's primarily classic psychoanalytic, and thus synchronic, vision of textual representation of gender
difference and, relatedly, heterosexuality and homosexuality. The
corrective work has depended on considering the ways texts participate in cultural change. In criticism, at least, the fixed, dichotomous
meanings of masculine and feminine have been undermined. Rather
than imagining masculine and feminine as comprising a set group
of attributes, we have begun to see them as differently configured
in different texts and contexts throughout history. Skepticism about
the value of naming appears more and more frequently in discussions of gender, and essentialism has acquired an almost purely pe-
jorative connotation so that references to "the feminine" can hardly
be made without qualification, explanation, or defense. Taking note
of the vigilant attitude critics now assume in relation to gender
stereotypes that just twenty years ago were treated by most as giv-
ens, one might be inclined to believe that few English professors
would refuse Gilles Deleuze and Félix Guattari's call for resistance
to "the social machine" whose "prime function . . . has always been
to codify the flows of desire, to inscribe them, to record them, to
see to it that no flow exists that is not properly dammed up, chan-
neled, regulated."[1]

However, the recent work of literary and film critics on masochism remains, for the most part, contained within the limits of an
earlier theoretical discourse determined by ahistorical interpretations of Freudian, Lacanian, or, for the more rebellious, early
Deleuzean descriptions of the psyche. The preoccupation of the ma-

jority of these critics with determining whether a scene or passage reveals "feminine," "erotogenic," "moral," "primary," or "reflexive" masochism suggests that the prevailing attitude toward masochism derives more from the spirit of taxonomy than that of epistemology. The existence of masochism as a recognizable state of being or set of behaviors is virtually unquestioned. I contend that rather than being an identifiable syndrome, disorder, perversion, or drive (as it is variously styled), masochism is an invention of the nineteenth century, created textually in response to the impact of specific developments in gender and sexual politics on the conventions of narrative poetry and prose.

The claim that masochism is no more than a textualized political convenience may seem exaggerated, even irrational, after the 1980s' explosion of interest in masochism. It would be difficult, given the present situation, to think seriously about interactions between culture and gender without also considering the role played by masochism. Yet, because I will argue that masochism has meaning only in reference to language, I will focus my investigation of it on its textual inscriptions and on some of the literary events attending its birth into history. In concentrating on masochism's existence as a term rather than a condition, the first thing one is likely to note is its terminological elusiveness. While the word *masochism* is probably more generally familiar now than ever before in history, it has no universally agreed-upon meaning.

Outside the academy, masochism has been and remains a major point of contention among feminists, with debate centering on whether or not lesbian sadomasochistic sex play can be compatible with feminism.[2] To those familiar with pornography aimed at masochists and its conventional depiction of the dominatrix as a feminist, it may seem odd that feminists have so far said very little publicly about the political significance of women sexually dominating men; however, dominatrix pornography is far from mainstream, and in popular culture masochism is associated with femininity. The picture most likely to come to mind when one hears the word *masochist* is probably of a bound and bruised woman, or more exotically a bound and bruised man in drag.

Even where the gender lines are not clearly drawn, the representations of dominance and submission current in Western culture delineate a figure readily recognizable as the masochist. From artistic parodies in novels like Kathy Acker's and films like Monika Treut's and earnest performances in leather bars and sadomasochistic sex clubs to their somewhat timid reflections in music videos and magazine advertisements, the proliferation of images of masochism continually reaffirms psychoanalytic theory's vision of the masochist as an actual, identifiable human type and of masochism as a definable neurosis.

Within the Psychoanalytic

As might be expected, academic writings on masochism do not simply reproduce popular culture's apparently unified picture of the masochist as a woman or an effeminate man aroused by receiving physical abuse. For many literary critics, masochism is diffused into a generally available relationship to language and art. Several critics view masochism as receptivity to the unsettling effect art can have on one's sense of a stable identity within a coherent cultural narrative. To Roland Barthes, the Marquis de Sade's evasion of narrative structure and transgression of linguistic boundaries "constitutes an outrage of meaning" resisted by the (nonmasochistic) victim, who "desires law, wants meaning, respects the paradigm." In contrast, "libertine poetics" cause in their practitioner the endless "diffraction" of subjectivity.[3] Masochism, then, becomes the choice to participate in a transgressive relation to language, recognizing the fluidity of meaning that undermines one's own identity. Leo Bersani explicitly defines masochism as the acceptance of this "shattering of the human subject" and equates it with both orgasm and the pleasure provided by art.[4] The ubiquity of this viewpoint is evident when Linda Williams begins a 1988 essay on the pleasures of reading by asking whether they can possibly derive from anything other than "erotogenic masochism—the offering up of one's self as a slave to the text" and concludes by urging the only feminist alternative: a more active readerly response modeled on "primary masochism."[5] By thus positing masochism as intrinsic to the experience of art, such theories undermine the term's traditional negative connotation, but they also blur its connection to sexual activity, a connection consistently made in modern and contemporary fiction, poetry, and films. Paradoxically, then, masochism has come to mean something in literary theory that often seems unrelated to the masochism we see represented in the art products about which criticism speaks. This disjunction is even more acute in feminist film criticism, which is becoming almost inseparable from discussion of masochism. Partly in response to Laura Mulvey's famous argument that classic film narratives are constructed to provide sadistic pleasure for male viewers,[6] feminist critics such as Linda Williams, Kaja Silverman, Tania Modleski, Parveen Adams, Gaylyn Studlar, and Carol Clover have extensively explored the masochistic pleasures specific films and film as a medium offer viewers of both sexes. Studlar has gone so far as to formulate an aesthetics of masochism.[7] Silverman, as a leading figure in the branch of gender studies focusing on male subjectivity, has taken on male masochism as one of her major topics. The meaning of the term *masochism* increasingly eludes us when these critics and others variously apply it to the intended or imagined response of a hypothetical film viewer, to the aesthetic that seems to inform a production or scene, to the position of an actress or actor within a production, and to both the behavior and the situation of a character within a film. Important distinctions seem effaced when theory uses the same word to describe, for instance, a character represented as angrily suffering a beating against his will and one depicted as the satisfied patron of a dominatrix.

The American Psychiatric Association acknowledged problems with the term *masochism* when they decided against including it in the revised version of the third edition of the *Diagnostic and Statistical Manual of Psychiatric Disorders* (*DSM*-III-R) in the late 1980s, substituting the phrase "self-defeating personality disorder," as a diagnostic description. This change makes sense as a strategy to avoid the accusation, frequently made by feminists, that psychiatrists and psychologists have used the concept of masochism to uphold the patriarchal fiction that women unconsciously seek sexual pain and humiliation in order to feel fulfilled. But as Gayle Rubin has pointed out, the official conflation of sexual masochism and "self-destructive personality patterns" works to demonize "low status sexual practices," like masochistic role-playing, which some people appear to choose freely and which, they assert, give them pleasure and increase their sense of self-esteem.[8] Of course, references to individuality and freedom of choice may sound naïve in the context of postmodern cultural critique. Still, the abundant evidence that participants in sadomasochistic subcultures do not perceive their own activities as in any sense defeating the self should trouble not only clinical definitions of masochism but also the definitions that literary theory has generated about masochism's explosive disruption of identity.[9]

If we wish to escape these linguistic difficulties by limiting the term *masochism* to a description of sexual pleasure in pain (what Freud calls erotogenic masochism), numerous problems in definition still arise. First, we face the mystery of the pleasure's source. Does it originate in sadism, which when frustrated in its Oedipal aim turns on the self (as Freud argues in "A Child Is Being Beaten"), or does it originate in the death drive, as he later asserts in "The Economic Problem of Masochism"?[10] Is the masochism manifested in certain ritualized sexual activities made pleasurable by identification with "the good mother" and rejection of the father, and, thus, is it antithetic to and incompatible with sadism, as Deleuze argues in his introduction to Leopold von Sacher-Masoch's *Venus in Furs*? Is masochism a retreat from natural sensuality into what Deleuze calls supersensual coldness?[11] Later, he and Guattari describe masochism differently, as a method of "bring[ing] forth a plane of consistency of desire." Is masochism then, as they claim, a process for "distribut[ing] intensities of pleasure and prevent[ing] them from being suffused by anxiety, shame, and guilt," a way of achieving a state in which the concept of lack is no longer meaningful?[12] Or, as Jessica Benjamin theorizes, in sharp contrast to Bersani, is it a strategy for establishing a safely structured connection to an Other within which the masochist can "abandon the protective false self and allow the nascent, hidden self to emerge"—a strategy always doomed to fail because all enactments of domination and submission make mutual recognition impossible?[13] Or, as Pat Califia has insisted, do both positions in the sadomasochistic scenerio subversively parody the roles prescribed by patriarchal society?[14] Of the current theorists on masochism, Mariana Valverde may seem the most flexible in her claim that masochists can be divided into five types.[15] Readers not permanently swayed by any of the competing theories on the topic may conclude that there are as many kinds of masochism as there are kinds of love.

This seems the right moment to ask whether a distinction can be made between masochism and love. An example of comic failure in that direction is provided in the psychiatrist Jean Clavreul's theory to explain the apparent happiness of couples he deems perverse either because of their homosexuality or their practice of acts associated with sadomasochism. He describes himself as troubled by their ability to speak of their love more eloquently than "normal" lovers can and even more disturbed by their perverse defiance of the psychoanalytic doctrine of disillusionment, as they continue through the years "as attentive toward each other as if they had just met for the first time." Most annoyingly of all, they often resist his helpful efforts to cure them of this "alleged love."[16]

A more generous vision of love's possibilities was provided for me one Valentine's Day by a florist's shop where I saw a display consisting of separately wrapped single roses. Some had real, red blooms, some had silk blooms, some had chocolate blooms (white or dark), and some had black leather blooms. The need for theory to explain why some customers chose the leather roses seems dubious. Yet for over a hundred years theory has tried to separate one kind of love from the others, not on the basis of object, as homosexuality is separated out, but on the more nebulous basis of the attitudes and activities the lover associates with romantic passion.

Before the term *masochism* was invented there were attempts to account for different preferences in erotic play, but they do not seem as governed by the totalizing impulse as the late nineteenth-century theories. For instance, in 1639, Johann Heinrich Meibom, a physician and writer on the Hippocratic Oath, published a Latin *epistola*, "On the Use of Flogging in Medical and Venereal Affairs: The Functions of the Reins and Loins." In it he recognizes that flagellation sexually excites some men, theorizes from his understanding of anatomy why this is so, and then, while condemning men who use this to prologue illicit activities, recommends such stimulation as an aid to procreative activity within marriage.[17] If 350 years later, we look from the most usual perspective in our society at this doctor, who appears eager to establish himself as religious and moral, we might be likely to find him insanely permissive in the latitude he grants patients who wish to act as men. Officially at least, we can no longer read the behavior of a man who asks his wife to whip him as the fulfillment of marital duties and the demands of adult masculinity, but only as an escape from manhood, as disavowal of his own gender. We are thus constrained because 250 years after the publication of Meibom's letter the formation of an official discourse that would separate the male seeker of erotic pain from masculinity began with a new word: masochism.

A Brief Escape into History

The term *masochism* was coined by Richard von Krafft-Ebing to describe Leopold von Sacher-Masoch, whose case history is given in *Psychopathia Sexualis*, 1886.[18] Sacher-Masoch was a popular writer whose work fit into a well-established late nineteenth-century genre.[19] Narrowly, the genre could be considered Victorian flagellation literature, but even if we only considered Sacher-Masoch's own works, which include many stories *not* featuring beatings, the context expands to one more accurately described as the literature of man's passionate surrender to the beloved woman. The question is then raised: Should all such literature be considered masochistic?

The implications of such a position are revealed in R. Howard Bloch's claim that male masochism is "inscribed at the core of Western eroticism."[20] Certainly, if we grant literature the status of a primary means of cultural inscription, this would seem to be the case in a retrospect informed by psychoanalytic theory. But to read all love stories as stories of male masochism, we must describe both love and masochism differently than we generally do. Keeping in mind some of the most authoritative official definitions of masochism, it is not particularly difficult to read all love stories as stories of masochism. Lovers have been classically seen, as in Plato's *Symposium*, as conscious of their own lack(s) and desirous beyond any permanent satisfaction that can be given on earth. Consequently, love becomes by definition a painful condition.

And whom shall we identify as the pained and consequently masochistic lover? In the period between Sappho and Charlotte Brontë, prestigious literary texts were mostly produced by men. In these

texts, men are more often than women represented as active subjects. We expect this focus on male activity, not only because the
societies from which the texts came were male-centered but also
because the authors would naturally partake of the general egotism
of human beings. When the topic is love, women most frequently
appear as the objects of passion rather than in the role of lover. In
this way we might read male masochism into the old tales of love.

If we go on to generalize about past texts' representations of
love, much material appears to support a retrospective reading of
male masochism as intrinsic to love literature. A certain amount
of generalizing is necessary to produce an overview of trends in representation. This strategy will have the unfortunate effect of eliding
the specific features of individual texts, the dissonance within texts,
and the textual marks of both development of conventions and resistance to them.[21] Yet a temporary blurring of small differences has
the advantage of bringing the larger, chronologically distributed
differences into focus.

In order to represent the pain of love metaphorically, writers have
followed various conventions. One of love's characteristic attributes
in literature is that it effects reversals in the usual hierarchy. Through
love, the high abase themselves to the low, and masters become en-
slaved to their slaves. In fiercely patriarchal societies, this may mean
simply that men bow to the will of women, as the medieval troubadour poets and Renaissance sonneteers, for instance, so often declare themselves ready to do. In much of this love poetry the
element of reversal in men's gestures of submission is somewhat
qualified by the difference in class status between the Lady and her
more humbly placed admirer. Still, the man's delighted response to
his subordinate position effects a reversal of expectation. He generally represents himself not simply accepting his social placement in
a dependent role, but eagerly desiring to serve his mistress to a degree that so far exceeds what the social contract demands that his
love seems to mock both the ordinary gender hierarchy and the specific social hierarchy intended to structure his relations with his aristocratic beloved.

A more fearful reversal can result from the supposedly emascu-
lating power of love, which threatens to reduce man to a sentimental and therefore womanly emotional state or even to a dependent

and thus womanly status. Some critics claim that by the Elizabethan period loving a woman could be more frightening to a man than loving another male because homosexual love "had fewer consequences and was easier to desexualize."[22] Within this trope of threatened gender identity, to love a woman is to risk everything in the most dangerous game available; but an especially daring man, such as Shakespeare's Romeo, can play with effeminization, visiting androgyny just as he visits Juliet's garden, the courage that makes the dalliance possible affirming the masculinity his love only seems to belie.

In addition, beauty, strongly associated with femininity, has traditionally been figured as a conquering force. It is cruel, potentially entrapping, and enthralling regardless of the personality of the woman who exhibits it. But it can also be used as a weapon in passive aggression, hence the "smiting beauties" and "stunners" who enthrall men in literature from the Renaissance on. Consequently, male pursuit of beautiful women can be read as a dangerous activity that gains a self-sacrificial aspect when it is motivated by love.

Women's suffering for love has traditionally been represented as passive rather than active and as belonging to domesticity rather than courtship. It is Patient Griselda, the wife, rather than a passionate Griselda, who remains, from the Middle Ages through the Victorian period, emblematic of women's acceptance of punishment for virtuous love's sweet sake. Up until the modern period, female characters who chase aloof lovers, begging, like Helena in *A Midsummer Night's Dream*, to be "used as you use your dog," are most often grotesques, comic figures in a world turned upside down; while male characters, like Pip in *Great Expectations*, whose love quest begins with being "treated like a dog in disgrace" may figure The Lover.[23] The pain love brings women has been naturalized as intrinsic to the biological female condition, just as woman's painfully subordinate position in society is naturalized. As women suffer in childbirth and then afterward love their dependent child, so they are most frequently represented as helplessly destined to love men, who are formed by nature to need but hurt women.

In contrast, the pain love brings men is frequently romanticized as a heroic source of incitement to action, analogous to the fearful ecstasy of religion or the terrifying exaltation of armed combat.

And at this point we arrive at the question raised by all of this generalization about our textual heritage: do any of the meanings of the modern term *masochism* seem appropriate to the description of an active, heroic masculine love? Within the context provided by an overview of past representations of love, it would seem that the articulation of desires to fall down in worship at the feet of the beloved, to be teased, or even struck by her must be considered just idiosyncratic variations of the role of lover, of no more diagnostic significance than desires to see her in a silk dress or to kiss her fingers.

The late nineteenth-century grouping of certain sexualized desires together and their later stigmatization as masochism stand out as milestones in the representation of male sexuality. Having passed these milestones, readers could never again see as a hero the lover who yields without reserve to his passion for woman. He could no longer be read as afflicted by the gods or fate, perhaps, but still courageous and seductively admirable. Before Freud, the sacrificial lover may be seen as a traitor to reason, as Dante describes Paolo in *The Inferno*. He may even be considered feminized in the social realm because he has given up some masculine privilege and voluntarily moved closer to the condition of woman. But still he faithfully obeys what are seen as the laws of the body; he remains a natural man whose plight arouses intense sympathy from sexually normal observers.[24] As Alexander Pope observes in "The Rape of the Lock," it was a commonplace that "mighty hearts are held in slender chains/ . . . Fair tresses man's imperial race ensnare,/ And beauty draws us with a single hair" (Canto II, 23–28). After Freud, the lover's willingness to cast himself at the feet of his mistress is read as a perverse total renunciation of masculinity. And the lover's every reiteration of his limitless subjection to woman is interpreted as an unconscious revelation of homosexuality as it is imagined by early psychoanalytic discourse, that is, as an immature state that disavows sexual reality.

However, I am not suggesting that Freud alone earns the blame for this enormous and rather strange shift in attitude toward the traditional figure of the lover. Instead, I would argue that Freud's discussions of masochism, embedded as they are in his concepts of romantic love and gender difference, belong to his time, in which both love and the lover were in the process of being redefined. Like Virginia Woolf writing in *A Room of One's Own* about the rise of a blatantly combative form of misogyny in the early twentieth-century novel, I assume that changes in the relative status of men and women in any society affect representations of gender in that society's literature. Therefore it seems worth briefly pointing out that the redefinition of the traditional, sacrificial male lover as an unmasculine pervert coincides with two major changes in the ways women participated in British, Western European, and American culture.

Because of my focus on English literature in the following chapters, I will look at the evidence of these changes in England, but I hope my readers will be mindful of similar developments in other countries. The most immediately apparent change in the situation of women in nineteenth-century England was the rise of feminism as a political movement (rather than merely a philosophy).[25] Despite all the well-documented evidence that women were oppressed in this period, we should not forget that they did make concrete gains. For example, as a result of the efforts of Victorian feminists, the Matrimonial Causes Bill of 1857 gave divorced and separated women some economic freedom that the Married Women's Property Act of 1870 (reformed in 1882) extended to protect wives from complete economic dependence on their spouses. The first women's suffrage society was formed in 1866. Girton, the first college for women, was established in 1870. Women's societies proliferated through the later part of the century, providing support for lectures and publications that furthered feminist goals.[26]

At the same time that English women were entering politics as actors rather than as victims to be defended or ignored by men, they were also gaining power as authors of literary texts. Victorian women writers such as Elizabeth Gaskell, the Brontë sisters, George Eliot, and Olive Schreiner played an acknowledged leading role in making the novel the dominant literary form of the century. The success of such writers as Elizabeth Barrett Browning and Christina Rossetti helped poetry become a respected mode of expression for women. Political and literary writings functioned as complementary sources of female authority. Whatever questions we raise about whether such writings actually represent female voices or only "speak for" women in male language (as some poststructuralist

feminist critics claim), they were understood by contemporary readers as articulating women's ideas and concerns. In fact, as many subsequent critics have noted, Victorian reviewers and critics were pre-
occupied with exploring the ways women's writings reflected both
their experience as members of their sex and the qualities considered
natural in their gender. Thus, Victorian men saw women acquiring
what must have seemed to be an unprecedented access to public
speech and control of cultural discourse.[27]

A great deal of what women's literary works had to say about
gender relations may have been as disquieting as feminist political
manifestoes, and ironically so, in that the novels seem most anti-
male in the very places where they most affirm a traditionally male
vision of love. While women's lyric poetry tended to reverse the
conventional gender roles in love by representing the female speaker
as the lover instead of the object of love, women's fiction most frequently reproduced the images, so common in prior texts by men,
of the self-abasing male lover and his exacting mistress. For example,
in *Wuthering Heights*, Heathcliff declares himself Cathy's slave; in
Jane Eyre, Rochester's desire for Jane is first inspired and then intensified by his physically dependent position; in *Middlemarch*, Will
Ladislaw silently vows that Dorothea will always have him as her
slave, his only claim to her love lies in how much he has suffered for
her. In several Victorian novels by women, men must undergo quasi-
ritualized humiliation or punishment before being judged deserving
of their lady's attention. For instance, in Olive Schreiner's *Story of
an African Farm*, the fair Lyndall condescends to treat her admirers
tenderly after one has been horsewhipped and the other has dressed
himself in women's clothes to wait on her. Although Victorian
women's novels do explore the emotional insecurity of the heroines,
their apparent self-possession is also stressed, in marked contrast to
their lovers' displays of agony, desperation, and wounds.

These texts also insist that the true measure of male love is lack
of volition. While the heroines make choices that define them morally, the heroes are helplessly compelled by love, and not judged to
love unless they are. In this respect Victorian women's fiction recovers the ethos so often expressed in medieval courtly romance that
love must be "suffered as a destiny [to be] submitted to and not
denied."[28] It also departs from the conventions of medieval ro-

mance in describing the helpless submission to love as an attribute
of true manliness, and thus Victorian women's fiction directly attacks the degeneration of chivalry into the self-conscious and controlled "gallantry" of eighteenth-century libertines.

Robert Corber has shown the influence on radical thought of
feminists such as Mary Wollstonecraft's denunciation of gallantry as
a means of dissimulating hostility toward women. Both radicals and
feminists emphasized choice in the libertine's chivalrous pose and
read it as flaunting aristocratic privilege. Interestingly, some radicals
associated chivalry with homosexuality,[29] apparently assuming that
such a false show must be hiding diametrically opposed desires. The
corresponding belief that the truly masculine man cannot help but
sufferingly worship the woman he loves might be read as a rather
transparently veiled early feminist prescription for more intense gestures of male submission to replace the cynically stylized forms of
the previous generation. Charlotte Perkins Gilman suggests as much
in her feminist utopia *Herland*. Of the three men who intrude upon
the matriarchal paradise, only Jeff Margrave can fit in. This sin-
cere and fervent "born worshiper" of women immediately becomes
"something of a traitor" to the other men, while "his worshipping
eyes, his grave courtesy" win him friends among the women. Although "his exalted gallantry" troubles him occasionally, since there
is no way for him to "serve" his self-sufficient female captors, they
find no fault with him. When the other men are expelled, Jeff remains, the narrator disgustedly remarking, "I never saw an alien
become naturalized more quickly than that man in Herland."[30]

If the major texts in Western love literature up until the Victorian
period can be considered as loosely constituting a monologue asserting man's passionate devotion to that beautiful silent object,
woman, Victorian fiction opens a dialogue that defines romantic
love as man's subordination to a woman insisting upon her right to
speak and act as a subject. Even when the female characters do not
make speeches that reverberate with popular feminist ideas (as they
do in the novels mentioned above), their participation in the dialogue of love always implicitly occurs within a society whose actual
women demanded and received more political power than they have
had in human memory. This development marked a major change,
because from the birth of the courtly tradition on, the narrative of

man's devotion to woman had unfolded within the narrative of
male ambition and achievement. The fiction that man's accomplish-
ments are all won as an offering to woman depends heavily on either
the silent acquiescence of women or the rigid separation of love and
marriage, since a complaining wife has considerable power to deconstruct the myth that men serve women in marriage.

Arthur Marotti's work on courtly love poetry as metaphoric expression of the political "realities of suit, service, and recompense,"
might be usefully considered from this perspective. Following Lauro
Martines's theory of the displacement of political ambitions into
romantic discourse in Petrarchan sonnets, Marotti claims that such
poetry also offered "ambitious men" in Renaissance England a form
in which to "fantasize a kind of mastery they lacked in actual experience." Marotti stresses reciprocity in describing the imagined
"love-match" that makes up to the poet for "the frustrations and
disappointments experienced in the public world" and allows him
to think of his self-abasement before the powerful as courtship
rather than toadying, preparation for "amorous mutuality," rather
than admission of inferiority.[31] But we might ask what else besides
his political situation must the poet be fantasizing about here? Given
the laws and customs governing marital relations, how much mutuality could have been possible in Renaissance marriages? Since
women today are still fighting for equal rights in marriage, it seems
unreasonable to assume that the Renaissance marriage could provide
a wife with power equivalent to her husband's.

Man's mastery in love is not exercised over the situation only, but
also directly over woman. Rather than compensating the poet for
the love-match which his ambition forbade him, the courtly poem
may have been a fantasy about what the love-match could have been
if man were able, as in fairy tales, to gain power by renouncing it,
and if woman, as in fantasies, was likely to demand from her lover
just what he wanted to give. Consequently, courtly poetry can be
read as a double lie, which romanticizes both man's (always subordinate) relation to political power and his (potentially dominant)
relation to female sexual power—a lie dependent for its continued
meaning on preserving both the situations it denies. As women began publicly to state their ambitions to rival men, the classic story
of love was disrupted. It was as if, after centuries, woman finally

took her lover at his word and responded to his offer to give her anything, with the demand that he give over power and authorship to her.

No wonder then, that, as the nineteenth century progressed, novels by men increasingly represented passionate love as a threat to male identity and antithetic to male creativity. Whereas the courtly tradition had often balanced love's pain against its capacity to inspire transcendent art and had read the ability to love a woman as a troublesome but positive sign of manhood, such writers as Dickens, Tennyson, Trollope, Thackeray, Meredith, and Hardy repeatedly dramatize "excessive" love's silencing and even castrating effect on men. Almost the only male writers in whose work the old love ethos sometimes appears uncolored by the new are Pre-Raphaelite rebels like Algernon Swinburne and Dante Gabriel Rossetti, who construct their own identities in opposition to the dominant culture's definition of masculinity. The context was consequently provided for the coding of male submission to woman as perverse to the point of effeminacy, the "feminine masochism" that Freud saw primarily in men.[32]

While some literary critics see Freudian theory as one of the forces undermining male authority in the twentieth century,[33] Jessica Benjamin seems right to emphasize the role that the "monadic self-interested ego . . . posited in classical psychoanalytic theory" plays in shoring up the phallocentric concept of individuality on which patriarchal society has been based.[34] At the very moment that English literature seemed poised between the old faith in objectivity and the emphasis on relativity characteristic of modernism, the image took form of the ego heroically fighting his way toward a dominating, self-centered masculinity.[35] At the end of the century, normative voices in Thomas Hardy's *Jude the Obscure*, for example, urge wife-beating and marital rape as *compassionate* solutions to the problems created by woman's dissatisfaction with her position in society and man's subversive desire to subordinate himself to her.[36] Masochism as a concept seems particularly suspect when we consider that it rewrites the traditional love story into a tale of man's failure to achieve sufficient masculine mastery of woman to make them both happy.

It is tempting to see the early psychologists' and Freud's interest in cataloguing deviations from a "healthy" male norm partially as a response to the decentering effect of woman's gaining a voice in narrativizing love. In the homophobic late nineteenth century, constructing a new story of love as domination of woman was made possible by the new sexology's nonsensical conflation of male homosexuality with submissively expressed male heterosexuality and its touting of female masochism as essential femininity. As I hope to show in the chapters that follow, this new love story was, not coincidentally, compatible with both the Victorians' redefinition of patriarchal marriage as the ultimate possible expression of love and their imperialist justifications of violent maintenance of paternalistic power.

Should we see the construction of masochism as a kind of misogynist cultural conspiracy? It does appear to have occurred under other auspices than those of chance or reason when we consider that resulting from a belief in masochism is the judgement that the more a man loves a woman in the ways that love has historically been understood, the more masochistic, ergo, the less heterosexual, he is. Belief in masochism definitely served a need, but perhaps one that we would prefer to see served no longer. I do not mean to suggest that belief in masochism has always and everywhere served the need of constricting masculinity into one allowed expression: brute domination of woman. Certainly love as it was formerly and more pleasantly understood has continued, and literary texts often record vigorous resistance to the most privileged post-nineteenth-century masculinity. But as long as man's domination of woman defines masculinity for theorists of gender, we can only think about resistance to it as an aberrant move toward effeminization.

To develop a description of the textual history of the concept of masochism, one must begin by avoiding subjecting literary characters to psychoanalysis, as if masochism had always existed as a definable state. Thus, we might follow the lead of psycholinguistic criticism and go deeply into language, treating it as the unconscious of the text. But even such a move finds itself ultimately circumscribed by the central paradigms of psychoanalytic theory, which limit the extent to which it can be critiqued from within. A special problem arises in the concepts of resistance and disavowal. These crucially important terms are generally understood in relation to the reality of castration. And the idea of castration as a basis of identity formation, whether in Freudian reference to the penis or in Lacanian reference to the phallus, masculinizes power. Female power becomes at worst a contradiction in terms, realized only in the fantasy figure of the phallic mother. At best it is relegated to the presymbolic realm of connection to the mother, what Julia Kristeva calls the semiotic, which we cannot inhabit as adults without losing access to the symbolic order, in other words losing language and what is commonly considered sanity. Within this model, female power that works openly in the world can only be understood as an illusion expressing resistance to reality. Employing such an interpretive framework means understanding stories of female power only in relation to the gendering of power posited as reality by psychoanalytic theory. However, when we see these stories in relation to prior texts and cultural discourses, that is, in relation to other fictions rather than to a presumed reality, a different pattern of resistance emerges.

Beyond the Psychoanalytic

It seems time to turn from treating the concept of masochism simply as a tool for understanding representation and begin investigating the history and politics of the representation of various acts and states of being now considered masochistic. If we believe that desires are affected, if not created, by official discourses, then how can it not matter that what we call male masochism has been understood and described differently throughout history? Even if one believes that official discourses only affect the speaking of desires, wouldn't the language of those discourses infiltrate the way the desire is represented? In order to understand masochism as a politically charged construct, we must look at the various descriptions of male submission to woman, the stories that contextualize such descriptions, and the language employed in different narratives of what we now call masochistic desire. Rather than analyzing descriptions of such desire as if they were case studies, we might more profitably attend to their status as fictions that participate in diverse literary traditions.

As I began by pointing out, the current practice of literary critical comment on the representation of masochism within texts often

uses psychoanalytic theory to diagnose the problems of fictional
characters. I prefer to consider characters and stories as responses to
questions implicit in conventions of representation. Therefore, I begin with a different set of questions than many now writing about
masochism. Instead of asking what theories of the mind's functioning are illustrated in a given text, I ask in what ways the text responds to theories of gender and power advanced in prior texts and
how the text addresses cultural discourses on this topic that were
popular in the period when the text was produced. In this approach,
I follow Deleuze and Guattari in *Anti-Oedipus* in treating articula-
tions of desire, at least as they appear within literary texts, as effects
of social conditions rather than the result of family history.

In his first and best-known discussion of masochism, *On Coldness
and Cruelty*, Deleuze works from a Freudian model in identifying
the actors in the masochistic drama with personages in the family
romance: the oral mother, the father, the child. However, later discussions of masochism written with Guattari in *Anti-Oedipus* and
A Thousand Plateaus work from a different model. In these antipsychoanalytic texts, Deleuze and Guattari argue for a new understanding of desire and sexuality. They reject the Lacanian concept
of subjectivity formation based on lack in favor of a Marxian theory
in which "everything is a machine."[37] The human body is composed
of machines that interact with machines in the world through flows
that include but go beyond the merely material, so that, for example,
an eye-machine might be described as receiving a flow of images
from a computer screen as machine. Thought itself is part of the
flow. In Deleuze and Guattari's system, "desiring-production" (synonymous with desire) is the primary force moving the machinery.
It is unrestricted, impersonal energy. Contrastingly, sexuality as we
generally know it is an expression of desire "territorialized" by the
codes of a specific culture; that is, desire has been organized, structured, and restricted in order to serve a society's needs. Capitalism
and psychoanalysis work together to personalize desire and organize
sexuality around an illusion of lack. In response, some transgressive
expressions of sexuality, like ritualized male masochism, deterritori-
alize desire by subverting the very social structures that negatively
determined the sexual expression's form in the first place. Socially
structured sexuality implodes, and the way clears for a pure flow

of desire and of creative thought. Deleuze and Guattari's vision of male masochism as both socially determined and in the purest sense antisocial, as a resistance structured by official power but in deconstructive excess to it, provides a useful framework within which we may read male masochism's interactions with culture. Their vision allows us to recognize both the ways definitions of masochism serve conservative social interests and the ways its actual expression can disrupt them. And above all, Deleuze and Guattari's work on masochism allows for politicization of masochism by shifting focus from the family to society.

The specific social conditions that concern this study are those that directly structure literary texts, that is, conventions arising out of the cultural dialogue that is the intertext, the place where meanings are made and in every sense reformed. Within intertextuality, male masochism realizes its most disruptive power. Attention to the revisionary response one text makes to others is crucial to this project, because it is only through such attention that one can follow masochism's widely divergent paths toward its current conflicting definitions.

In the chapters that follow, I look at various representations of male masochism in literary and film narratives within the context of both the interpretive and critical literature that has built up around them and the narratives' own references to other texts. I consider literary traditions in the representation of male love as service and ordeal as well as discussing the ways in which modernist and postmodernist writers respond, within their own works, to earlier writers'—including psychoanalytic theorists'—depictions of behaviors labeled masochistic. I will not proceed chronologically because the concept of male masochism has not developed in a unified linear way. Instead of a single coherent narrative of masochism, literary texts present us with many competing tales of submission and domination as likely to ignore as to refine the patterns of valuation and demonization of romantic attitudes shaping other stories told during the same period. In fact, I hope to show that some of the word *masochism*'s elusiveness results from the branching out of different strands of narrative toward the assignment of contradictory meanings to masculinity and love. Consequently, each of the chapters of this book is organized around a cluster of texts that seem to be engaged in dialogue with each other about a problem in the figuration of masochism directly relevant to one particular narrative of gender identity. Each chapter highlights ways that various texts, created at different historical moments, reenvision a specific narrative tradition's representation of love.

In the initial two chapters, I will look at revisionary response as a register of resistance. In each case, one text writes against the underlying assumptions of a discourse of masochism that has gained authority because it serves the interests of socially conservative groups: in the first case imperialist powers and in the second supporters of a return to Victorian domestic ideology. The first chapter presents the feminist argument against equating male masochism with male advocacy of women. This persistent argument appears in the responses Mary Webb's novel *Gone To Earth* makes to Thomas Hardy's *Tess of the d'Urbervilles*. The subtlety of Webb's little-known text is revealed through its exploration of ways men's colonialist impulses have paradoxically been expressed masochistically. Her position on male masochism, at first seemingly conservative, not only clearly derives from early modernist texts in defense of woman, it also closely parallels much recent feminist theory on imperialism's construction of gender difference. The second chapter expands the analysis of masochism's role in the formation of modern gender politics. It foregrounds the anti-Freudian dialogue about the social and cultural functions of male masochism implicit in *Ulysses*'s responses to Leopold von Sacher-Masoch's *Venus in Furs*. James Joyce's defiant portrayal of masochism as the only route out of sterility not only challenges the most fundamental psychoanalytic definitions of perversion as escape from sexual maturity into fantasy, it goes in the opposite direction from Webb and Hardy in accounting for the pleasures masochism offers men in their everyday lives.

The next two chapters examine ways that modernist and postmodernist literary representations of male masochism build on different earlier traditions of portraying romantic passion. The third chapter, beginning with a new reading of Liliana Cavani's film *The Night Porter* and going on to discuss ritualized male submission in D. H. Lawrence's *Sons and Lovers* and *Women in Love*, and Iris Murdoch's *A Severed Head* and *The Sacred and Profane Love Machine*, continues exploration of an apparently deliberately counterpsychoanalytic tradition. But here the representation of male heterosexual love as necessarily sacrificial does not focus on what men have to gain through giving up power to women, but instead on how the demands of Eros work mystically in the service of justice.

The fourth chapter provides an entirely different perspective on narratives of male masochism by concentrating on the pleasure attributed to the woman in the scenario of female dominance of men and on the tradition of representing such pleasure as necessary to reciprocal love. The first section of the chapter traces, through analysis of Daniel Defoe's *Moll Flanders*, Jane Austen's *Pride and Prejudice*, and Jonathan Demme's film *Something Wild*, depictions of courtship as an education in submitting to women's desires. These diverse texts form part of a tradition that modifies Deleuze's description of the role of the dominatrix in the literature of male masochism as enacting the man's desire without reference to her own. The second half of the chapter scrutinizes Stephen Frears and Christopher Hampton's revisions of Choderlos de Laclos's *Les Liaisons dangereuses* in order to reveal some of the process through which representation of the erotic is shaped by conventions of cultural "master" narratives that assign historically determined moral values to sexual behavior.

The final chapter surveys how literary texts have worked both with and against the writing of masochism into official discourses of sexuality. It comments on the various ways masochism in Victorian novels can be seen taking form as a social problem and on the influence of these texts' narrative patterns on psychoanalytic theory. It ends by considering the resistance to conventional readings of male masochism offered by Kathy Acker's and Angela Carter's postmodernist revisions of Victorian classics such as Charles Dickens's *Great Expectations*.

Because my purpose here is to call into question the ways masochism has been read and, through the process of interpretation, created as a perversion of love, I focus on representations of male masochism in which dominance is overtly associated with women or the feminine. Part of the process that has demonized male masochism has been the attribution of masochistic attitudes and behaviors to oppressed groups. Masochism has been deemed unnatural in members of the culturally dominant group—white heterosexual males—at the same time that it has been naturalized as essential to the character of all women, homosexual men, and male members of subordinated minority groups. For this reason, it would seem that discussion of the putative masochism of members of oppressed groups must address very different issues than those central to discussion of the putative masochism of white heterosexual men. My focus is not meant to suggest that, in the study of masochism, no topic other than a privileged man's submission to a woman is worthy of serious attention, but rather it is meant to help prepare the way for the discussion of other activities and attitudes classified as masochistic by clarifying how erotic submission has come to be seen as unnatural in one particular situation, the very one in which it once signified love.

1

MARY WEBB'S
RETURN OF THE NATIVE TESS
Male Masochism and the Colonialist Impulse

> It is unmanly, it is effeminate, it is inartistic to gloat over
> pleasure, to revel in immoderation, to become passion's slave.
> "Reticence in Literature," Arthur Waugh

LITERARY CRITICISM USUALLY describes the relationship between femininity and male masochism in one of two general
ways. The first way of reading the masochistic figure comes from
classic psychoanalytic theory. Following Freud's discussions of erotogenic masochism, one must conclude that any masochistic male
character, despite his apparent masculinity (that is, the masculine
gender explicitly attributed to him in the text), occupies the feminine position in a gender-bound power dynamic reflecting the binary structuring of patriarchal culture. In other words he embodies
what Freud called feminine masochism. The second way of reading
the male masochist is through feminist narration of social history.
Reading along these lines, one interprets male masochism as a de-
fensive move. The masochistic male character functions within a patriarchal myth of woman's cruelty and man's vulnerability that
justifies woman's being violently repressed.[1] In either case, male
masochism translucently masks an image of woman abused and violated; all the eroticized pain in depictions of masochism is thus
(dis)placed on the feminine side.

While such readings are feminist in that they expose the misogyny concealed beneath the appearance of extreme deference to and
service of woman, they can also be misleading in that, by empha-
sizing patriarchy's debasement of the feminine, they turn attention

away from the masochist's pleasure in *his own* pain and, more importantly, they turn attention away from the roles that may be played by specific female figures in the interactions that produce his pain and code it as pleasure. Narratives about these interactions provide surprising revelations about how members of a dominant group can satisfy their submissive desires without undermining their power or identity, and also about how members of a subordinate group can be destroyed in the process. Consequently, while it might seem that a focus on the suffering that male masochists experience as men would lead us away from feminist concerns, it may instead help us follow earlier writers' explorations of them.

These literary excursions have been often overlooked, probably in part because psychoanalytic discourse has so authoritatively defined male masochism that competing descriptions of men's strategies for receiving romantic pain have been ignored. An added problem is that our understanding of the dialogue between past texts on this topic is distorted by the lack of canonical status or even the unavailability of so many of the ones authored by women. Often what began as a dialogue now has the appearance of a diatribe in which only texts authored by men are heard.

Although the literary canon has become not only a site of conflict but a passionately contested concept and gynocritics has won considerable respect for recovering forgotten women's texts,[2] books by previously popular and recently rediscovered women writers continue to go rapidly out of print. If for no other reason than their usefulness in providing contextualization, such books should interest theorists of culture and language and feminist critics of all sorts. Why, then, are these books disappearing almost as soon as they reappear?

One line of argument articulated by many feminist critics asserts that the structure of the academy and the training of English professors exert an influence on our judgments so that we apply, often unconsciously, heavily biased "received standards of greatness and even goodness."[3] In other words, our aesthetics are colonized by the dominant discourse. What is not as generally acknowledged is that our rejection of certain books as inferior and unworthy of serious attention can as easily proceed from unexamined *feminist* standards. Books that have enjoyed popular success often did so because they offered sensationalism derived from a strong mixture of sex and violence, while avoiding outraging their public by at least overtly upholding the most prevalent contemporary ideology. For obvious reasons, such books are unlikely to delight feminist readers immediately, perhaps especially when their authors are women. Yet, though feminism and institutionalized misogyny are in unlikely alliance against them, these books deserve careful attention in context—rather than as part of the project of contextualizing "classics"—because reilluminated in this way, they shine with a surprising power of their own.

Mary Webb's *Gone to Earth* is a case in point. In this chapter, I will look at Webb's novel's exposure of how male masochism, forbidden direct expression in the modern world, collaborates with colonialism. Webb's depiction of male masochism subtly recognizes that repression of any sexual expression, including one that society already deems perverse, will twist the expression into a new form. The particular form her understanding of this process takes more closely resembles the ideas of Deleuze and Guattari than those of Freud. While throughout his works Freud repeatedly decribes maturation as dependent on desire's movement from diffused expression with no object or goal to an expression that shores up patriarchal domesticity, Deleuze and Guattari just as insistently claim that any sublimation or channeling of desire perverts and maims its expression. Because their view exposes the perversity of domesticated sexuality, it is useful to feminism even though their theory of desire is far from being explicitly feminist. Ironically, one of the reasons that Webb's brilliant investigation of masochism is not read no doubt results from its potential interpretation as misogynistic.

Just when the predicament of Hazel Woodus, the heroine of *Gone to Earth* seems to allow for no resolution, Webb ends the novel by dropping her into a hole. By what might be considered a sort of poetic justice, Webb, as author, has been in danger of suffering the same treatment from readers for some time now. Despite the seductively beautiful paperback editions of her books published in the late 1970s and early 1980s, Webb remains unfamiliar even to most professional readers. The current lack of interest in her work is understandable because Webb's elegiac vision of a pastoral England and often expressed admiration for Thomas Hardy inspire comparison of their novels. And those judging by anything akin to formalist standards will rank Hardy much higher, because despite all the criticism Hardy has received for carelessness, his novels are decidedly better if better means more smoothly plotted and linguistically sophisticated.

Since all readers do not judge by such standards, we might ordinarily expect to find numerous appreciations of Webb among the works of the Anglo-American feminist critics engaged in the construction of a women's literary canon. Unfortunately, Webb repeatedly dramatizes masochistic female behavior while her narrators assert its naturalness.[4] Faced with a "minor" novelist whose work might be regarded as supporting the old critical assessment of women writers as conservative and imitative, and, even more troublingly, might seem to substantiate psychology's past claim that women are naturally masochistic, even scholars of women's literary traditions may be inclined to let her drop back into obscurity. Yet it is a pity for Hardy's novels to eclipse Webb's, because hers have their own virtues, among which is the illumination their revisionary responses to his shed on the ways modernist texts in defense of woman connect *male* masochism and the colonialist impulse.

In *Black Skin, White Masks*, Frantz Fanon warns "those who take it on themselves to describe colonialism . . . that it is utopian to try to ascertain in what ways one kind of inhuman behavior differs from another."[5] Writings championing women, from the Victorian period on, have commonly avoided at least this sort of relativism, substituting a metonymy in which all appropriative urges are read as colonialist and the oppressor of individuals as a figure for imperial power. This metonymy is exemplified in the phrase "white slaves" for prostitutes, which not only asserts woman's lack of autonomy and her enslavement to the satisfaction of male desires, but paradoxically, because of the differentiating qualifier "white," insists upon the lack of significant difference between her condition and that of the black slave. She is only a slave of a different color. Also, by introducing the idea that skin color has an important relation to enslavement, the phrase places the analogy historically and geographically. Prostituted woman, as white slave, is not like the conquered person of ancient times or the Oriental odalisque. Her condition mirrors that of slaves of African heritage, whose slavery reifies the status of their group in relation to imperialist powers.

Uncle Tom's Cabin, for example, has as the center of its horror that Simon Legree buys refined, pious Emmeline of the "white, delicate hands" to be his sexual slave.[6] Stowe envisions blacks and women as spiritually superior to the brutal white patriarchs who use the system of slavery to enable the satisfaction of lust that the natural purity of their victims would otherwise forbid.[7] In such a vision, all enslavement is sexualized; fear of sex and fear of subordination feed upon each other. As Karen Sánchez-Eppler shows, for "feminist-abolitionists. . . . the particular horror and appeal of the slave woman lay in the magnitude of her sexual vulnerability," and, consequently "antislavery stories written by women who appear to have no intention of questioning marital or familial relations constantly employ rhetoric or depict scenarios that jar against their benign assumptions about women's proper domestic place."[8] The importance to feminism of consciously recognizing the colonized condition of all women is emphasized by Trinh T. Minh-ha's powerful rejection of the separation of women's issues from racial issues. She points out that focusing on the difference of "third world" women or "women of color" from white women aids the interests of the dominant group. "It is the very kind of colonized-anthropo-logized difference the master has always happily granted his subordinates."[9]

In *A Room of One's Own*, Virginia Woolf makes a series of connections similar to Stowe's and Trinh's. To illustrate her concept of gender difference, she writes that male instinct "murmurs if it sees a fine woman go by, or even a dog, Ce chien est à moi. . . . It is one of the great advantages of being a woman that one can pass even a very fine negress without wishing to make an Englishwoman of her."[10] In this passage, not only is male desire represented as contemptuously equating, while still maintaining, differences of race, gender, and "even" species, it is also represented as transformative in intent. Woolf imagines male desire as an impulse simultaneously to possess and to change its alien object into someone familiar, to make her part of the group that gives identity to the self. The pairing of objectification and appropriation makes what at first seems an exogamous urge into a movement toward quasi-incestuous gratification. And in such a longing to make the other into the sister/mother and mate there is a hint of masochism, since the angel in the house is always potentially the avenging angel, the angel of death.[11]

Current feminist criticism and gender studies have made extensive metaphoric use of colonialism to describe the relations between the patriarchal discourse and its subjects. An early and no doubt influential appearance of this metaphor, in a note to Hélène Cixous's "The Laugh of the Medusa," generously recognizes the harm done on both sides of the colonizing encounter.

> Men still have everything to say about their sexuality, and everything to write. For what they have said so far, for the most part, stems from the opposition activity/passivity from the power relation between a fantasized obligatory virility meant to invade, to colonize, and the consequential phantasm of woman as 'dark continent' to penetrate and to 'pacify.' . . . Conquering her, they've made haste to depart from her borders. . . . The way man has of getting out of himself and into her whom he takes not for the other but for his own, deprives him, he knows, of his own bodily territory.[12]

That all writers who used anticolonial rhetoric to protest the oppression of woman saw such implications in it is unlikely, mainly because colonialist actions were rarely seen as expressions of masochism. Except in texts asserting that self-sacrificing imperialists deliberately took on a "white man's burden" of suffering by submitting to cruel savages, colonialist impulses appear more obviously connected to sadism than to masochism. Of course, imperialist guilt can be expressed in public confessions like George Orwell's "Shooting an Elephant" and "A Hanging," or Joseph Conrad's *Heart of Darkness.* In Rudyard Kipling's fiction, colonial conquest is sometimes inextricable from punishment through the feminine, as for example, in "The Man Who Would Be King" and "Without Benefit of Clergy." But in these cases masochism comes into play only in its broadest sense. It seems to lack the element of sexual pleasure popularly seen as its definitive ingredient.

Two texts that explicitly connect colonialism and a man's voluptuously endured suffering at the hands of woman are Jean Rhys's

Wide Sargasso Sea and Angela Carter's "Black Venus." Rhys locates *Wide Sargasso Sea* in the land of Bertha Rochester, the Other of *Jane Eyre*, and examines through this Other's eyes the story of Rochester's sufferings that will later morally legitimate his adulterous desire for Jane. With our reading of Rhys's novel always retrospectively informed by *Jane Eyre*, Rochester's trip to the West Indies and his conquest there of "Bertha" (as he names her) take on the sinister appearance of a journey to justify his later attitude that he is entitled to possess whatever woman he desires and discard any woman he no longer wants. Throughout *Wide Sargasso Sea*, Rhys demonstrates that such attitudes spring from the same sources as those that inspire colonialism. Man pursues and possesses the Other as a (potentially enriching) burden he can choose either to groan under or to cast off.

Carter's "Black Venus," a fictional biography of Jeanne Duval, Charles Baudelaire's Caribbean mistress, also stresses the ways that woman can be repeatedly rendered Other, that Otherness can be written upon Otherness until she is so distanced from recognizable humanity that she can be treated not only as a thing but as an idea making artistic creation possible. Carter shows the ways that Baudelaire's poetry makes Jeanne emblematically female, black, and without language, and so the ultimate topic/subject of language. Brutally reduced to a black hole, she becomes the unattainable, indescribable extreme toward which poetic language always strains. Covered by his projection of Otherness, no longer present even to herself, she becomes a living embodiment of that prelinguistic state Julia Kristeva calls the semiotic, the symbol of the lost, unqualified human presence, that which cannot be recovered but which art hopelessly and painfully strives to recover. Carter dryly remarks, "The greatest poet of alienation stumbled upon the perfect stranger," but, as she shows us, the discovery of the stranger, like all discoveries by conquerors and colonizers, always depends upon estranging what is discovered.[13]

Such depictions of the colonizing project raise the question of what exactly is being estranged when another is designated Other. If we are looking at textual representations of masochism as literalizations of projection in which the subject's discomfort with his own incoherence is played out through first disowning a trouble-

some part of himself by taking another being as the sign for it and
then recovering it/her as subordinate, what we are actually seeing
would seem to be a sadomasochistic drama of which it makes no
sense to ask to whom the pain is attached. From the beginning there
would be only one (self-torturing) subject in view. It is this sort of
drama that best fits Deleuze's description of masochism as a dialectic of "transpositions or displacements" in which the masochist escapes the limitations of self and approximates "the impersonal
Ideal" by treating his mistress as a mirror or parrot, "the personal
element turning by reflection upon itself into the impersonal."[14]
However, the entire scenario becomes far more complicated when
we turn our attention from the inside of the masochist's psyche to
the ways fictions of masochistic encounters represent the masochist's
interactions with another being in the world.

The first problem one encounters in attempting to elucidate the
literary connections made between masochistic impulses and any
others is the slipperiness of the term. As a result of the popularization of modern psychological theory, masochism is rarely linguistically differentiated from sadism. The usefulness of distinguishing
between the two has increasingly been recognized by literary critics
in the last few years.[15] Theorists of masochism have separated the
terms in the interests of interpretive precision, or of better understanding the psychological circumstances of textual production, or
of disclosing the unconscious of the text. However, in the process
of deconstruction attendant upon the separation of masochism from
sadism, we might also consider the role a historically specific ideology has played in their fusion.

The conflation of the sadism and masochism seems to have begun
with what Paul Robinson sees as the characteristically modern negation of distinctions in Havelock Ellis's concept of sadomasochism
as one of many "erotic symbolisms" for ordinary sexual desires.[16]
This modernist normalization of sadistic and masochistic desires
also implicitly supports as natural the sexually charged social hierarchies coming under attack in the early part of the twentieth century. While writers like Woolf, whom we might retrospectively term
culture critics, insisted on both the connection between sadism and
imperialism and their perversity, more respected theorists of sexu-

ality argued that masochism was actually merely the result of a mis-
direction of the normal aggression associated with maleness.[17] The
popularization of Freudian psychology completed the process of
embedding the two terms within each other so that neither condition could be thought of separately.

Although by 1920 (in *Beyond the Pleasure Principle*) Freud was
considering the possibility that "there *might* be such a thing as primary masochism," and in 1929 (in *Civilization and Its Discontents*)
he rather dubiously acknowledged that masochistic and sadistic instincts could "appear in isolation from each other," the psychoanalytic community (and modern discourse) seem more profoundly
influenced by his earlier assertion (in the 1915 revision of "The Sexual Aberrations") that the "sadist is always at the same time a
masochist."[18] Unlike Robert Caserio, whose recent reading of "erotogenic" masochism in Freud and Laplanche rightly questions the
general understanding of sadism and masochism as alternating expressions of the same perversion, or as forming "an unbreakable mo-
nad," I remain unpersuaded that the popular concept of sadomasochism goes against the spirit of Freud's writings on the
subject.[19] Throughout his work, Freud uses the terms sadism and
masochism primarily to differentiate between the foci (self/other)
of impulses to control and destroy. The conflation *sadomasochism*
troubles me, not because it simplifies Freud's extraordinarily convoluted discussions of sadism and masochism but because it avoids extreme qualitative differences in the attitudes toward authority expressed through sadistic and masochistic pleasure, fantasy, and
ritual.

Although, in *The Forms of Violence*, Leo Bersani and Ulysse
Dutoit follow Freud in considering sadism "a derived and projected
masochism," Bersani earlier provided a suggestion of what masochism can mean in relation to imperialist ideology with his insight
that Freud's lack of consistency in assigning meanings to the terms
"pain" and "pleasure" in his discussions of masochism may indicate
a movement toward regarding sexual excitement as incompatible with
"the structured self."[20] According to this reading, masochism, in its
excessive surrender to sexual excitement, would become a particularly powerful force against the concept of unitary selfhood. One

might go even further and say that masochism deconstructs the binary opposition between pain and pleasure and consequently renders meaningless hierarchies that depend on punishment.

It seems worth noting that epistemological problems only arise
when Freud tries to account for masochistic pleasure; sadism is easy
enough to explain. As Angela Carter has shown in her searching
critique of the novels of Sade, a masochistic drama is not simply a
sadistic drama in which subjecthood is transferred to the one being
tortured, it is (at least potentially) an attack on hierarchy through
the freeing of erotic energies from the dichotomies subject/object,
victim/victimizer, and good/evil that structure them in the sadistic
drama.[21] The reason for my parenthetical qualification will become
apparent in the discussion of *Tess of the d'Urbervilles* that follows.
Deleuze's analysis of Masoch's novels points to a structure in masochistic ritual—rather than the dissolution of structure Carter sees
in masochistic pleasure—but one "animated by a dialectic spirit."
According to Deleuze, through appropriation of the voice of power,
the masochist parodies the law. And through his chosen ordeals,
punishment is transposed from its auxiliary function "into a condition that makes possible the forbidden pleasure."[22] The absolute
identification of pain with pleasure in masochistic discourse makes
it the ideal medium for a narrative of the ego's triumph over that
ultimate colonizer, the superego. But what of the texts, other than
Masoch's necessarily definitive products, in which such narratives
appear?

Edmund Bergler, who has produced an extensive body of work
on masochism, describing it as the wellspring of all neurosis, sees
artistic creation as "*anti*-masochistic" because of the artist's implicit assertion of freedom from dependence on the powerful and
punishing mother of infancy.[23] Here it seems necessary to separate
author and text, impulse and representation of impulse. Since we
cannot know about intentionality, except through the mediation of
texts, including in this case those within psychological discourse, it
seems useless to describe an author's aesthetics as masochistic or
antimasochistic based on the sort of therapeutic role his creative
activity may (or may not) be meant to perform. In the keynote address of a symposium on masochism, Arnold Cooper, despite his
intention of following Bergler's model, adopted a more promising

approach in focusing on cultural artifacts. Implicit in his conclusion that "all cultures value most those achievements that are fired in pain. . . . The hero is someone who has suffered" is the idea that what is generally called heroism involves the conscious choice of suffering.[24] To this extent all literature exists in reference to an intertext that connects masochism with a kind of idealized masculinity.

Once again, such masochism does not seem sexual; heroes have rarely been imagined as willing victims of sexual abuse. But it is at the nexus of cultural constructions of masculinity as the urge to conquer/control and as the urge to be subjected to control that the strange figure of the supermasculine masochist becomes sexualized. His masochism manifests itself as eroticized sexual frustration.

In *The Use of Pleasure*, Michel Foucault connects this masochistic inclination to specific beliefs about the attitudes appropriate to each sex. It may seem that if masculinity is connected with activity and femininity with passivity, the promiscuous man would be considered especially virile and the celibate, or only moderately sexually active, man would be considered effeminate. However, Foucault argues that when the ability to take control, at will, of the sexual, including one's own sexual appetites, constitutes an essential indicator of manliness, abandoning oneself to sexual pleasure must be seen as effeminate. But by denying himself all the sexual activity he wants, a man does not necessarily deny himself erotic pleasure. Nor, when woman stands for sexual uncontrol, need a celibate man miss the pleasure of controlling her. On the contrary, as Foucault notes, if a man believes that controlling his desires is the most masculine of sexual activities, exercising such control can be intensely, erotically pleasurable.[25]

It can also become the informing principle of a particular type of art that displaces woman as sexual object by leaping from male sexual desire, the representation of which is the text's ostensible object, over the sex act the narrator/protagonist is denied, into creative fulfillment. Perhaps the best known example of this sort of text is "To His Coy Mistress," a "seduction poem" that seems calculated to repulse, through mocking and belligerent insults, the woman it pretends to seduce, while allowing the poet his solitary ecstasy of creation. In the concluding lines word play substitutes for sex play: "Let us roll all our strength and all/ Our sweetness up into one ball,/ And tear our pleasures with rough strife/ Thorough the iron gates of life/ Thus, though we cannot make our sun/ Stand still, yet we will make him run." Images of rape and war simultaneously open the significative power of the "ball" to allow a vision of a transcendent virility defeating even time itself—and to warn her to close her thighs lest she be torn open. As Francis Barker has convincingly shown, the poem's rhetoric is saturated with the political and moral ideology of its time, most apparent in its insistence that "[g]oods are to be got, ultimately, by effort, and [that] pleasure . . . must be *torn* from inhospitable circumstances by struggle and amid conflict." In this battle to colonize the woman's body, male pleasure occurs simultaneously with destroying the possibility of sexual intercourse; it arises in the midst of the textualized dismemberment of the woman's body.[26] Although not all artistic treatments of male sexual frustration are such perverse, narcissistic pleasure machines, ecstatic male renunciation of sexual activity occurs throughout classic and modern texts. Its very omnipresence in our culture makes it hard to read as a perversion of normal sexual expression. Still, we might avoid the mistake of advice columnists who term the eroticized renunciation of sex "true love."

We could consider Webb a victim of the same delusion, because her major theme is the progression of heroines from submission to brutes who do not deserve them, to acceptance of the rule of renunciatory Christ-figures who do. But a very different view of male masochism's meaning is offered in the only one of Webb's works that does not end with a woman giving herself up to her "rightful" male ruler.

From the beginning to the end of *Gone to Earth*, the heroine, Hazel Woodus, devotes herself to protecting her partly domesticated pet fox, the only living being she unambiguously loves. She perceives her family, father, aunt, and amorous cousin, for the most part, as distractions from her intense sensual pleasure in nature. And her two serious suitors, the squirely Jack Reddin and the minister Edward Marston, are hardly more to her. She marries Marston in order to secure a safe home for the fox, which her father threatens to drown, and sexually submits to Reddin because instinct moves her against her will. To rephrase my earlier characterization of its conclusion with all the friendliness I feel towards the novel, *Gone to Earth* ends with its untamed heroine's death as the only possible escape from the two men fighting to experience pleasurable sexual suffering through control of her body. Although Webb's treatment of Hazel can be read as a dismissal of her importance and even as advocating female quietism through reinscribing the conventional inefficacy of feminist protest in the novel, it might better be understood as an incontrovertible rejection of exterior definition and control.[27] In fact, Hazel's death is the hinge on which *Gone to Earth* swings away from *Tess of the d'Urbervilles* toward the anticolonialist aesthetic from which Webb's revisionary responses come.

Gérard Genette's term *métatextualité* probably best describes the primary relationship of Webb's novel to Hardy's because, although *Gone to Earth* never quotes *Tess* and makes few direct allusions to it, on almost every level of meaning Webb's novel provides a critical commentary on Hardy's.[28] That Webb saw an interest in sadism and masochism in Hardy's works is suggested paratextually by her dedication to him of *Seven for a Secret*, the novel in which she deals most explicitly with these topics.[29] That she also saw a connection in *Tess of the d'Urbervilles* between such sexual impulses and the urge to establish control over "primitive," "virgin" territory is indicated by the way she develops Hardy's sexual themes in her own work.

The two novels are quite similar structurally. Like Hardy, Webb places a triangle at the center. The basic actions that create the triangle are almost identical. In each story a "natural," passionate but innocent country girl is first courted and then forced into her first sexual experience by a rural libertine. She seeks refuge with an idealistic, philosophical young man who loves her, or at least his image of her as a figure for purity. Because she cannot fit this image, due to the perfidy of the woman-chaser who continues to hound her, she is destroyed. The stories are narrated in chronological order, for the most part, with the heroine's periods of sexual activity or chastity determining the other actions.

Often changes in the heroine's sexual condition are marked by changes in setting, as when Tess is brought to Tantridge to lose her virginity and, having lost it, next appears on the road away from Tantridge, resolved to be chaste; or when Angel Clare's refusal to consummate their marriage puts her on the road once more. In *Gone to Earth*, Hazel jumps like a yo-yo between Undern, the valley home of low Reddin, and the parsonage of high-minded Marston, on "God's Little Mountain." Her vertical movements parodically translate Tess's long, agonizing pilgrimages into literal leaps at blessedness and tumbles into sin. The slapstick rapidity of Hazel's moral movement fits the tone the book derives from its abundant transcriptions of Hazel's comically innocent philosophical musings. As a natural skeptic unfamiliar with the Christian doctrines or the Edwardian mores governing most of the other characters, Hazel clownishly illustrates morality's connection to place with her absolute inability to recognize that, wherever she is, each of her lovers expects her to live according to the rules of his social circle. Her moral mobility visibly demonstrates the moral slippage unsettling the power of both the novels to name love.

Both novels occupy a liminal position between the most characteristic textual attitudes toward sex of the Victorian and High Modern periods. Victorian texts tend to concern themselves with a taxonomy of love, manufacturing evidence to illustrate the dire consequences of purely sexual love. While the Victorians were often surprisingly forgiving about sexual transgression when it was ameliorated by love, lust without love is almost universally condemned in Victorian texts. There is very little difference in the wages of lust in texts otherwise as dissimilar as *Adam Bede*, *Vanity Fair*, and *David Copperfield*. In contrast, texts otherwise as diverse as *Mrs. Dalloway*, *Ulysses*, *The Awakening*, and *Sons and Lovers* present, as valuable in themselves, moments when one person reciprocates in kind another's sexual desire. In the early twentieth-century novel, reciprocal lust does not make an aperture in the fabric of wholesomeness through which evil enters the world, but instead provides a little secret breathing space for bodies oppressed by the almost unbearable overlay of social readings of their desires. In *Tess of the d'Urbervilles* and *Gone to Earth* lust in action forces the participants into a waste of shame too dreary to be Shakespearean. But both novels seem to yearn wistfully for a world in which a good man could act on his lust without moral confusion. "Bad" love remains safe in its Victorian category, a Pandora's box that must never be opened. Webb and Hardy easily identify the man who opens it as a scoundrel. "Good" love, however, is sliding over the threshold into modernity, and we scarcely know by what name to call Marston and Clare.

Transtextuality is most evident in Webb's characterizations, her three main characters bearing a parodic relation to Hardy's. While Tess is "backward," Hazel is positively antisocial. Tess appears primitive to Alec d'Urberville and Angel Clare because she lacks the affectations of their social class, but as Hardy insistently tells us, she is a true aristocrat. In her occasional flashes of anger she partakes of the frightening and austere viciousness of the "barbarian" upper class Matthew Arnold describes in *Culture and Anarchy*. The overbearing passion that causes her to murder d'Urberville places her in, rather than separating her from, the structuring classifications of her social world. And in the end she acquiesces to its laws. Thus, Tess follows the tradition of the noble slave created by texts like Aphra Behn's *Oroonoko*. Although Tess's motivations are sometimes maddeningly unclear, her actions and others' actions involving her can be understood in relation to traditional texts such as ballads.[30] Hazel is a young savage incapable of obeying or even understanding any law except nature's. Because she acts outside all familiar systems of meaning, Hazel's actions are explicable only by reference to instinct.

She is far more savage than noble. Her pragmatic, self-absorbed personality closely resembles that of the pet fox which Webb rather heavy-handedly lets us know represents her wild soul. Without religion and utterly impervious to socializing forces, Hazel seems incapable of understanding the mores that govern the other characters. In her solitary and generally companionable life with her father: "There was nothing filial about her or parental about him. Neither did they ever evince the least affection for each other."[31] The tragedy of Hazel's subjugation does not, as in Tess's case, derive from our sense of an inversion of the normal order of things, but from our perception of her as displaced into a system in which she can see no meaning. Bowed down under the law of the fathers—when fatherhood is an empty word to her—the personification of noncomprehension, she recalls the ghostlike natives that so horrify Marlow on his entrance into the Belgian Congo in *Heart of Darkness*. The special nature of her suffering, like theirs, makes us know how colonialism negates the concepts of law and criminality by rewriting the social contract as a bill of sale only the owner can read.

By placing her "pure woman" permanently outside the social world the men in both *Gone to Earth* and *Tess of the d'Urbervilles* inhabit, Webb highlights the source of both heroines' attraction: the allure of the primitive. In Hardy's novel, the urge to possess a daughter of nature seems almost interchangeable with the urge to enter a country perceived as primitive. A seemingly reflexive projection of uncomplicated primitivism onto Tess is revealed in d'Urberville's continual astonishment that social rules affect her at all and Clare's fantasy that she grew up innocent as the first woman. D'Urberville's most socially correct plan concerning her is that they go together to Africa. Clearly there is something in his passion for her incompatible with "civilized" life. Clare's passion is distinctly similar. When he learns of Tess's "sin," he recoils from her not only because he knows it will allow the social world to criticize his love and marriage but also because the marriage will redefine as a fall his rejection of his family's social life. In despair of achieving an entrance to the natural, edenic, presocial world through marriage, Clare runs away to the wilds of back-country Brazil.

Both Hardy and Webb emphasize the high-minded man's unconsciousness of this need to escape the demands of civilization. Like all British colonialists-in-good-faith, Clare and Marston believe that they are possessing primitive woman in order to lift her out of darkness. Clare begins his courtship of Tess with an offer of a course of instructive reading. He means to give her the "social assistance" of instruction in his more refined "manner and habits," "speech and phrases," and "likings and aversions" before they set out on their new, "colonial" life.[32] Webb's reading of Hardy reveals the extent of the destruction in the wake of a masochism that allows man glorious suffering in resistance to society only at the expense of his colonization of woman. Like lands conquered by social rebels, the beloved woman becomes the ground on which man enacts his defiance of the parent-country. But he is glamorized as an outcast in inverse relation to her forced repression into conformity. As much as Clare rebels against his parents' social world and its system of mundane laws, he seems to see himself as an emissary of the higher, cultural aesthetics that determine the social laws. Marston simply turns Hazel over to his mother to be made into a lady. *Tess of the d'Urbervilles* achieves its most hopeful mood when Clare begins his education of Tess. *Gone to Earth* seems most ominous when we hear that, while Marston bravely battles against his own and his community's prejudices and received ideas, Hazel will be left under the instruction of his mother, "one of nature's opiates, and she administered herself unconsciously to everyone who saw much of her. Edward's father, having had an overdose had not survived" (58). In her characterizations of Mrs. Marston and Hazel's aunt Mrs. Prowde, Webb exaggerates the apparently wholesome bourgeois propriety of the elder Clares into a deathliness that blights every life it touches.

The parody and exaggeration in Webb's text comes to directly contradict the prior text in her revision of Hardy's depiction of Tess alienated from nature after her impregnation. When Tess wanders the "lonely hills and dales" imagining herself "a figure of Guilt intruding into the haunts of innocence," we are made to perceive her emotions as doubly ironic, first because d'Urberville has taken her for (and taken her because he believes she is) a sort of human animal to whom instinct must be the most binding law, and secondly, because she has not, as she weakly believes she has, broken any "law known to the environment in which she fancied herself such an anomaly" (134–35). Hardy implies that both her problem and her anguish result from misreading her character. She cannot recognize her own nature or her place in nature, but Hardy, as omniscient artist, does.

The subject-object relationship of male author-female protagonist is reinforced as we are shown that to the educated eye Tess should figure not guilt but modernist alienation. And as such a figure she must always be denied the perspective allowed to prescient males like her creator and Clare, who suffer from but do not represent the condition. Her entrapment by social rules, through which Clare learns and the narrator explores the inescapability of the antinatural world, earns more pity because she submits to it ignorantly, the more foolish because if her morality were in harmony with her understanding she would repudiate her social definition as fallen. We feel *for* her to the extent that we do not share her perception; our sympathy must be mingled with a sort of contempt. The opposite is true when Webb parodies this section of Hardy's novel by showing the trees and flowers weeping as "they foreswore [Hazel's] company for ever" (205).

Hazel's alienation from nature, after Reddin takes possession of her body, appears in the form of a battle between the domestic interior and wild exterior of his house, as the room that contains her comes under attack by personified plants and fills with nature's "subdued complaints and whisperings" (204). "It was almost as if the freemasonry of the green world was up in arms for Hazel . . . [because she] had now been plunged so deeply into human life that she was lost to it" (204). "Human" here seems to mean domestic, while nature is allied with art. "For the spirits of beauty and magic are (as the bondsman of colour knows and the bondsman of poetry) inimical to the ordinary life and destiny of man. They break up homes" (205). As the medium for an overarching vision that, could she attain it, would reconcile Tess to unwanted pregnancy, Hardy's art claims alliance with both nature and sexuality as forces that domesticate woman. It seems to aspire to build homes after the traditional pattern. And, in fact, Hardy's novels often have at their hearts romanticized cottages where quiet acceptance of gender roles seems synonymous with the natural life. In contrast, Hazel is out of harmony with nature because she has been raped and abducted into domestic bondage. She suffers because her vision is artistic, natural, and so, transcendent. We are invited to sympathize with her to the extent that we, like the narrator, share this antidomestic aesthetic.

The difference between the two passages can be partially understood in terms of historically bound concepts of the relationship between nature and art. Webb recalls the romanticism of Shelley and Keats, as well as the early Yeats, in her insistence that art, vision, and nature are one. Hardy's narrative pose in *Tess* is like that of Clym Yeobright in *The Return of the Native:* the new artist escaping from the cities—perceived as effeminizing—and coming back to a manly life in nature to create through his sophisticated, anatomizing, and ultimately colonizing gaze a landscape invisible to those who have always inhabited it. In Hardy's text, the artist knows nature because he is separate from it, and this difference enables his knowledge. The gendering of this difference, subtle in Hardy's novel, is emphatic in *Gone to Earth.*

Hardy tells us that Tess mentally constructs the landscape that contains her, but it is a "sorry and mistaken creation" since "she was making a distinction where there was no difference" (134–35). As a championing of unwed mothers against conventional moral condemnation the radicalism of this passage should not be underestimated. Nonetheless, it also implies not only the inferiority of Tess's creativity to the narrator's, but that the cause of this inferiority is her failure to recognize that her biological destiny negates her pretensions to autonomous desire. The passage suggests that if only she could accept her unwanted defloration and pregnancy as part of nature's great plan, she would be content as the "skipping rabbits" and "sleeping birds" that surround her.

Nature has no such plans in *Gone to Earth*. Hazel's perfect empathy with the natural world is lost because in her "sexual meeting" with Reddin, she is "merely passive," lacking the "passion pure and burning" that would accord with nature's spirit (205). As represented by Webb, this spirit always opposes anything that reinscribes the feminine sex role. Hazel's mother "had born her in bitter rebellion, hating marriage and a settled life and Abel Woodus as a wild cat hates a cage. She was a rover born for the artist's joy and sorrow" (12). Apparently for Hardy, nature and woman are properly and most happily intertwined specular objects of the (male) artist.[33] Webb counters with a vision of natural female artistry continually threatened by men who, in attempting to possess it through possession of the woman, actually stop it at its passionate source.

Webb aligns herself with Hardy in showing considerable sympathy for men like Marston and Clare who initially revere woman-in-nature, who only intend to improve on paradise a little for its own good. These men, like Conrad's Kurtz before his fall, exemplify colonialism as the dissemination of cultural ideology as an act that masks unconscious flight from it. But the villainous d'Urberville and Reddin are depicted simply as imperialist exploiters. Although neither man travels to foreign lands, each finds, in England, a country/woman to colonize. Their women become means of (re)production. That Tess's body functions as a piece of fertile ground is expressed indirectly through the harvest scene that frames our first view of her as a mother and explicitly in the narrative statement that "a field woman is a part of the field" (137). D'Urberville reveals his utilitarian attitude toward Tess when his initial courtship of her takes the form of employing her and teaching her to serve his mother. Despite his lack of interest in Tess's "product," their child, d'Urberville does take possession of the field-woman and makes the once virgin land bear for him. Reddin seems to be literally after what he can get out of Hazel. Webb rarely mentions Reddin's desire for Hazel without also mentioning his desire for a son. Like the land he farms and even more like the woods in which he hunts, Hazel represents to Reddin a wild territory to be invaded and made, in both senses of the word, to yield.

Webb's narrator describes Reddin as sadistic and conventionally enough attributes his sadism to an "over-virility" that characterizes "the most rabid imperialists" (256). But this narrative classification seems unreliable because it is only in action that his conquest and possession of Hazel look sadistic. At the level of his urge to possess, he appears, like d'Urberville, markedly masochistic. Each finds the woman attractive in proportion to how seriously she demonstrates contempt for him, and all evidence that her coldness can never change inflames him further.

Part of d'Urberville's complexity comes from his readiness to reveal masochistic leanings that seem inappropriate to his bullying style. We might remember that before Tess, his favorite was "a dark virago, Car Darch, dubbed Queen of Spades" (110). Here Hardy anticipates Havelock Ellis in suggesting that both behaviors express the same drive; lust for conquest shows its reverse as "devotional passion" (383). D'Urberville seems fond of using the language of submission to Tess; "I have no right but to obey" (397). That these courtly tones are not ironic seems clear from his perception of his own passion for her as a force to which he must "give way" (401). Both his and Reddin's impulses toward conquest are inextricably connected to their impulses to lose control. As much as they want to enter primitive and unknown territory they apparently need it to receive them savagely. The woman's insurmountable resistance seems necessary to preserve the boundaries between them. By dwelling on what Hardy omits, the grotesque domestic life of the imperialist-seducer and his conquest, Webb stresses the interplay of male needs that depends on repressing female desire.

Where Hardy's characterizations of the two male rivals suggest a natural connection between masochism and sadism, Webb's suggests that the connection is a socially constructed evil. It is in the treatment of the would-be altruistic colonialist impulse that Webb's novel best provides a commentary on Hardy's. Although Hardy has much to say about inevitability in *Tess of the d'Urbervilles*, he has made it difficult for the reader to avoid feeling Tess's tragic fate directly results from Clare's foolish decision to leave her after the marriage. We are shown that Clare wants Tess to be an unapproachable goddess, "Artemis, Demeter," and thus is most moved by her when she has "the cold gleam" of northern light on her face (187). This attitude seems to inform his decision to "make a confession to her" before consummating their marriage (291), thus setting the stage for a penitential approach to the marriage bed. It may also inform his decision not to consummate the marriage at all, because in denying himself sexual satisfaction, even though on the grounds that she is unworthy, Clare ensures the prolongation of his excitingly tormenting desire.

Webb is much more emphatic than Hardy in blaming her heroine's tragedy on the man who denies himself sexual pleasure. Although the narrator praises Marston's "altruism," Webb dramatizes his behavior through the imagery of masochistic ritual. She makes masochism look simultaneously ridiculous and seductive as Marston rejects "the norm," his previous love of "ordinary things," "Church and State," and "the letter of the law" in favor of a voluptuously intense, self-torturing celibacy in which his Bible becomes an anthology of erotica, full of "sweet, frank love-stories . . . that would, if written by a novelist, be banned" (127–30). While she concentrates on showing the sorry results of masochism's misuse, Webb suggests its potential for deliciously disruptive pleasure. Because of Reddin's active sexuality, Marston tells him, "You are not a man . . . you are nothing but sex organs" (274). Marston ecstatically affirms his own male identity, on his knees before the bridal bed he will never enter.[34] Even when he realizes that, as we are told, "it was his own love that had destroyed them both," or rather, as we are shown, his particular way of expressing it, Marston still continues to deny himself and his wife sexual intercourse (265). Yet, as Webb repeatedly tells us, were it possible for Hazel to survive as a woman without a master, Marston's remoteness from his bride might benefit her, giving her remarkably unsocialized responses to life room to develop. As in

Deleuze and Guattari's account of desire's territorialization into sexuality, the culturally predetermined structure of the patriarchal family, not the unusual desires of Marston and Hazel, appears as perversity. The novel's implicit defense of male masochism makes space for feminist critique. It is not simply the self-denying masochism of the men around her that oppresses Hazel but its combination with their impulses to control and possess her, impulses that function to bring them back into harmony with social and religious law.

In Hardy's novel, d'Urberville tells Tess he is giving up his evangelical mission for her sake because "I thought I worshipped on the mountain, but I find I still serve in the groves" (402). In *Gone to Earth*, Marston's parsonage is on "God's Little Mountain" and Reddin's house is set in a cherry grove. Tess and Hazel are claimed both according to the laws of nature and the old gods and according to the Judeo-Christian tradition and the social laws it has created. Yet, no matter where the heroine is placed by the men who desire her, no matter whether she is sexually possessed or only legally owned, she remains cold, distant, Other, colonized, at the insistence of the coupling of the men's masochistic needs with their need to conform to social law.

Hardy tells us that in their sexual histories Tess and Clare are "doubles" (291–92). But in their sexual needs, he implies, they differ fatally. In the final section, entitled "Fulfilment," we last see Clare with his sister-in-law, 'Liza-Lu, presumably intending to offer her the protection of marriage, as Tess has requested. We can also assume that the marriage will be unconsummated because he has previously said that sex with her would be incest. Appropriately, she is a "spiritualized image of Tess, slighter" (488). This conclusion perversely hints that men find their fulfillment in celibacy, which in this particular case is brought about by the desiring woman's execution.[35] Tess acquires meaning through the complicated game of male desire and self-denial in which she is a counter taken for a goal. As a human colony, she has her meaning only in relation to man, the colonizer's, masochistic sexual economy.

Tess is woman as a trope for victimization. Almost every contact she has with others inscribes her victimization. She takes victimhood beyond gender in her roles as peasant to aristocrat, worker to employer, and child to parent. She even lends it to whatever man enters her life. But then she genders it feminine again, for if she is, as Hardy names her, a pure woman, her story defines pure womanhood, that is, female essence, as victimization. Such troping of womanhood, as many feminist critics have shown, silences real women's voices. Even though Hardy obviously means to defend Tess and actual women like her from the misreading of a misogynist culture that would call them impure, "the revaluation of the *figure* of the woman by a male author cannot substitute for the actual participation of women in the literary conversation."[36] Hardy's apparent advocacy of Tess actually accomplishes what Gayatri Chakravorti Spivak calls "translation-as-violation," a feature of imperialist ideology. As Spivak points out, "not only the power but also the self-undermining of the man may be operated by the troping of the woman," but still the writer from the dominant group effaces the specificity of his subordinate in order to speak for her group, the language of which is always read as inadequate to the project of political change.[37] As a figure for victimization, Tess perforce cannot speak or even think on her own behalf. She is always already colonized, not as Hardy would tell us, by her oppressive society, but by Hardy's actions as her interpreter. Her motivational opacity helps create her iconic purity.

Tess's idealization has much in common with the "compassion as contempt" which, in an otherwise often annoying account of Western leftism, Pascal Bruckner claims postcolonialists extend to their former subjects. Here, as in the type of rhetoric he attacks, masochistically harsh criticism of one's own group depends upon denial of subjecthood to the supposedly defended victim.[38] As Renato Rosaldo more perceptively shows, the confessional posturing of the servant of imperialism, when struck by nostalgia for what he has helped destroy, originates in the same "ethic of masculine heroics" that inspires colonial conquests in the first place.[39] Agonizing (voluptuously?) over the loss of the beloved, the male subject appears more a hero than before. The workings of *Tess of the d'Urbervilles* are in many ways similar to those of the novels that, according to John McClure, set out "to discredit the romances which serve imperialism," only to attain moral authority by reducing the

indigenous people of the "other" land to "signs of the sacred."[40]
Part of the sublime pathos of Hardy's novel's conclusion is that
Clare's life continues to mean something after Tess is gone. When
we have nothing left to wonder about Tess, we still see Clare and
must take him as the tragic center of what story is left.

Such later modernist anticolonial novels as Rhys's *Wide Sargasso
Sea* and Doris Lessing's *The Grass Is Singing* similarly rely on continuing the reader's interest in the conquering male to lend additional meaning to the story of his colonization and destruction of
a woman. As a response to *Jane Eyre*, Rhys's novel, whatever it says
about its protagonist, must always also answer the question posed
by the prior text, "what does his first marriage reveal about Rochester?" The murder of Lessing's female protagonist is framed by
visions of the devastation of each man who loved her and presented
through a young male colonist whose responses to the new land will
be determined by her death. Although both novels make important
feminist points, they still assign woman the role of sacrificial victim
whose death helps us to better know politically empowered man
and the world his imperial presence defines.

Gone to Earth answers Hardy's novel in a way that reminds us
that "[t]he history of colonialism, whether within or outside a na-
tion state, is not a history of the uncontested superimposition of a
coherently unitary metaphysic upon an opposition inevitably perceived as inarticulate," and that, as Diana Fuss argues, focusing on
an "always already" extant power relation closes off the possibility
of a historicization that recognizes difference*s* as well as difference.[41]
Marston's inner debate over whether or not Hazel is "pure" is con-
ducted in language that excludes her own, but ultimately ends in
his recognition of her authenticity as constituted outside his symbology. "He did not know how this could be. He only knew it was
so" (270). Hazel's defiant idiosyncrasy stands against her lovers'
moves to read her as a symbol. And Webb allows nothing to stand
beyond her. Just as, early in the novel, Hazel refuses to see sacred
meaning in self-sacrifice and declares "if so be any's got to die; I'll
die for myself," Webb refuses to continue her novel beyond the record of Hazel's absence. Hazel's death does not let us see through
our cathartic tears what has been left behind; it obliterates the world
that had held her. The earth and sky freeze, "the righteous men of

the hunt cease to be people of any class or time or creed" (288). The systems that make meaning roll away.

Webb's novel provides a defiant vision of a female Otherness that cannot be appropriated to satisfy male needs. Webb suggests that while, from Hardy's masculine perspective, the negation of female specificity may enable art, providing a space for the masochistic desire of the masculine subject to leap into narcissistic fulfillment, for the woman artist, it is ultimately the desiring female subject who matters, who signifies, and without whose presence there can be no art. Webb's revision reveals not only her judgment that Hardy's novel is in a sense a critique of colonialism, but also that its own aesthetics, because of their basis in a masculinist masochism deeply invested in domesticity, are colonialist. While Hardy's vision of female biology as feminine destiny places woman in a condition of victimhood in relation to which man can only be *sado*masochistic, Webb evaluates a range of male masochisms in relation to the figure of woman as natural artist. Webb's own aesthetics are anticolonial, stressing the primacy of meaning of the colonized land/woman. Hardy's gods take up another fly, but Webb's game ends when the vixen has gone to earth.

2

THE MASOCHIST AS EXILE
BETWEEN TWO GODDESSES
"Venus Metempsychosis" and
Venus in Furs in *Ulysses*

With the boy the result is not entirely satisfactory; the feminine
line is not given up, and the boy is certainly not "on top" in his
conscious masochistic phantasy.
    Sigmund Freud, "A Child Is Being Beaten"

He who aims by women to be prized,
First by the men, you see, must be despised.
    William Wycherley, *The Country Wife*

MARY WEBB'S *Gone to Earth* opens a little space for a dreamlike
vision of male submission as an expression of love that might
foster female independence, but her novel's conclusion retreats from
the idea that such relations can be sustained within the English society of her times. The behavior of her exemplary male masochist
remains contained within the frame of the early twentieth century's
construction of an imperialistic sadomasochism that forces victimization on women. Marston longs for another mode of being, but
he must long in vain. Consequently, the novel's tone is elegiac; the
depiction of Marston at his most self-abasing becomes an act of
mourning for what love was but can never be again. In comparison,
both Leopold von Sacher-Masoch and James Joyce look forward in
eager anticipation to the changes in gender relations that ritual male
submission can bring. Few literary rather than purely pornographic
texts showcase male masochism as enthusiastically as Sacher-
Masoch's *Venus in Furs* and Joyce's *Ulysses*.

That *Ulysses* quotes from and alludes to *Venus in Furs* is well known. One way of understanding this intertextual connection would be to see it in classically Freudian terms, in fact exactly as Freud sees sexual masochism in men, as an erotic communication between men that traverses the image of woman. Of men's fantasies of being beaten by a powerful woman, Freud writes, "The phantasy which . . . is conscious or can become so, is not a primary one. It possesses a preceding stage which is invariably unconscious and has as its content: '*I am being beaten by my father*.' " Freud goes on to explain that in this fantasy, which cannot become conscious, "the being beaten also stands for being loved (in a genital sense)." The imagined presence of the woman is thus read as a psychic ruse by which the man can "evade his homosexuality."[1] This reading of masochism renders the presence of actual women negligible in the male masochist's life and, against the grain of his fantasies, insists on the powerlessness of women. However, the Freudian vision has proven not at all antithetical to some feminist approaches.

One of feminism's earliest and most useful moves was to deconstruct paternalistic protectiveness. By exposing the self-interest inherent in man's placement of woman on a pedestal, early feminists could assert themselves not only against open misogynists but also against men who professed to speak on behalf of women, only to essentialize and silence them. A deep suspicion of the motives of men claiming to speak in the interest of women has remained a major feature of contemporary feminism, as was reflected in the 1980s debates over the entrance of male scholars into feminist criticism. Most contemporary analysts of gender and culture, including some who would probably not call themselves feminists, are now rightfully skeptical about all male gestures of deference to women. Consequently, male masochism, the most exaggerated gesture of them all, shows itself, as in Webb's novel, to be complicitous with the patriarchal power it seems to subvert. Certainly as a strategy for empowering women male masochism begs to be despised. But before concluding categorically, as Christopher Newfield does, that "masochism cannot serve . . . as a basis for men's support for feminism,"[2] we might consider the implications of masochism's relation to authority, in which the begging for scorn goes much further than a pose before woman.

To be a woman's man has always meant to be outcast, since man's birthright of masculinity with all its privileges, including a subjectivity equated with essential humanity, can only be claimed through identification with other men and against women. When male masochism takes the form of desire for sexual contact with a dangerous, objectified female Other, the masochist may appear as a hero tormented by Eros, and like Odysseus, no less masculine because his journey back to reclaim his patrimony involves striving against (the attraction of) woman as well as fate; but the masochist who expresses his sexuality solely in response to a woman's desires becomes an exile, still identified in reference to his paternal heritage but no longer able to claim it.

Ulysses is a text of exile. The very vividness with which Dublin and "Bloomsday" are conjured up attests to their distance in space and time, for distance creates the perspective necessary for precise focus on details. It is axiomatic that to be too close to material causes the writer to see it in a blur. In *Ulysses* Joyce moves back from Dublin in order to achieve a new vision of it. And *Ulysses* is not only removed from the world of Dublin, June 16, 1904. The novel also speaks its exile from conventional, especially realist, prose through parodic quotations. Positioned between *A Portrait of the Artist as a Young Man*, a text of departure, and *Finnegans Wake*, a text that begins already having departed from literary conventions, *Ulysses* occupies the ambiguous, and perhaps quintessential modernist position of the exile, removed from the past but not cut off from it: looking back, vacillating between longing and repulsion, alienated from but contemplating something that was or could have been home. Many theorists describe male masochism as a state that suggests such exile in that it simultaneously acknowledges and moves away from paternal power.

Frances Restuccia implicitly connects exile and masochism by applying to *Ulysses* Gilles Deleuze's commentary on *Venus in Furs*, *Masochism: An Interpretation of Coldness and Cruelty*. Deleuze takes issue with Freud's view of masochism as a sublimated expression of desire for the father. As described by Deleuze, masochism is a (male) strategy for receiving sexual pleasure without experiencing the castration anxiety that results from identification and rivalry with the father. The masochist gives up paternal/phallic power by contract to a woman who then acts as his agent to punish him *as* a representative or impersonator of the father; "what is beaten, humiliated and ridiculed in him is the image and the likeness of the father."[3] In Restuccia's reading, father and land are conflated in the figures of sadistic and castrating actual fathers and priests who create the "repressive patriarchal atmosphere" of Joyce's Dublin. As Restuccia convincingly shows, a concurrent evocation/mimicry and distancing renunciation of the authoritative father(land) figure characterizes *Ulysses*'s style. Restuccia closely follows Deleuze in seeing Molly as given the voice of linguistic play, which "punishes Joyce . . . [b]y dismantling his realism," but only as "a cipher" through whom Joyce can torment and assault (another aspect of) himself.[4] In this vision, the masochist's exile is a sort of solitary confinement; connection with woman, let alone entrance into her sphere, becomes impossible because she is only a mask through which he speaks. While this is obviously true of all characters in fiction and thus might explain Joyce's own position as a masochist, exile, and author, the Deleuzean paradigm of the authoring masochist and puppet dominatrix presents problems when applied to representations of male masochism within the narrative of *Ulysses*.

As Thaïs Morgan has shown, "the most widespread feminist interpretation of the dominatrix . . . as a man's mind in a woman's body is deeply misogynistic" in its Freudian denial of both the gender identity and subjectivity of aggressive women.[5] Freud's and Deleuze's readings of male masochism have in common erasure of female agency and presence. If one agrees with Restuccia and such prominent feminist scholars of women's modernism as Sandra Gilbert and Susan Gubar that *Ulysses* is a thoroughly misogynist text in which the purpose and effect of Joyce's representations of women's voices is to condemn woman, and especially female creativity and literary production, then we can read the cruelty of Molly and other female characters as constructed by Joyce's need to assert himself against the fathers. We can then agree that "the reality of women remains ignored; fetishistic disavowal allows textuality or free play even as it provides the security of a dominant position— only the son's (disguised as the mother's) rather than the father's."[6] By extension the mock-heroic movements of the two main male characters, Leopold Bloom and Stephen Dedalus, must be charted

solely in reference to patriarchal power, with the narrative's apparent representations of female power read as misleading signs veiling
masculine presence. But must we read the women out of *Ulysses?*

In analyzing a text's representation of gender, it is obviously important to examine closely how it genders language and how differently gendered discourses work within the text. But considering the
direction literary criticism has taken in the last decade, it seems un-
necessary to make a case for doing so. Instead, I want to urge that
we not ignore the manifest content of narratives directly confront-
ing problems of gender. *Ulysses* tells a story about the politics of
sexuality and especially sexual reproduction and, like *Venus in Furs*,
it places its main characters in a world in which conscious "fantasy"
and "reality" have the same truth status so that one does not metaphorically represent the other. This is of vital importance to its
antipsychoanalytic vision of gender relations.

As Ronald Bogue notes, a central event in the development of
Deleuze and Guattari's theories was Deleuze's recognition that in
Venus in Furs "the ideal [figured in the masochistic drama] represents, not a separate world beyond the sensible world, but a contest-
atory force of violent disequilibrium within the sensible world."[7]
Such a representation of truth calls into question the utility of such
concepts as the reality principle and disavowal that are deeply implicated in the politics of gender. At the very least it problematizes
interpretation of what actually happens in the text on the plot level.
For this reason alone, we cannot offer readings of either *Venus in
Furs* or *Ulysses* that assume plot details are unimportant to its representation of gender or can be agreed on without comment.

To the extent that it can be read as a story about representative
modern lives, one of *Ulysses*'s major concerns is the struggle between
creative and destructive drives. The struggle is placed in relation to
the characters' ordinary activities on a long, but apparently typical
day. Because of the narrow and specific placement of this concern
within the characters' daily lives, in which the pursuit of sexual pleasure features as a far more engrossing preoccupation than any other
activity, creativity is conflated with procreation. Bloom's masochism
could then be interpreted as one of many obstacles that the fertility
inherent in life encounters.

Following this interpretation—a mainstay of Joyce criticism—

one might conclude, as many critics do, that Joyce used Sacher-Masoch's novel as his model for depicting masochism as one distraction from the procreative business of life. According to such readings, masochism plays only a minor role in *Ulysses*, and the female characters seem mere conduits through which men can or cannot, depending on their sexual aggressiveness, reproduce themselves. But, if procreation is a major theme of *Ulysses*, men's submission to women who express desires of their own must also be considered a major theme, because Joyce's passionate interest in both shapes not just Bloom's character but the entire novel. Yet a consideration of the relationship of masochism to fertility in *Ulysses* logically begins with Bloom and his marital problems with Molly. Following the lead Joyce provides, we might begin to read the characterization of Bloom by looking at how his dialogue with Molly serves as a foundation for interpreting his life.

When Bloom tries to explain metempsychosis to Molly, he initially correctly defines it as reincarnation, but the examples he provides confuse it with metamorphosis.[8] At the end of the day, in Molly's mind, the term has become both eroticized and religicized—"that word met something with hoses in it and he came out with some jawbreakers about the incarnation" (620). By then the word's true meaning hardly matters, because metempsychosis has been connected to the central problem of Bloom's day: whether or not he will be able to create a new version of himself in a new body. "Venus Metempsychosis," as the goddess who may preside over this miraculous enactment of the ordinary, is well entitled to her place in the new Bloomusalem, beside those other representatives of Bloom's ability to see the divine in mundane forms of love, Venus Callipyge and Venus Pandemos.

The Venuses that adorn Bloom's reformed dream-Dublin are all "naked goddesses"; Venus in furs does not appear among them, yet one might feel that she too deserves a place of honor, for she is invoked again and again throughout *Ulysses* (400). Does the presence of the Venus of masochism preclude that of the Venus of procreation? The standard psychoanalytic answer would be yes. Freud repeatedly suggests that male masochists are generally impotent and that masochism in men frustrates procreative instincts, even while he contradicts himself by admitting that "the real-life performances of masochistic perverts" can "serve to induce potency and lead to the sexual act."[9] Unlike other kinds of foreplay, masochistic play is stigmatized by psychoanalytic theory as a hindrance to the act it paradoxically enables, so that the potency of the "pervert" must be achieved both in spite of his performance and by means of it.

A brief look at some of the Joyce criticism on Bloom's masochism reveals the tendency of critics to eliminate even the slight ambiguity of the psychoanalytic condemnation of male masochism as a perversion of normal sexual aims that arises from Freud's grudging admission that male masochists can include vaginal penetration and ejaculation in their performances. Most Joyce critics seem to believe that male masochism is synonymous with impotence/sterility in sexual relations. The factual status this idea has for them influences their readings of *Ulysses* so that they believe Joyce makes the male masochist a figure for sterility. William York Tindall is typical in finding Bloom's role as "happy cuckold," "womanly man," and "masochistic pig" and his role as "husband and father" mutually exclusive.[10] Stanley Sultan says that Bloom can return to "the full manhood of earlier years," only by "subjugating" the women who would dominate him.[11] In contrast, Hugh Kenner argues that the masochistic rituals of "Circe" are necessary to Bloom because he has defied "the injunction laid on his people to be fruitful and multiply" and so "needs to undergo purgation by pity and terror."[12] Richard Brown agrees that Bloom's sexual degradation is necessary to the success of his journey back to Molly, but only because Bloom's masochistic experiences reinforce the "feministic recognition of female strength," which helps him overcome his potentially destructive jealousy.[13] Rejecting the Freudian representation of male masochism as inapplicable to a novel written prior to Freud's texts on the topic and by an avid reader of Havelock Ellis, Brown views fertility and masochism as approximately equal threats to Bloom's happiness and sees Bloom's "onanistic concept of sexuality" as the virtue ultimately protecting him from destruction in nighttown (Brown 88).

However, Bloom and Molly seem more disturbed by their sexual relationship's irregularity than Brown acknowledges. Bloom himself seems to consider his ordeals in "Circe" punishments for his inability to "do a man's job" (441). To Molly, Bloom's masochism is just

another one of the many "cracked ideas" of "man man tyrant as
ever," who will never "let you enjoy anything naturally," one among
a multitude of annoying idiosyncrasies, all involving intellectualiz-
ing pleasure, like his "explaining and rigamaroling about religion
and persecution" when Molly just wants to sing a folk song (639,
635, 634). Here Molly's understanding of male masochism anticipates Freud's: both see it as replacing a type of sexual behavior they
presume is more natural.

In *Three Essays on the Theory of Sexuality*, Freud's discussion of
sadism and masochism betrays, in his typical fashion, his anxiety
about the incompatibility of male masochism with "normal" masculinity as he imagines it. He claims that the "roots" of sadism "are
easy to detect in the normal. The sexuality of most male human
beings contains an element of *aggressiveness*—a desire to subjugate."
Masochism in males, "further removed from the normal sexual aim
than its counterpart," seems most comfortably (for Freud) accounted for as "nothing more than an extension of sadism turned
round upon the subject's own self."[14] In her unpretentious way,
Molly seems to be predicting the Freudian position when she groups
masochism with other ways of distancing oneself from direct, natural experience. Male aggression is natural, male masochism is
twisted, "turned round." But Molly's judgments, despite their placement at the end of the novel, are hardly final.

Leo Bersani criticizes *Ulysses* for giving the texts to which it
parodically alludes the authoritative status of "cultural artifacts."[15]
Claiming that "a whole set of conventional psychological and moral
significances coexist quite comfortably in Joyce with a radical skepticism concerning the validity of any move whatsoever beyond or
behind the signifier," Bersani compares Joyce's use of language to
that of Lacanians whose semiotic approach to Freud "has in no way
affected the normative status, in their thought, of the psychologi-
cally and morally specific referent of a phallocentric heterosexuality"
(27). One might question, however, whether such a referent is vali-
dated in *Ulysses*.

Admittedly, Molly's speech has a certain referential flatness in its
quotation of the cultural commonplaces that would later inform
Freud's view of masochism. It cannot be taken to represent a consciousness that is uniquely her own. Rather, it is dialogic in its trans-

mission of a discourse that fuses the biases of ordinary "phallocentric heterosexuality" with psychological theories of sexuality. But
this very fusion challenges the authority of psychology's (and subsequent psychoanalytic theory's) description of masochism, especially as the psychological "insights" are presented within a context
that insists on the independence of language from "the moves of
an individual consciousness" (Bersani 27). Both Freudian and ordinary folk wisdom explanations of masochism are put at a remove
from experience. Masochism, as revealed to us during the course of
Ulysses's day, is assigned multiple causes, results, and even forms, by
a variety of speakers who represent competing cultural visions, and
only by considering them all can we glimpse the complex relationship Joyce suggests exists between Venus Metempsychosis and Venus
in furs.

The presence of the latter goddess is the most obvious in "Circe,"
in which she is mentioned by name in Mrs. Bellingham's complaint—"He addressed me in several handwritings with fulsome
compliments as a Venus in furs"—and implicitly in the contents of
Bloom's hallucinations, which often parodically parallel Sacher-
Masoch's novel (360). Richard Ellmann locates several points of
similarity between Bloom's experiences in nighttown and Severin's
with Wanda: each man wants to wear "his lady's livery" and act as
an (abused) servant, each awakens her latent sadism, puts her shoe
onto her foot and feels that foot on his neck, "attends [her] at her
bath," agrees to be her slave, and ushers in her new lover.[16]

There are some errors in Ellmann's description of correspondences between the two novels that subsequent critics seem not to
have judged worth noting. Yet if we can assume that Joyce is deliberately drawing on Sacher-Masoch's novel for his depiction of masochism, the changes he makes in modeling Bloom and his main female tormenter Bella Cohen on *Venus in Furs*' central couple should
be read as revisionary responses to Sacher-Masoch's representation
of the male masochist and his partner. To look at this sort of response means thinking of the relation between texts in terms of
revision rather than of influence. It means focusing on the conscious
level of mimicry rather than the unconscious one, and so highlight-
ing ways that a given text's transmission of a previous text's depiction of gender norms expresses resistance and even refutation.

While both novels depict masochistic experiences antipsychoana-
lytically as meaningful in themselves, as events rather than symbols
and as truths rather than clues to truths, the enactment of the masochistic drama is treated differently in each text. What might be
considered Sacher-Masoch's pathologizing of Severin contrasts with
Joyce's refusal to portray his masochist as suffering an illness.
Severin and Bloom do not, as Ellmann claims, both request and
enjoy the "privilege" of "being birched" (369). While Bloom prefers
"the spanking idea. A warm tingling glow without effusion. Refined
birching" (382), nothing so mild appeals to Severin, who is obsessed
with martyrdom and whose mistress begins his torments with a
whip "like those they use in Russia on disobedient slaves."[17] Bloom
is threatened with a vicious flogging that, because of the timely
arrival of Davy Stephens, never occurs; he undergoes a calm and
apparently sensationless martyrdom "amid phoenix flames"; the
punishments he receives from Bella/Bello are humiliating but relatively painless (406). He suffers no physical agonies comparable to
those of Severin, who is beaten unconscious repeatedly throughout
Venus in Furs.

Adding to its impact, Severin's story is told in a realist mode with
an additional internal narrator standing in for the reader. This narrator frames the tale by reading Severin's manuscript, increasing the
effect that one is reading a true account and experiencing the voy-
euristic sensations it provides. In his fantastic affair with Wanda,
Severin may be dreaming, but as he says, it is with his "eyes open"
(124) and in front of a witness. Bloom's experiences of being tortured are distanced by their presentation as dreams/fantasies. Sacher-Masoch's technique challenges doctors of sick minds to move
in for the cure because it insists that masochistic performances are
violent, painful events enacted in the real world. One can understand why Sacher-Masoch's writings provoked first Richard von
Krafft-Ebing and then Havelock Ellis to offer analyses of male masochism in order to help men like Severin/Sacher-Masoch overcome
"compulsions" to behave in ways that the analysts themselves would
prefer not to. In contrast, *Ulysses* neatly deflects paternalistic analysis
of the male masochism represented within "Circe" by marking it as
merely fantastical, a playscript, yes, but only in the sense of closet
drama. With its talking objects and painless tortures, "Circe" is not

a play that could ever actually be staged on earth. Bloom's masochistic fantasies are events that unsettle his world, but they are also
fantasies that leave no marks on him for doctors to heal.

Ellmann's suggestion that Wanda and Bella are equivalent characters is even more misleading than his paralleling of Bloom's and
Severin's desires and fantasies, for in contrasting these two domi-
natrices Joyce once again anticipates and deflects the moves of
analysis. Bella is introduced as a middle-aged, "massive whoremis-
tress" with a mustache and a dark, heavy face (429). She metamor-
phoses into the nightmare hermaphrodite Bello when she enters
Bloom's fantasy. Severin's Venus is "twenty-four at most," and
seems extremely fragile with her "graceful and poetic figure," "pi-
quant" face, and "skin so delicate that her blue veins show through"
(Sacher-Masoch 127, 131). Ellmann also neglects to mention the
most glaring difference between Severin's and Bloom's chastise-
ments: Bloom is dressed, addressed, and offered to men as a woman,
while Severin at his least conventionally manly moments is always
identified as male.

These contrasts position the two novels very differently in relation to the development of psychoanalytic theory on masochism.
Sacher-Masoch's inversion of gender norms harmonizes with *fin de
siècle* concepts of role mobility across a dichotomized field of traits.
He anticipates psychoanalytic theory in his repeated assertions that
human nature together with social conditions, specifically the political powerlessness of women, determine that all heterosexual contact must enslave one partner but that men and women have equal
potential to play the dominant role. In Krafft-Ebing's judgment
that masochism is natural only in women, an idea preserved in
Freud's term "feminine masochism" for sexual masochism, as well
as Ellis's view that "in the normal sadism which occurs throughout
a large part of nature it is nearly always the male who is the victim
of the female,"[18] the common factor is certainty that masochism and
sadism have fixed genders that naturally correspond to biological
sex. Bloom's fantasy about Bella seems to attempt a slavish, as it
were, adherence to this dictum, but Joyce's farcical manner of letting us know this casts a scornful sideways glance on the whole business of gendering masochism.

If, as Paul Robinson claims, Ellis's interpretation of masochism and sadism is "a remarkable piece of sexual apologetics" in which his "subjects emerge as relatively normal human beings," Ellis is also remarkably patronizing in his assumption that men whose deepest sexual desire does not involve dominance of women must be in some way physically deficient.[19] Joyce's comments, provided obliquely through *Ulysses*, on *Venus in Furs*' male masochist figure have a decidedly different tone. Male masochism in the "Circe" chapter becomes, as it is in Sacher-Masoch's novel, the sign of too much sexual feeling, "supersensuality," as Severin calls it. Under the enchantment of "Circe," Bloom's sexualization of all his experiences, a characteristic of his personality plainly apparent earlier in the day, opens him to a whirling flood of images that unfix all the commonplace ideas, current in his culture, about the ways biological sex determines appropriate behavior.

"Circe" seems conceived in opposition to psychological theories of latency and the subconscious that it lays out only to satirize ruthlessly through exaggeration.[20] As Bersani points out, "It is the episode which most openly invites a psychoanalytic interpretation, at the same time that it compels us to acknowledge impenetrable resistance to any such interpretation" (17). "Circe" is packed with sexual mothers and blatant homosexuality from the moment when Bloom joins Stephen in the whorehouse until both rush out into the street. Zoe, urging Bloom to follow her up the stairs, is both whore and mother with "[t]he hand that rocks the cradle" and at a touch reduces Bloom to his baby-self (408). Her allure becomes masculine as well as feminine when Bloom appreciatively notices rising from her skirts "the lion reek of all the male brutes that have possessed her" (409). A moment later, motherly again, she cries out "Hoopsa!" as she catches him on the stairs, and so echoes the midwives in "Oxen of the Sun" (409, 314). Florry, the prostitute Bloom seems to find most appealing, has a charm compounded of masculine and motherly elements, as she is "[o]bviously mammal in weight of bosom" and, according to Virag, probably the possessor of a "potent rectum" (418). Again female promiscuity, maternity, and male homosexuality flow into each other as Bloom's musings on the attraction and repulsion between women and serpents lead him to think of unmilked cows who "seek out the saurian's lair in order to entrust their teats to his avid suction," and Virag responds "Who's

dear Gerald?" (421). We learn later that Gerald introduced Bloom
to the pleasures of cross-dressing.

Within this atmosphere, Bloom's apparent inclination to assign
masochism a fixed feminine gender seems particularly absurd, and
in the scene between Bloom and Bella the confusion of genders and
roles reaches its apex. *Ulysses*'s quotations from George Meredith's
The Ordeal of Richard Feverl suggest an allusion to the Bella in that
novel who uses the lure of cross-dressing to seduce the hero, who
later extravagantly claims that she "taught [him] how devils love."[21]
The demonic hovers on the feminine side of the hermaphroditic
figure in both Bloom's and Richard Feverel's imaginations. Despite
"a baritone voice" and male attire, Bello is more a "ma'amsir" than
a man (432, 434). Bello, the "suckeress," threatens Bloom with
phallic but feminine high heels, "glistening in their proud erect-
ness," and "thrusts out" for his kisses both "a figged fist and foul
cigar" (436, 433). S/he refers to herself as a lady and tells Bloom to
call her "mistress" although the stage directions assign Bello the
male pronouns.

Likewise Bloom, as self-declared woman, has "large male hands
and nose" (437). Bello taunts Bloom for urinating sitting down and
commands him to "Do it standing, sir!"—and a moment later
"bares his arm and plunges it elbowdeep in Bloom's vulva" (438,
440). Bloom's relationship to Bella is as changeable as their respective genders. As the ottoman to a very solid cigar smoker and *Ga-
zette* reader, Bloom seems to be a literally downtrodden wife. Re-
named Ruby Cohen (after the heroine of the sadomasochistic novel
Ruby of the Ring and after Bella Cohen herself), Bloom seems to
have been adopted by his tormenter, who mockingly describes his
domestic economies as "[l]ittlejobs that make mother pleased"
(437). Owned with the "ruby ring," Bloom is a fiancée awaiting
"the night before the wedding" but also a "maid of all work" (439–
40). Finally he is a "male prostitute" offered by Bello to other men
(442). Transvestism here does not have the effect of normalizing
gender roles, though it can when the cross-dressing simply emphasizes man's inability to play woman's role except as farce. Because
the ridiculousness of the roles Ruby/Bloom plays is independent of
gender, the absurdity of society's urging women to assume them is
highlighted.

If Bloom were the only masochist in *Ulysses*—and "Circe" the whole of the text—Joyce would have achieved little more than a proleptic deconstruction of Freud's concept of feminine masochism. But masochism is not played only as farce in "Circe," let alone the rest of *Ulysses*. In the representation of Stephen's masochism, Joyce goes beyond simply resisting psychology's interpretations of male submissiveness and offers his own interpretation. Stephen's hallucinations counterbalance a delicately drawn anguish to Bloom's orgiastic dreams. Unlike Bloom's visions in form, Stephen's are very similar in content. In his drunken babble of "Circe's or what am I saying Ceres' altar," Stephen confuses, as Bloom does, the "laughing witch" with the fertile mother (408, 411). Stephen's pronouncement, "Blessed be the eight beatitudes," summons a procession of eight of his drinking companions in which Mulligan is the seventh named (415). The semicoherent recitation of the British beatitudes that follows reminds us chiefly that the seventh is "buggery" and also perhaps of Stephen's train of thought on the beach, as looking at Mulligan's big shoe on his own little foot, he thinks "you were delighted when Esther Osvalt's shoe went on you . . . *Tiens, quel petit pied!* Staunch friend, a brother soul: Wilde's love that dare not \ speak its name" (41). Reinforcing the impression, "beautiful Best" makes a brief reappearance.

Florry's request for "Love's old sweet song" brings another convoluted string of associations on the same themes (422). The Siamese twins recall Stephen's joke in "Oxen of the Sun" in which the fleshly union of the live twin with a dead thing is compared to the "sacred" union of man and woman (336). This joke suggests a connection between Bloom and Stephen because the former is inextricably bound by nature and religious law to his wife and the latter to his mother, of whom he is the "image" (541). For both, these bonds are a source of pain.

The second appearance of the twin motif adds resonances. As "Oxford dons" they are reminiscent of Mulligan, with his "manner of Oxenford," but also of "donnish" Stephen (178). As Tindall speculates, "maybe they have Matthew Arnold's face to suggest Hebraism and Hellenism or Jewgreek" (212). Like the metamorphosed dog on the beach in "Proteus," they are also "dogsbody" and "unattired" buck at bay, persecutor and persecuted united in one flesh, as they argue and insult each other (38–39). When Kitty's recitation of the tragic tale of Mary Shortall and Jimmy Pidgeon inspires Stephen to remember a sacrilegious joke, the twists of levity and pain form an even more elaborate knot as his hallucination ties together in one identity: mismatched twins, the Virgin Mother, a diseased whore, and the man who enjoys being victimized sexually by another. This bizarre identity then names the Holy Ghost as its betrayer and the (indirect) murderer of his own son (424). Florry's insistence that Stephen is "a spoiled priest" sparks a vision that suggests that Stephen feels he has ruined himself. Stephen's hallucination of himself as "Simon Stephen Cardinal Dedalus" seems inspired by Flaubert's description of the Queen of Sheba appearing in a vision to tempt Saint Anthony.[22] The actions of the dwarves recall not only those of Flaubert's "Douze négrillons crépus" but also Lynch's repeated efforts to get a "nickle dime bumshow" from the whores (348). Father and son, tormenter and tormented, religious figure and whore once again unite in one being that Stephen claims as self.

Bloom accepts punishment as a romping charade, and his two immolations are playful rituals from which he emerges to begin casually again, but Stephen, like Severin, seems driven toward real torture and real annihilation. When he gives his hand to Zoe and "chants to the air of the bloodoath in the *Dusk of the Gods*," he smilingly but seriously contracts himself to the Venus who "Macht uns alle kaput" (457). Zoe's mocking pronouncements, "Blue eyed beauty," "No wit," "Woman's hand," remind Stephen of the devastating punishments he suffered at school when his palms were beaten, but despite his denial of courage he urges her to "Continue. Lie. Hold me. Caress" (457–58). The pathos of Severin's situation, banished in the broad comedy of Bloom's ordeals, reappears in Stephen's briefer, quieter visions. Because Bloom and Stephen are Siamese twins of a sort, mystically connected, Stephen's more profoundly experienced pain gives tragic shadings to Bloom's comedy.

When both men look into the mirror together they see, in the image of Shakespeare that appears, the past, present, and future of vulnerable man bound to changeable woman. Shakespeare's garbled speech comments on the situation that obsesses each of them. Of course, Bloom shares an obvious problem with the cuckolded

Shakespeare, and as the hallucination that directly precedes this vision demonstrates, Bloom realizes that he has played the roles of both Iago and Othello, "bawd and cuckold" (174). He has, in fact, exceeded Othello in one sense: his Desdemona actually is an adulteress. But "Thursdaymomun" suggests someone other than the (on) Thursday moaning, adulterous Molly (463). Stephen has told Zoe that he was born on a Thursday (458). He has also argued that Anne Hathaway was the inspiration for Desdemona and through a series of associations mentally connected guilty Anne to his own innocent mother. May Dedalus is the Thursday *maman* that he fears he has killed, a sacrifice to his pride and his "unremitting intellect" (174). However, Stephen does, as he claims, "have reasons" to take on the role of Hamlet because May, like Mary in his joke, has been corrupted by "the sacred pigeon," who, in Stephen's view, resembles Claudius, in being a poisoner of pious ears (170). And in a horrible echo of the comic scene in which Bello tries to sell Bloom to "the Caliph Haroun al Raschid," May offers up her son to the "corpsechewer" (440, 474). Stephen rejects union in "love, grief and agony" with "The Mother" as Christ and escapes into the street to seek in physical pain some relief from his emotional pain (475).

Stephen's contemptuous taunting of the soldiers and Bloom's crawling to Boylan and Molly (in his hallucination) are such obviously different modes of behavior that they seem to arise from diametrically opposed attitudes, but both reflect and comment on aspects of Sacher-Masoch's vision. In *Venus in Furs*, Wanda and Severin consider moving to a country where slavery is legal but decide against it because the essence of their shared fantasy is that the slave be compelled to submit out of love "not by law, right, or power" (Sacher-Masoch 165). Bloom, in "flunkey's prune plush coat" masturbating as he watches his dream-vision of Boylan and Molly, and Stephen, declaring "*Non serviam*" to church and state and, determinedly weaponless, accepting meek martyrdom to the representatives of Britain, both enact roles that Severin finds compatible (461, 475). Theodore Reik's description of the masochist seems applicable to all three:

> He exhibits the punishment but also its failure. He shows his submission certainly, but he also shows his invincible rebellion, dem-

onstrating that he gains pleasure despite the discomfort. . . . He
cannot be broken from the outside. He has an inexhaustible capacity for taking a beating and yet he knows unconsciously that he is
not licked.[23]

By telling the basic story of all "flagellation literature" simultaneously in a farcical and a heroic form and then interweaving the two
so that they comment continuously upon each other, Joyce opens
out *Venus in Furs* to tell us more about the pleasures within and the
compulsions behind masochism than can Sacher-Masoch, the realist
mode of whose story demands that he treat it seriously.

But "Circe" is positioned within *Ulysses* as far more than a reinterpretation of Sacher-Masoch's novel. It is the climactic chapter
of the novel, the chapter in which Bloom and Stephen move as close
as they will come on that day to resolving their problems. The masochistic themes, which reach their dramatic culmination in "Circe,"
run through all of *Ulysses*, as do allusions to *Venus in Furs*. And it
is at the site of these allusions that the text stresses the importance
of women's active agency to affect the interchange between men's
masochistic and procreative desires.

Ellmann mentions one instance in which Joyce uses a detail from
Sacher-Masoch's novel not limited to "Circe." "The marble statu-
ette that Bloom takes home in the rain, and . . . the nymph, 'beautiful immortal', whose 'classic curves' are pictured above his bed,
are paralleled in the 'stonecold and pure' plaster cast of Venus to
which Severin prays in *Venus in Furs*" (Ellmann 370). Deleuze's interpretation of *Venus in Furs* centers on Severin's worship of the
statue of Venus. In the frozen figure of the marble goddess, Deleuze
sees the masochist's "ideal," a female who appears "cold—maternal—severe" (Deleuze 45). The combination of coldness and cruelty with maternity links it with death. Deleuze agrees with Edmund Bergler in finding "the specific element of masochism is the
oral mother, the ideal of coldness, solicitude, and death" (Deleuze
49). One might certainly question whether Wanda, in *Venus in Furs*,
ever appears in this guise. Cruel yet maternally solicitous Wanda
is, but deathly she is not, unless one brings to bear on the novel
Freud's (and Bergler's) interpretation of masochism as a manifesta-
tion of the death drive. The cold nymph in *Ulysses*, like the ghost

of Stephen's mother, signifies denial of sexuality, not ideal satisfaction. As in *Venus in Furs* where the active, desiring as well as desirable, and ultimately uncontrollable Wanda replaces the statue on whom Severin projects his fantasies, in *Ulysses* willful, fertile, lascivious Molly vanquishes the image of the pure nymph and her deathly decree, "No more desire" (450).

Rather than functioning to preserve and affirm the authority of all their prior texts, *Ulysses*'s quotations of *Venus in Furs* intensify the rebellious questioning of the authority of canonical texts that is intrinsic to Sacher-Masoch's aesthetic. This aesthetic prominently structures *Venus in Furs*' biblical references.[24] For example, the novel's epigraph is, "The Lord hath smitten him by the hand of a woman," and Severin, pondering the passage, cannot help "envying the heathen Holofernes." After some further reflection about how "unchivalrous" the language of the Old Testament is, Severin wonders, "What must I do for him to smite *me*?" (129) The masochist's impudent negation of the law by transforming punishment into pleasure could hardly, it seems, be more clearly expressed. Yet Joyce's reworking of this material extends its rejection of religious authority into a critique of the paternalistic principles underlying it. Sacher-Masoch's continual references to "a small woman's hand" as a symbol of her transcendent power are echoed in Stephen's belief that he collapsed, after leaving the whorehouse, because of "the reapparition of a matutinal cloud . . . at first no bigger than a woman's hand" (545). The biblical Elijah, in the midst of his battles with Jezebel and her priests of Baal, prays for rain, which comes when "a little cloud [arises], out of the sea, like a man's hand" (Kings 18:44). Jezebel, of course, is later defeated, but the feminization of the hand as sign in Sacher-Masoch's and Joyce's elaborate systems of woman worship suggests that there is no power above woman's to strike man or lift him into new life.

Nonetheless, *Venus in Furs* ends with an apparent repudiation of female dominance and a return to ordinary gender relations. Severin declares himself "cured" of his desire to be whipped, a cure he demonstrates by berating and threatening his peasant mistress for bringing him improperly cooked eggs (228, 125). Still, his admissions that his story is written with "the red blood that drips from his heart" when he remembers Wanda (126) and that thoughts of even his most extreme sufferings with her continue to bring irrepressible smiles to his face, undermine the moral that he says he has drawn from his experience. The conclusion further undercuts our sense of the cure's value with Severin's explanation that his desires have been tamed through substitution of a new cynicism, in which women are no more than "the sacred wenches of Benares" and man "Plato's rooster," for the passionate mysticism that had made both "images of God" (229). We are shown not a return to gender norms and the family that they have traditionally been credited with making possible, but instead a sour, sterile isolation in which Severin must always reject the eggs his woman offers in order to keep her under his control.

Thus it seems particularly odd that many critics have read a new gender hierarchy and the promise of another pregnancy in Joyce's repetition of the eggs theme with Molly's annoyed opening remark, "Yes because he never did a thing like that before as ask to get his breakfast in bed with a couple of eggs" (608). Sultan, for instance, believes that Bloom asks Molly to make his breakfast because "he has recovered his manhood" and consequently "wants uxorial service from her" (402, 420). Fritz Senn's interpretation, that Bloom did not ask for eggs in the morning but that Molly simply misunderstood his "somnolent mumblings," seems more sensible.[25] In Molly's astounded view, Bloom seems to have turned into hardly less of a tyrant than the "cured" Severin, but Bloom's last thoughts before falling asleep completely lack Severin's affected harshness.

Masochism, as Sacher-Masoch depicts it, is the choice to be martyred in the name of love. He shows no romantic choices other than absolute submission to vicious tortures or brutal domination. But Bloom, returned to "Ithaca," having appropriated "the viscous cream ordinarily reserved for the breakfast of his wife Marion (Molly)" but also having "kissed the plump mellow smellow melons of her rump" seems to have reached a level of self-assertion he finds satisfactory (552, 604). Because in *Ulysses*, men's passionate, swooning surrender, such as Bloom experienced "under wild ferns on Howth," appears as an end in itself that need not be followed by the infliction of torture (although Bloom is perfectly willing, at least in fantasy, that it be), there is no need to show a reversal of power in which woman is trampled back to her usual place as part of a representation of masculine self-assertion (144).

Instead, in contrast to Sacher-Masoch, Joyce insists on the compatibility of the desire to submit to the will of woman with (hetero)sexually active masculinity. Although not attracted, as Bloom is, to the idea of physical pain, Stephen seems equally unattracted to the role of sexual aggressor. He seems to long to be "ravished" as thoroughly as Bloom was on Howth. He interrupts his theory of the marital woes of Shakespeare, "overborne in a cornfield" and forever "undone" with the surprisingly envious (silent) comments "And my turn? When? Come!" and "Wait to be wooed and won. Ay, meacock. Who will woo you?" (161, 157, 173). If Shakespeare "left her [Anne Hathaway] and gained the world of men," Stephen remains skeptical about that gain, commenting, "But his boywomen are the women of a boy. Their life and speech are lent them by males" (157). Faced with the choice between exile from woman into the world of men or exile from the world of men because of the overpowering presence of a woman whose life and speech are her own, Stephen chooses the latter, or rather begs to be chosen. "Touch me. . . . Touch, touch me" is Stephen's erotic litany, reflected in Bloom's "We are their harps" (41, 223).

Neither Molly's monologue nor Bloom's reminiscence indicates that Bloom was more masterful with Molly in the early days of their marriage than he is when the novel opens. In fact, while she was still "dying to find out was he circumcised," his way of getting her to grant him a sexual favor was to threaten to "kneel down in the wet" (615). Yet Bloom impregnated Molly twice. Joyce seems to be suggesting that submissiveness, even masochism, far from presenting an impediment to procreation, can be a way to express virile passion, that a "real man" can be "strong to the verge of weakness" and even beyond (532). To this extent Joyce does seem "close in spirit" to Ellis, as Brown says (85), especially to the spirit expressed in Ellis's claims that while

> masochism is commonly regarded . . . in man as a sort of inversion of the normal masculine emotional attitude . . . this view is not altogether justified. . . . In a minor degree, not amounting to a com-

plete perversion of the sexual instinct, this sentiment of
abnegation, the desire to be even physically subjected to the adored
woman, cannot be regarded as abnormal. . . . It may, indeed, be
said that passion in its more lyric exaltations almost necessarily involves some resort to masochistic expression. (111–12)

Joyce's transmission of this theory is central to *Ulysses*'s rebellion
against the newly forming norms of sexual behavior because, as
James Kincaid shows, Ellis goes against modern values in naturalizing the connection between erotic pain and love.[26] And he goes further in suggesting that male submission belongs by nature to
courtship ritual.

The two imperatives that come to Stephen in the library—"Act.
Be acted on"—are shown to be not inherently contradictory; yet,
neither Bloom nor Stephen seems capable of acting with a woman
on June 16th in any way except to avoid contact with her (173). Both
are haunted by the knowledge that men who act with women often
do so violently and against their own best interests. Stephen notes
that Othello "acts and is acted on. Lover of an ideal or a perversion,
like José he kills the real Carmen" (174). They see in male erotic
action a circuit of self-torture in which man places woman between
two aspects of himself and then kills her to insure "that the moor
in him shall suffer." Their solution is to tighten the circle by exclud-
ing her (passionately desired) presence. Neither man acts to satisfy
his much-reiterated longing for loving contact with a woman. And
this avoidance of the thing desired is also a kind of masochism.

While *Ulysses* may seem to present many variations of masochistic
behavior, it actually divides masochism into two types: the eroticization of pain and the eroticization of denial.[27] The first, in all its
infinite variety, is shown to be not incompatible with procreative
sexual activity. The second must be, because it depends on strict
avoidance of sexual intercourse with a responsive woman.

Joyce gives us many clues to the mystery of why Stephen "*Auton-
timerumenos*" spends his time toadying to men he despises and
drunkenly entertaining whores who repel him and why Bloom has
not had "complete carnal intercourse, with ejaculation of semen
within the natural female organ" in eleven years (173, 605). In addition to desire, both men feel toward women a complex mixture

of contempt, pity, and guilt. David Hayman conjectures that Molly is "the ultimate siren" in "Sirens," but that paradoxically "Ulysses-Bloom" would be saved if he could go to her rather than staying away, "paralyzed by fear and guilt."[28] Still, since Bloom's guilt seems to arise from his sexual neglect of Molly, his fear seems to be the deciding emotion. Both Bloom's and Stephen's fear of women and reluctance to have reciprocal sexual contact with them might be explained by their belief that women are in some way evil, contemptible creatures.

Their contempt for women is conventional; indeed, it is the most conventional sentiment each man shows during the course of the day.[29] Ellmann finds a great difference between Stephen's and Bloom's thoughts about women. He writes, "For Stephen women are distant creatures, changeable as the moon and to be seen mythically as great sources of fertility and corruption. . . . Bloom has a different view. . . . Women, not woman, interest him" (Ellmann, *Ulysses* 47). While this is generally the case, Bloom's is not always, as Ellmann calls it, a "kindlier vision" (Ellmann 48). Stephen's references to "woman's unclean loins, of man's flesh made not in God's likeness, the serpent's prey" and "Eve. Naked wheatbellied sin. A snake coils her, fang in's kiss" sound less like Bloom than Deasy, holding forth about Cassandra, Eve, Helen, and MacMurrough's wife, each "a woman who was no better than she should be" (12, 163, 29). And Stephen's cruel image of his mother as Ireland, the feminized betrayer—"thou hast suckled me with a bitter milk . . . thou hast left me alone for ever in the dark ways of my bitterness: and with a kiss of ashes thou hast kissed my mouth" is less like Bloom's vision of the Promised Land as "the grey sunken cunt of the world," through no fault of its/her own, than like the citizen's pronouncement that a "dishonoured wife [is] the cause of all our misfortunes" (322, 50, 266). However, Stephen's ungrateful description of the prostitute he had in Fumbally's lane as having a "shefiend's whiteness" seems as much like Bloom's characterization of Gerty as "that little limping devil," as it is like Lenehan's reference to Molly's breasts as "Hell's delights" (39, 303, 193).

In Bloom's case the contempt often seems to result from his resentment of his own situation as husband to a wife who "wears the pants." Bloom's oscillations in attitude toward women often seem

to strategically assert male subjectivity, to remind himself that he
chooses to submit. An early morning exchange with the cat reveals
how quickly Bloom can pass from wounded pride to contempt:
"Wonder what I look like to her. Height of a tower? No she can
jump me.—Afraid of the chickens she is, he said mockingly. . . . I
never saw such a stupid pussens. . . . " Still these insults are framed
by his naturalization not only of her viciousness—"Cruel. Her nature"—but also of the masochistic response he projects onto her
prey—"Curious mice never squeal. seem to like it"—and his serving
her breakfast as generously as he does Molly's, before he has his own
(45). At one point the thought of a married sailor's return home
reminds Bloom of going "into the house of bondage," but elsewhere this destination seems to him simply part of his heritage, his
subordination part of "what life is after all" (310, 101). His angry
response to the nymph's rejection, that he has never gotten a "stud-
fee" but put in "sixteen years of black slave labour" without hope
of "five shillings alimony" is followed by some arrogant posturing
toward Bella, but he soon settles into another fantasy of ecstatic
servitude (452). Bloom's recognition that the "Flower to console"
him has a pin that "cuts lo" does not seem to put him off (216). As
he tells his aristocratic threateners, "I love the danger" (381).

  For Stephen contempt is clearly a direct response to unbearable
pity and guilt. Where Bloom vacillates between scornful resentment
of women, as enslaving slaves, and veneration of them as cruel goddesses, Stephen's position is fixed; he is paralyzed between sympathy
and repudiation. If he is ashamed of praying for a look under a
widow's skirts, he makes her a "squaw," or of shouting "*naked
women*" he defiantly asks, "What else were they invented for?" (34).
Haunted by the memory of his dying mother weeping over "love's
bitter mystery," knowing that "someone killed her," and that he
has denied her last request, Stephen must reduce her from the one
who "had saved him from being trampled under foot" to an "all-
woombing tomb" (8, 5, 28, 40). On the beach, the "shellcocoacol-
oured" waters make him think of his failure to save his mother, and
later, drinking rich cocoa with Bloom, he remembers his sister, Dilly,
"waiting for some weak Trinidad shell cocoa that was in the soot-
coated kettle to be done so that she and he could drink it with the
oatmeal water for milk" (30, 507). But he has deserted her, despite

his knowledge that "[s]he is drowning" in the same element that took May, the oppressive patriarchy of Dublin, in which women are brutally and inescapably reduced to their biological functions (200). After leaving Dilly to her fate, Stephen is next seen drunkenly arguing that birth control devices should never be used and that if a woman's life is endangered in childbirth, "that earthly mother which was but a dam to bear forth beastly should die" (319). The professor's comparison of Stephen to Antisthenes, who was full of bitterness because "he was the son of a noble and a bond woman," may be more apt than it seems at first (122).

Bloom, less bitter than Stephen, has no lack of sympathy for women. The rumor that Mr. Power keeps a mistress makes Bloom think "Not pleasant for the wife" (77). The greyness of John O'Connell's beard (a sign of "temper getting cross") brings a sympathetic thought of Mrs. O'Connell (89). Bloom is sorry for skinny, ragged Dilly and worn-out Mrs. Breen. His vengeful fantasy of Molly old and abandoned, "Big spanishy eyes goggling at nothing" ends with a snap of honest recollection that "too much happy bores" him (278). Nevertheless, this compassion for the generally vulnerable position of women does not seem to keep Bloom from seeing them as possible sexual partners. He successfully reminds himself "be on your guard not to feel too much pity" for Gerty and, through the alter-ego Virag, checks his sympathy for Kitty (308).

Like Stephen, Bloom is most profoundly affected, even paralyzed by his pity for mothers. His response to the knowledge that Molly has cuckolded him and to the teasing threats of the girls in "Nausicaa" to "give it to him" on his "beetoteetum" is defiantly virile, but he becomes impotent after overhearing Mrs. Purefoy's screams in childbed (219, 290). In "Hades" Bloom's thoughts of "women dead in childbirth," the way women must be kept from thinking of death "to conceive at all," the "mother and deadborn child . . . buried in the one coffin," and the "love that kills" blend in with the other musings on death (86, 89, 90, 94). But he does not leave this theme behind in the graveyard. Of Dedalus, Bloom thinks "Fifteen children he had. Birth every year almost," and later, "Wore out his wife: now sings" (124, 225). His confusion over Mrs. Purefoy's name ("Mrs Beaufoy, Purefoy") seems to come from a similar judgment (305). Philip Beaufoy is associated in his mind with "the mas-

terstroke" and with the sort of sentimental and romantic literature
that inspires Gerty's dreams of marriage in "a nice snug cozy little
homely house" where a kind, sober, hardworking husband gives "his
dear little wifey a good hearty hug" (130, 289). Thinking of the
romantic pleasures of girlhood, Bloom decides "Sad however because it lasts only a few years" (305). His next thoughts are of Mrs.
Dignam's bereavement, "Mrs Beaufoy, Purefoy," and Mrs. Breen,
"once like that too, marriageable," all of whom have been knocked
low by the masterstroke from "the lord and master" (305, 129).
"Matcham often thinks the laughing witch. Poor Mrs. Purefoy"
(230). The masterstroke brings agony, "belly swollen out," then the
difficulties of childbirth of which Bloom thinks "kill me that
would" (132). As the day passes with Bloom "woman's woe with
wonder pondering," it becomes clear that although he wanted and
still wants "a woman who can deliver the goods," he does not want
to sentence Molly to "Life with hard labour" or even to another
fruitless ordeal like her last pregnancy (318, 232, 132).

Molly, herself, despite her "Gea-Tellus" posture in the bed and
ardent love of nature seems by no means eager to have another baby
(606). She wishes men could know "what I went through with
Milly," and thinks of Mr. Purefoy, "not satisfied till they have us
swollen out like elephants" (611). Her memories of her girlhood
fears of being left "with a child embarazada" inspire hostile
thoughts about men and pleasant reminiscence of how she "tormented the life out of" one of her suitors (626). Her fear about
menstruating too early is balanced by relief that "anyhow he didnt
make me pregnant" (633). Thoughts of the devious ways of men
cause her to think of the deformed babies in "the Aristocrats Mas-
terpiece" and to comment "as if we hadnt enough of that in real
life" (633). The one time that she considers allowing Bloom to impregnate her, her phrasing—"suppose I risked having another"—
suggests that his sexual practices have not frustrated any maternal
desires on her part (611). In fact, her comment on Rudy's death—"I
knew well Id never have another"—implies that she decided then
not to become pregnant again; not an unusual decision for a mother
in her situation to make (640). Since she and Bloom had "normal"
sex just "5 weeks previous, viz. 27 November 1893, to the birth"
there seems to have been no reason for her to have known that preg-

nancy was no longer a possibility unless she had decided to tell Bloom to begin avoiding ejaculating inside her vagina (605).

Sultan has taken the line in Joyce's March 22 letter to Frank Budgen, "am working hard at *Oxen of the Sun*, the idea being the crime committed against fecundity by sterilizing the act of coition," to mean that Joyce was strictly opposed to contraceptives (285–95). But, as Brown points out, fertility in "Oxen of the Sun" seems to be as much of a curse as a blessing (70–78). When Bannon and Mulligan arrive at the hospital, the latter entertains the crowd with some boasting about his willingness to impregnate all attractive women "the poorest kitchenwench no less than the opulent lady of fashion," and Bannon regrets being without his "cloak" (condom) when he was with Milly in Mulligar (329, 331). Mulligan's belly has "never bore a bastard" and never will, but fifteen-year-old Milly's can, as the discussion of the problems with birth control devices that follows reminds us (330). Bloom's reminiscence of his first sexual experience also implies that human sympathy opposes fertility in some cases. All the while Mrs. Purefoy screams, trying to give her child life, as Bloom insists, "at the risk of her own" (343).

Certain word choices in the parodies also give the scene in the maternity hospital unpleasant reverberations. In a novel with as many references to Shakespeare as *Ulysses*, Bannon's complaint about traveling without his cloak seems intended to bring Sonnet 34 to mind—"Why didst thou promise such a beauteous day/ And make me travel forth without my cloak"—a sonnet that has much to say about "disgrace," "shame," "loss," and "offense." In the passage that parodies Victorian raptures on the birth of a child, Joyce's choice of the name "Doady" for Mr. Purefoy is even more ominously suggestive because it is Dora Copperfield's nickname for her husband (343). In Dickens's novel, Dora's baby dies just after birth: "The spirit fluttered for a moment on the threshold of its little prison, and unconscious of captivity, took wing."[30] Afterward Dora weakens and dies herself. Opposed to Dickens's sentimental vision is the nighttown apparition of maternity as Black Mass: "On the altarstone Mrs Mina Purefoy, goddess of unreason, lies, naked, fettered, a chalice resting on her swollen belly" (469).

Both Stephen and Bloom remember a line from Meredith's *The Ordeal of Richard Feverel*: "The sentimentalist is he who would enjoy without incurring the immense debtorship for a thing done" (164, 337). In this novel, as in Dickens's, the sweet young heroine also dies because she is too weakened by childbirth to face the problems of her marriage. If Joyce differs from Sacher-Masoch in depicting male submission as potentially harmless, he represents female submission as horrific sacrifice, all the more terrible because it is generally celebrated by society and in literature. Stephen and Bloom have seen the mothers eviscerated on the altar. And, unlike the Victorian voice of "Oxen of the Sun," who praises Purefoy for "knock[ing] another child out of her," they are not sentimentalists, and they know that their love, even if it is submissive rather than aggressive, aims to recreate their own lives at the expense of their beloveds' safety and romantic dreams (334).

One alternative to incurring this immense debt is to avoid sexual contact with women. As Deasy says of the Jews, they cannot be persecuted if they are never "let in" (30). "Eunuch. One way out of it," notes Bloom (67). Less extreme escapes are offered by the bachelors who "Unwed, unfancied, ware of wiles . . . fingerponder nightly each his variorum edition of *The Taming of the Shrew*" (175). Perhaps the most seductive alternative is offered by the sailor of "Eumaeus," whose once painful physical memento of Antonio "a Greek" recalls Severin's ultimate sexual encounter with the Greek who, at least temporarily, whips him past all desiring (516). But Stephen as well as Bloom "pointedly turn[s] a deaf ear" not only to "six sixteen," "Antonio and so forth" but to all the day's enticements away from union with woman (527–28). "Both admitted the alternately stimulating and obtunding influence of heterosexual magnetism," and both obey its pull (544).

Bloom makes his choice in "Hades" and spends his day moving circuitously, back to "a woman . . . Life, life" (74). He rejects the sterility of the antisexual nymph but accepts his role as "Adorer of the adulterous rump," and glories in "divaricated thighs" even when they are not spread for him alone (432, 450). Stephen rejects the sterile adoration of death offered by the ghost mother but accepts "the pain of love," "the bitter mystery" that the live mother knew and, as he regains consciousness, relives the moment when he tried to give her comfort (5). At the end of "Circe" the ruby that has haunted Bloom throughout the episode is out of the circus ring and placed on Rudy's breast. The men's evasive rituals of sterile masochism are over and the painful and pleasurable submission to and responsibility for the act of procreation must begin.

Nothing seems settled at the end of *Ulysses*, but progress toward some sort of interchange with a woman has been made. Bloom has returned to the womb not that bore him but to the one that can, and might if it pleases Molly, bear more of his children. Stephen, in contrast, has rejected "the Oedipal mate" who could help him "fill the void left by his mother's death" (Hayman 35). Possibly he does so because she could never be "*sua donna*" or answer his inner plea "*Amor me solo*," nor could she give him a child that he could acknowledge as his own (173, 199). Molly fantasizes about a shining clean poet like "those fine young men I could see down in Margate Strand bathing," a Buck Mulligan, in fact, with whom she could while away some lonely hours (638). Stephen is moving not toward adultery but toward marriage, that terrifying place that has almost finished Bloom and may "immolate" Stephen, "consenting," the only place where the pain of love can result in joyously welcomed new life (567).

In its many and concluding suggestions that women are most important to men as potential mothers, *Ulysses* is no feminist novel. Yet in its persuasive representation of submissiveness as the most appropriate attitude for a man to adopt toward the woman who can give him children, *Ulysses* seems hardly as misogynistic as some critics find it. While Joyce's, as well as Bloom's and Stephen's, focus in relations between men and women is placed firmly on the man's search for identity, as the novel's title suggests, a masculinity that can combine passionate heterosexuality with empathic recognition of and deference to the needs and desires of women is continually disclosed as an ideal.

Ulysses appeared at a crucial historical moment when the homophobia which, as Eve Kosofsky Sedgwick has shown, had been increasingly deployed in literary, legal, and medical texts to regulate all relations between men[31] was extended, by pseudoscientific psychological theorizing, to radically constrict possibilities in men's romantic relations with women, as well. Allied with Ellis and against Ellis's precursor Krafft-Ebing and his successor Freud, Joyce offers an alternative reading of the male masochist as a man well suited to act heterosexually, marry, beget and raise children. Idealizing male masochism on these grounds is hardly synonymous with championing the cause of women's liberation. Still it creates a model for marriage that offers women more space to voice their own concerns than exists in the male-dominated marriage that psychoanalytic theory would describe as healthier and more normal. And it challenges psychoanalysis's implicit categorization of gentle, yielding husbands as gynophobic latent homosexuals.

Joyce recovers his ideal of male submission to woman from the stigmatizing label "masochism," through the most masochistic of strategies. He centers the narrative on two masochists who refuse to be cured and vigorously applies to them the very discourses that should mark them as perverse. This intertextuality evokes prior texts and cultural voices only to inculcate in the reader a salutary sense of exile, for if normality must mean the opposite of what Bloom achieves, how could anyone who ever hopes to love endure a return to it?

3

SEVERED HEADS
AND WHITE ROSES
Masochism and the Sacrifice of Men
in D. H. Lawrence and Iris Murdoch

When we love, we forgive and forget everything, for we have no
choice. . . . We are driven by a gentle and mysterious power that
deprives us of all will and reason, and we are swept along with no
thought for the morrow.

>   Leopold von Sacher-Masoch, *Venus in Furs*

The sea is streaked red with Adonis
The lights flicker red in small jars.
Wheat shoots rise new by the altar,
    flower from the swift seed.

>   Ezra Pound, Canto XLVII

IN *ULYSSES* COMPLETE heterosexual contact with woman, imagined as including recognition of her autonomous feelings and
needs, is equated with masochism, since such closeness to woman is
seen as inevitably bringing the (male) lover pain. However, the
lover's pain is not accounted for psychoanalytically as arising from
fear of feminization through contact with woman. Instead, the
painfulness of love is attributed to love's power to make man aware
of the injustice of woman's position in society and acutely concerned with helping her. In a sense then, one might say that Joyce
represents masochism as part of the sacrificial nature loving has for
men. To love is to refuse one's masculine birthright, the power of
a Simon Dedalus who uses his wife like a bondslave until she dies
and then goes on his way blithely singing, and instead to choose,

like Leopold Bloom, to return to the house of bondage, where society keeps woman immured, and to serve her. Conventional masculinity becomes a sacrifice, offered up in the name of love.

Other texts construct images of more extreme masochistic sacrifices than that of officially defined masculine identity and depict
male masochists who go far beyond recognition of the Other. Their
gestures of resistance to the social and cultural forces that make her
Other approach something like redemptive self-sacrifice. In these
images the holy and the transgressive touch, as they do in the image
of the white rose, which has traditionally been an icon, according
to context, of both sacred and profane love.[1]

Because psychoanalytic theory privileges the family, its vision of
masochism includes Freud's reinterpretation of religious experience
as repressed memory of oceanic connection to the mother or as worship of an imago of the father as omnipotent. As a result, the in-
teraction of masochistic desire with religious/cultural ideology is
obscured. Jessica Benjamin and Gilles Deleuze and Félix Guattari
have recognized the cost of obscuring this connection and have, in
very different ways, argued against classic psychoanalytic under-
standings of masochism's dynamics. Benjamin sees in the theory of
the Oedipus Complex a "sanitized" version of authority that "denies the fear and submission that paternal power has historically inspired," and, moreover, that affirms the cultural edict demanding
"rejection of femininity" as a precondition to attaining mature masculinity. She believes that in so doing, psychoanalytic theory continues cultural ideology's project of sanctifying actual fathers as representatives of divine omnipotence, and demonizing actual mothers
as representatives of the forces of repression, illusion, and loss of
identity. Benjamin sees masochism as an expression of the "desire
for recognition," which she believes psychoanalysts misconstrue as
renunciation of identity and disavowal of reality. She attributes this
misunderstanding to psychoanalysis focusing on a "hidden inner
world" structured by early childhood familial relations and ignoring
"the mystifying outer world of power and powerlessness."[2] In the
two volumes of *Capitalism and Schizophrenia*, Deleuze and Guattari
move beyond the Freudian perspective that had earlier informed
Deleuze's discussion of masochism in his commentary on *Venus in
Furs*. Deleuze and Guattari argue for a social reading of masochism

that sees neither the father nor the mother as the primary cause of the desire to be beaten or forced into sexual submission, but rather sees the parents as "subordinate agents of transmission or execution" of "the group fantasy." Masochism itself is read as a process through which some "bring[ ] forth a plane of consistency of desire," and thus attain "an achieved state in which desire no longer lacks anything but fills itself and constructs its own field of immanence."[3] Deleuze and Guattari compare this process to those characteristic of religious mysticism. Although Benjamin sees the failure of the standard psychoanalytic approach in its refusal to recognize the affinity between patriarchal religion and the Oedipal Complex, and Deleuze and Guattari see its failure in its lack of attention to the successful mysticism of masochism, both approaches examine sexual masochism as a quasi-religious response to society and culture.

Behaviors that would now be considered masochistic have been part of religious rituals at least as long as they have been a part of courtship rituals. Yet the psychological theories most frequently drawn on by literary critics have had relatively little to say about the connection between sexual and religious pursuits of pain. Freud was silent on the subject of what he might have labeled religious masochism. There is only a hint of his characteristic criticism of Christianity in his description of "the moral masochist" as one who "always turns his cheek whenever he has a chance of receiving a blow." Theodor Reik extensively discusses what he considers masochistic elements of Christianity. But, like Freud, he carefully distinguishes between sexual masochism and the masochism that, in Freud's words, "is chiefly remarkable for having loosened its connection with what we recognize as sexuality"—Reik calls it "social masochism."[4] For him, "the sexual masochist" and the socially masochistic "martyr or saint" represent different poles of experience.

In contrast, Georges Bataille deconstructs this dichotomy, arguing that "all eroticism has a sacramental character" and that "the sanctity of transgression" attached to sacrificial acts derives from the metaphoric connection between human sacrifice and sexual intercourse. But in his insistence that historically "the female partner in eroticism was seen as the victim, the male as the sacrificer," Bataille determinedly ignores the evidence that the sacrificial victim is most frequently imagined as male, evidence he himself has provided in a number of the illustrations of his book and in the example of Christianity,[5] not to mention Egyptian, Greek, and Roman mythology and fertility ritual. Film and modern literary representations of sacrificial masochism have not so scrupulously maintained the divisions between saint and sinner or masculine and feminine, although, as in Bataille's otherwise daring work, a normative impulse toward phallocentric binarism often manifests itself concurrently with the deconstructive strategy.

By closely examining texts that place masochistic ritual at the center of their troping of poetic justice, we can see how the erotic and the sacred can meet in the image of male sacrifice. The concept of poetic justice is in its essence mystical and predicated on belief in divine providence. In some ways a metaphysical approach to male masochism is ideally suited to the demand Modernism puts on narratives to create plausible characters without resort to nineteenth-century Realism. Having abandoned the Victorian approach to characterization, which relied on an exhaustive recounting of every social, familial, and even genetic detail of the main characters' lives that might explain their behavior, Modernists and their successors have tended either to provide clues for a Freudian reading of motivation or to represent motives as arising from chance and circumstance. As Deleuze and Guattari point out, the popularization of psychoanalysis in our time has relentlessly labeled naïve any explanation of human motivation that does not return to the Oedipal theory.[6] Modern and contemporary texts often struggle out of the grip of Freudianism into a passionately naïve embrace of mysticism about where impulses come from, gesturing toward an eros that turns over the world's hierarchies and rights its wrongs, not always in carnivalesque play but also in terrible earnest.

Just as in *Civilization and Its Discontents* Freud had to imagine an Eros powerful enough to stand against the Thanatos that he imagined transcending men's lives and acting as the Unseen Mover behind such horrors as fascism, the anti-Freudian authors often seem driven to conjure up an Eros that can break them out of the Oedipal box into history and the world. For these writers metaphysical representation of masochism functions textually similarly to the way Deleuze and Guattari say the enactment of ritual does for masochists, to clear away the mapping imposed on desire by the domi-

nant culture and thus to allow the emergence of another sort of
vision, one that enables resistance.

Before going on to discuss D. H. Lawrence's and Iris Murdoch's
complex resistances of psychoanalytic construction and contextualization of the masochist, I will look at the simpler and more sche-
matic representation of sacrificial male masochism in the much-re-
viled film, *The Night Porter* (dir. Liliana Cavani, 1974). The film has
received most of its negative criticism on the grounds that it por-
trays the heroine, a concentration camp survivor, as a masochist.[7]
This interpretation is debatable, first because the role of Lucia is
played by Charlotte Rampling so nearly without affect that she often
seems in a state of shock rather than masochistic, and second because the narrative line is almost entirely concerned with the transformation of her lover, Max (Dirk Bogarde), from a Nazi into the
consenting victim of a fascistic society that forces him to choose
between dying and renouncing his pleasurably agonizing love.
Merely to dramatize such a choice as the demand of society calls
into question the Freudian concept of masochism as an expression
of a primal death drive or a response to social restrictions on love,
e.g. the incest taboo.[8] The *Liebestod* retains its masochistic shading
in *The Night Porter*, but through its opposition to Freudian readings
of "sadomasochism," it gains a dimension of political resistance.

The film begins by following Max through his duties as the night
porter in an elegant small hotel in Vienna. Until the arrival of Lucia,
the hotel seems entirely occupied by aging former Nazis for whom
Max exhibits weary contempt but whose eccentric desires he pa-
tiently gratifies. Caught in a sort of existentialist hell, he seems compelled to go on forever performing the same ludicrous and disgusting rituals, serving these grotesque bullies to whom he once pledged
himself. But we soon learn that he is only in purgatory. He is awaiting his trial, an ironically inverted secret procedure through which
the former SS officers who use the hotel, and not incidentally who
also occupy positions of power in the new Austria, are confronted
with carefully gathered documentary evidence and eyewitnesses of
their crimes, that are afterward "filed," that is, destroyed. While the
"judges" sanctimoniously explain to Max that the trial is a sort of
talking cure, its purpose being the attainment of self-knowledge
that will relieve guilt, he insists on its true function: the erasure of

the living evidence that the positive identities of the empowered are gained at the expense of excluded others.[9] Before Lucia comes on the scene, the film recalls Kafka's *The Trial* with its soul-sick protagonist and its claustrophobic setting within a world of bureaucratic evil. The crucial difference is that we are always aware that Max's misery is not without explanation, and that his sufferings are emphatically not cause to question divine justice. However, his interactions with Lucia do much to redefine traditional concepts of how poetic justice is achieved.

Brought back in contact with him by chance and seemingly as surprised as he is to find that she desires him, Lucia instructs Max in a masochism that is shown to redeem him. A performance of *The Magic Flute* by her conductor-husband provides a musical background suggestive of the battle for men's souls between the rational fathers and the Queen of the Night, as Lucia and Max are overwhelmed by a flood of flashbacks that disclose the history of their relationship, a love so mysterious, terrifying, and, in many ways repellent, that the viewer may well wish to turn away as the lovers themselves have done in the years in between and look into the darkness that frames them. Nagged by his persecutor/patrons about his refusal to take a government job, Max explains that his position as a night porter allows him to avoid the daylight in which he is too ashamed to walk. The scene focusing on Lucia almost hidden in the shadows of the theater more subtly suggests her affinity for the nightworld. Lucia's Queen of the Night aspect is one of the strangest things in this odd film. It inheres in her mysterious love for Max. Critics follow the usual analytic path when they account for the love by calling Lucia masochistic, but the film emphasizes the dark, obscure, enigmatic quality of her inner life, so that is always possible to see her as loving Max despite his cruelty rather than because of it.[10] And perhaps most disturbingly of all, it is possible to imagine that she loves Max because she secretly shares his desire to inflict pain, but since her inner life is virtually defined by its elusiveness, we cannot place Lucia on a sadomasochistic spectrum.

From their first meeting, when Max films her but never the other prisoners around her, his obsessive need to separate her out and project a meaning onto her is repetitively dramatized. As a disembodied bored voice asks the other prisoners their names and religion, Lucia appears from Max's point of view as a somnambulist Juliet, as if the Capulet's party were staged already in the tomb.[11] The film's and Max's camera together capture an image of her, but she remains remote, elsewhere, nameless. The scene defines her lack of power and consequently of identity in the actual world. In equating Max's vision with the director's, the film also paradoxically prepares the viewer for Lucia's later ascendency over Max, because, as we soon see, Max's mastery over Lucia can only parody the director/camera's control of what is seen. The power of a character within the frame can never meld with the power of the controlling intelligence outside the film, so to suggest their convergence draws attention to their divergence and ultimately opens gaps through which we become aware of the constructedness of the film's vision. Lucia's battered body remains an object onto which meanings are visibly and imperfectly projected.

Carol Clover's analysis of the representation of the look in horror films is particularly pertinent to what happens when Max turns his camera's eye onto Lucia. Clover elaborates on Kaja Silverman's idea that in film the eye and the gaze have a relationship analogous to that of the penis and the phallus in Lacanian theory, that is, "the former can stand in for the latter, but can never approximate it."[12] Clover contends that in the horror genre "the theme of failed gazing" is so pervasive that "*whenever* a man imagines himself as a controlling voyeur . . . some sort of humiliation is bound to follow, typically in the form of his being overwhelmed, in one form or another, by the sexuality of the very female he meant to master" (emphasis Clover's). And while *The Night Porter* is not technically a horror film, it works as Clover claims horror films do, by creating identifications that resist our current cultural tendency to "naturalize sadistic violence as a fixture of masculinity."[13] Because the film aligns the erotic with transgression of all paternal laws while it insists on the traditional equation of subjectivity, masculinity, and active love, it affirms the heroic masculinity of a lover who undermines paternal power by consenting to his own destruction.

Susan Sontag and Michel Foucault both see in the film evidence of a movement to eroticize fascism based on the irresistible allure of power. Sontag describes the film as exemplifying a "solemn eroticization of fascism [that] must be distinguished from a sophisticated playing with cultural horror."[14] While I agree with Sontag that fascism has been appallingly eroticized since the 1960s, *The Night Porter* does not seem to me part of the reactionary aesthetics Foucault dubbed "the retro movement" in film.[15] Rather than valorizing power, the film exposes the inadequacy of the naked exercise of power as a means to erotic satisfaction. In this sense, Cavani's vision has a certain affinity with Benjamin's. Benjamin claims that domination always ends in disappointment because "a slave who is completely dominated loses the quality of being able to give recognition" (58). Such a critique of the relationship between fascist power and eroticism is implied in Max's ultimate game with Lucia in the camp.

In recalling the incident, Max says that he had "cast" her as Salome. After she gives, at his command, a song-and-dance performance reminiscent of Marlene Dietrich's in *The Blue Angel*, Max presents her with the severed head of a prisoner about whom she had complained. His explanation of the scene makes clear that Lucia participated unknowingly in the terrible charade, thinking that he would simply have the man transferred. Symbolically overdetermined, the scene can be read as his last attempt to differentiate himself from her. The scene tells us that he has full directorial responsibility; he is the auteur who arranges and literally executes, while she is the actress moved like an object through his fantasy. In the drama he stages, he exercises power while she is the uncomprehending, volitionless figure for erotic power. But the other symbolic contents of the scene overflow the narrow narrative container he has created. Her opacity that keeps us or him from knowing whether she feels pleasure prevents him from claiming the power he has been given by the SS as something that belongs to him. Thus the subjectivity the film assigns him works perversely to undermine our sense of his relative power.

In her analysis of the relationship between pain and imagination, Elaine Scarry offers a description of the dynamics of torture that clarifies how it becomes eroticized by its agents. According to Scarry, political torture depends, in large part, on "the translation of all the objectified elements of pain into the insignia of power." To successfully dominate his victim, the torturer must deny the reality of the other's suffering, driving out his consciousness of it with an all-consuming consciousness of his own motives.[16] While this description closely fits torture scenes in works by the Marquis de Sade because of their putative didactic function, it should alert us to the profound difference in torture scenarios that focus on masochistic pleasure. As Deleuze points out, the masochist's dream torturer, the "realization of [his] fantasy" is very different from the sadist whose pleasure partially depends on ignoring the feelings of the victim.[17] Max, like such classic masochistic protagonists as Sacher-Masoch's Severin and unlike Sade's philosophical libertines— or Max's fellow SS men—does not claim to be acting according to principle but instead confesses his confusion and sense of being compelled from within. While he seems to be trying to author a story of his own power and control, it unravels around him as his attention is continually coopted by his need to know whether or not Lucia feels pleasure.

In fact, the Salome scene is a flashback presented to us already deconstructed by a prior scene in which Lucia ferociously, triumphantly claims the struggling and terrified Max as hers on the floor of her hotel room. This scene allows us to interpret the Salome scene differently from the way Max seems to intend it and to read the climactic moment in which the severed head is displayed to the girl in dominatrix regalia as a gendering of blood sacrifice. Our sense that a man has arranged the tableau is effaced by the frozen horror of the spectacle of male death shown forth as the proof of female power. And as Max draws back, the camera moves in closely to show Lucia's smooth mask of a face.

Like a bland votary of Eros, Lucia indifferently accepts the violence mixed in with Max's love, but he succumbs utterly to the violence of her passion. Here the film most complicates the analytic picture of masochism. Where psychoanalysis looks at erotic masochism in terms of misdirected and degrading sexual desire, the film's occasional moments of dignity come from its insistent interest in masochism as a transcendent form of love. Within the film, desire dictates games, but love asks more. As long as Max simply desires Lucia, her psychic impenetrability is just an intriguing irritant to him, part of the way she passively feeds his pleasurable obsession. But when he loves her, when he falls, literally knocked to the floor by her inexplicable reciprocation of his interest, he must begin a new course of action. His behavior toward her changes: he puts away his camera, and his would-be dominating gaze is replaced with a look of ecstatic suffering attention. Bogarde's performance in *Death in Venice* (1971) is brought to mind, but here it is reiterated in a context of reciprocity. After Max and Lucia's reunion in the hotel, her unconditional acceptance of him releases him from the solitary confinement in alienation that his guilt had previously decreed, but it also teaches him, or, in behaviorist terms, models for him, what he must do. So he walks on broken glass to please her, defies his Nazi patrons to keep her, and finally, to her evident delight, escorts her out to meet the death he unequivocally prefers to the loss of her.

From the moment we are told that Max "amused himself" by pretending to be a doctor in a concentration camp, the audience must want to see him die. But his death, unlike that of the real prosecuted war criminals, does more than simply rid the world of another Nazi—it puts the final seal on his rejection of the protection he is, and men like him are, offered by fascistic systems that rationalize away the pain of the oppressed. By the end, his unease has clearly begun to infect his former associates whose previous murderous solipsism has been replaced by an anxiety to know what effect they are having on others, as is evidenced in their questioning of both Max and Lucia. Max is depicted as a man of very limited virtue, beyond question unable to pass from love of the one to compassion for the many, and certainly too late the hero. Yet in the end Max renounces worldly power and walks to the place of sacrifice in the name of erotic love.

If there is such a thing as a fully realized revolutionary work of art, Cavani's *Night Porter* is not one. The film could be considered reactionary for several reasons, for instance that a middle-aged woman and an effeminate homosexual man figure banal, narcissistic evil. But *The Night Porter*'s representation of male sexual masochism as the driving force behind the kind of sacrifice needed to renew the world makes it, in its own odd way, an act of resistance. Among the forces it resists is a psychoanalytic discourse which, when wedded to political analysis, denies the possibility of changing the patriarchal power structure. Cavani appears to agree with Freud's speculation, in *Civilization and Its Discontents*, that masochism and sadism are differently directed manifestations of the same basic drive, but she apparently disagrees that the basis of both is "the death drive."

Sadism is depicted here, as in Deleuze's and Bersani's writings, as a strategy to connect with the Other through the subject's own power—a strategy always doomed to fail. But masochism appears as another form of subjectivity, one that can be saturated with an eroticism that dismantles the sadistic/paternalistic power structure. The reification of Max's role as debased servant of the Third Reich in his taking on the identity of the night porter and his costuming in a uniform parodically reminiscent of the Gestapo are such masochistic dismantling gestures. His ultimate choice to close the gap of Otherness between himself and Lucia through ritualized self-sacrifice undermines the fundamental assumption behind the other former Nazis' staging of trials: that all acts performed by the powerful serve to consolidate their power. Rather than woman functioning as a link between the male masochist and the father, as in Freud's reading of masochism in "A Child Is Being Beaten," the fathers, in their blind cruelty, work to bond Max to Lucia.

The paradigm governing most feminist analyses of masochism, including Benjamin's, seems to be that domination is always coded masculine and submission feminine. Thus men's masochism can occlude but never challenge the distribution of power along gender lines. In contrast, stories like *The Night Porter* dramatize apparent male sadism as a thin covering over the lover's intrinsic urge to subordinate himself to woman. They suggest that this urge, indistinguishable from love, can erupt forcefully enough to destabilize patriarchal power. Such representations of male masochism seem to posit a primary female power that compels the allegiance of male lovers. One might even go so far as to say that their deification of the erotic also feminizes Eros, locating the matriarchal goddess not in some distant unrecoverable past or in the unconscious but as a vital player in the drama of love.

In *Sons and Lovers* and *Women in Love*, D. H. Lawrence, most frequently seen as a masculinist writer,[18] stresses the importance of male sacrifice, while he also vividly illustrates some of the anxieties occasioned by this concept of gender relations. Sandra Gilbert calls Lawrence "the archetype of the male modernist . . . who implicitly believes in the Great Mother's power even while he explicitly dreads and rejects it." Gilbert's fascinating reading of Lawrence's *The Ladybird* reveals some of the ways that mythology of mother goddesses served by Dionysian consorts informs many of his texts. Gilbert emphasizes the heroine Daphne's creativity and the men's "helpless dependence on her maternal stitchery" to effect their "resurrection." The symbolism of the two male protagonists' first names, Basil and Johann, to which Gilbert glancingly refers, suggests that Lawrence does more in *The Ladybird* than show that "the mysteries of the blood . . . are the rites of female creativity." If Basil Apsley's first name makes us think of "the pot of basil in which Keats's Isabella kept the severed . . . head of her lover" then Johann Psanek's should call to mind John's head being presented on a plate to Salome.[19] Consequently *The Ladybird* relates female mysteries of the blood as much to the destruction of men as to their resurrection.

Benjamin writes in psychoanalytic terms of the relations between maternal power, destruction, and resurrection as they determine possibilities within sadomasochistic exchanges. Benjamin believes that there can be no mutual recognition within the sadomasochistic exchange because it is also marked by "a polarization of subject and object," which, even when men and women reverse roles, continues to code the masochistic role as feminine. She attributes this inescapable gender coding to our culture's repression of female, and specifically maternal, subjectivity. Because "only someone who fully achieves subjectivity can survive destruction and permit full differentiation," and because maternal subjectivity is denied, we can only vacillate between terrifying feminine identification with a mother who cannot be seen as a complete person and contemptuous masculine rejection of her (81–82). While this description certainly fits many ordinary sexual/romantic relationships, I question its applicability to female-dominant sadomasochistic relations. Benjamin's analysis of these relations fails to consider the most deep-rooted cultural reasons that men are so frequently made uneasy by "the mother's assertion of her own separate selfhood." Benjamin attributes this unease to narcissism, and also, through rather circular reasoning, to cultural biases against the feminine (82). Lawrence's *Sons and Lovers* provides a different perspective, one more closely connected to mythic and religious representations of male sacrifice in the name of an all-too-complete and powerful mother—or Mother.

Part of the energy of Lawrence's novel comes from its engagement with and resistance to Freudian concepts of gender and sexual differentiation, especially the Oedipus Complex theory.[20] Both in the narrative and the structure of the novel's first chapters, Gertrude Morel is accorded primacy. She is the first character introduced; Walter Morel is introduced as "her husband."[21] Walter Morel does not fit Freud's description of the "stronger" parent destined to win the son's allegiance away from the mother as soon as the child begins to understand the "dangers which threaten it in the external world,"[22] a parent so strong he will eventually be perceived as threatening to castrate his son. Instead, even before his son's birth, Walter has come to resemble nothing more than a detumescent penis. His confrontations with his wife cause "a slight shrinking, a diminishing in his assurance. Physically even, he shrank, and his fine full presence waned . . . as he sank from his erect, assertive bearing, his physique seemed to contract along with his pride and moral strength" (26). Walter is reminiscent of the male consort of that figure for matriarchy, the queen bee, and one might pause to remember that Lawrence called his wife, Frieda, The Queen Bee. Having performed his biological function, Walter is spent, disposable, while Gertrude's stature and influence increase. For the protagonist, Paul, to identify with her is to share in her creative power. "His life-story, like an Arabian Nights, was told night after night to his mother. It was almost as if it were her own life" (113). In this and many similar passages, mothers and creative artists are equated. Sacred maternal power makes and unmakes, while men watch in awe.

Separation from the mother, brought about by awakening heterosexual desire, entails a painful and frightening loss of agency and identity. Paul's first "sweetheart," Miriam, controls his sexuality almost completely for years. He is "impotent against" her spiritual, "religious" rejection of eroticism (178). Lawrence describes Paul as one of many men who "could easier deny themselves than incur any reproach from a woman; for a woman was like their mother, and they were full of the sense of their mother. They preferred them-

selves to suffer the misery of celibacy rather than risk the other person" (279). The narrator's philosophizing here and in similar passages has most often been interpreted as supporting Freud's
Oedipus theory, but this interpretation can only be made by disre-
garding Lawrence's furious opposition to Freud, later reflected in
his books *Psychoanalysis and the Unconscious* (1921) and *Fantasia of
the Unconscious* (1922).[23] Extratextual evidence of Lawrence's disagreements with Freud is not strictly necessary to dismiss the Freudian reading of the above passage, however. One might simply look
at the way mothers are represented here. It is not the mother who
is taboo but the sense of separation from her occasioned by her unhappiness or reproach. Only if we assume that all women dislike sex
can we say that Paul feels that sex is impossible because it would
necessarily offend the mother. And far from standing for all women,
Miriam is repeatedly described as unusual because of her lack of
sexual feeling.

In their sexual encounters, Miriam's submissiveness repels Paul.
That she lies naked before him, "as if she had given herself up to
sacrifice . . . like a creature awaiting immolation" causes Paul to lose
his erection (289–90). He must "shut his eyes . . . to her" in order
to regain it (290). A combination of recognition of the other person
and sexual pleasure depends, for him, on a woman's power to demand his sexual performance as a tribute to her. His fantasy is that
Miriam will "hold him and [claim him], with joy and authority"
(418).

Paul longingly watches his brother give himself up to a woman.
William dies still enchanted by the "witch-woman" whose "beauty
seemed to hurt him" (129). Then Paul, himself, comes under the
sway of Clara who "remind[s] him of Juno dethroned" (262) who
is called "the Queen of Sheba" (270), whose "strong form . . .
seem[s] to slumber with power" (270), whose hands, he notices,
are larger than his, "and powerful looking" (273). He is intensely
aroused by his sense of her "towering in her force above him" (331).
The success of their lovemaking seems attributed to her dominance,
that he can be "her boot-boy for the time being, and nothing else"
(311). "He looked at her with a little pain, and was afraid. He was
so humble before her" (338–39). His submission is "her recognition"
(339). Having been judged inadequate by Clara—"you've never

given me yourself"—and been severely beaten by her husband, Paul gives her up (363). After the death of his mother and a final failed effort to get Miriam to show any sexual aggression, Paul is left "derelict"—as the final chapter is entitled—walking away from an almost unbearable sense of his own loss of identity.

In *Sons and Lovers*, male masochism appears mutedly, half-sublimated into secretively gloated-over emotional pain and little rituals of service, but also as an ideal of passion against which ordinary male-dominant sexual relations appear utterly unsatisfying. In *Women in Love* masochism is much more explicitly represented and even more uncompromisingly freighted with moral values. The love story of Rupert Birkin and Ursula Brangwen, at the center of the novel, posits as the ideal the achievement of "an equilibrium, a pure balance of two single beings."[24] This achievement is problematized, as in the earlier novel, by the text's insistence that antagonism cannot be eradicated from the relationship between the sexes. Unlike the women of *Sons and Lovers*, who are often gentle and yielding, the women in *Women in Love* are so consistently fierce and aggressive yet so strongly attractive that the men are faced less with the choice of dominating them or not than with a choice between endlessly fighting them or bowing down to them. Birkin, who gradually becomes the narrative's exemplary lover, oscillates between the two attitudes.

The characters Gerald Crich and Gudrun Brangwen serve as foils for the main couple. Their love affair illustrates alternatives to the attitudes assumed by Birkin and Ursula. But Gerald and Gudrun, repeatedly associated with the "river of dissolution" and the destructive aspect of sexuality, also represent alternative drives within or possible identities for the generally more positive and creative Birkin and Ursula. Through this dichotomy in the novel Lawrence works out his ambivalence about female power and male submission to it and reaches a tentative solution, at least on an artistic level, to the problems posed by sexual antagonism.

As in *The Night Porter*, the solution comes through a masochism charged with mystical religious feeling and explicitly linked to redemption. From the beginning of the story, Birkin is presented as the more romantic of the two main male characters, the one who identifies himself more in relation to women. Despite his rebellion against the Magna Mater in "Moony" and his taunting rhetoric about the female animal's need to submit, Birkin reveres Woman religiously. In explaining to Gerald his desire that a woman be "the centre and core" of his life, lest his life be "nothing," Birkin says that there is no other alternative "seeing that there's no God" (58). The knowledge that Ursula not only desires him but wants to sexually dominate him reduces Birkin to enthralled obedience. "By her tone he could tell she . . . was subtly gratified that she should have power over them both. He gave himself, in a strange, electric submission" (176). He capitulates to her demands over and over, as he does in their first love scene, which ends with him "murmuring [the words she has commanded him to speak] in a subtle voice of love, and irony, and submission" (154). Birkin irritates Ursula's more conventionally masculine father by saying, "it's much more likely that it's I who am at the beck and call of the woman, than she at mine" (258). Her "abuse" of him, he admits is "all for the good" (310). The "balance" he ultimately attains with her derives from the very limited resistance to her power, which he exorcises by verbally expressing, but not acting on, his independent desires and ideals. In this way he avoids being completely subsumed by her.

In contrast to Birkin's abstract devotion to Woman, quick capitulations to a specific woman's authority, and intellectual resources of retreat, is Gerald's misogyny and more physical and extreme masochism. The first woman we see him court is the "Pussum," who attracts him by cutting open another lover's hand. She loses Gerald when she submits to him. In the indomitable Gudrun, Gerald finds a mate who can hold his attention to the death, that is, to his death. Their first love scene prefigures their subsequent relationship. He challenges her with "a *faint* domineering smile" (170; emphasis mine). She responds by hitting him in the face with the back of her hand. In answer to his angry remark that she has "struck the first blow," she says, "And I shall strike the last. . . . He was silent, he did not contradict her." Then, like "the masochist's sadist" according to Deleuze, she stresses the relationship between her cruelty and his desire: "It's you who make me behave like this, you know." Overcome by passion, he can only stammer, "I'm not angry with you. I'm in love with you" (171). Believing, as he does, in "education through subjection and torment," seeing himself as "only this, this being that should come to her, and be given to her," he cannot draw away from the "torture she inflict[s] upon him" (205, 239, 446). "Her fingers had him under their power. The fathomless, fathomless desire they could evoke in him was deeper than death, where he had no choice" (332). For him the only satisfaction is "to suffer when you are with a woman," to find her "so perfect . . . it tears you like a silk, and every stroke and bit cuts hot" (440). Gerald succumbs to this desire and so loses first autonomy and then life.

Both Birkin's and Gerald's desires are put into perspective by references, like those in *Sons and Lovers* (and many of Lawrence's other works), to female masochism as disgusting and repellent. Gerald abandons the Pussum because of "her inchoate look of a violated slave" on the morning after they have sex (80). Birkin's first mistress, Hermione, never appears more completely inferior to Ursula than when she reacts to the proud young woman's refusal to submit to Birkin with the secret thought "Ah, if only he would have made this demand of her!" (294). There is nothing in the novel so fearsome as the apparent submission of women. Mrs. Crich submits to her husband, "let[s] him take what he want[s] and do as he want[s] with her," but she becomes "like a hawk," or a wolf who secretly devours him (217). Her very "subjugation . . . dominate[s] as by a spell," ultimately destroying him (218). Images like these naturalize women's power over men as something that can no more be overcome through force or cajoled away than a wild animal's fierceness.

These images also oppose Freudian interpretations that particularize the mother figure as an imago of the subject's actual mother. As Deleuze and Guattari point out, Lawrence's texts show his recognition that "psychoanalysis was shutting sexuality up in a bizarre sort of box painted with bourgeois motifs . . . making of it . . . the dirty little family secret, a private theater rather than the fantastic factory of Nature and Production" (49). Like Artaud, praised by Deleuze and Guattari for attacking psychoanalytic theory's attempts to contain desire within a narrative of the family, Lawrence creates a theater of cruelty in which masochistic desire ritually affirms natural and cultural forces larger than the personal and familial.[25]

As Virginia Hyde has shown, references to diverse religions, religious rituals, and "centers of worship" abound in *Women in Love*, complementing the novel's philosophical concern with cosmology.[26]

The narrative contextualizes female domination of men by repeated visions of woman as "Mother and substance of all life" (344), an image in which the natural is conflated with the sacred. Thus Ursula and Gudrun both appear as terrible earth or fertility goddesses when they are at their most seductive. Gudrun's fetishization of the deep scratches she and Gerald receive from a rabbit bring him "underworld knowledge" so that they are "initiated" into mysteries of the flesh (241–43). Gudrun's caressing of Gerald's body is referred to as "harvesting" him, a description that evokes the sacrifice of the Corn King (332). Birkin experiences his supreme sexual experience when, after Ursula has disciplined him and forced him to acknowledge her possession of him, she awakens him to a deeper satisfaction than phallic eroticism can provide for either of them. This new relation with Ursula is consummated between Sherwood Forest, "where Biblical and Druidical association converge in the novel's one sacred setting," and Southwell Minster with its notable carving of the pagan, sacrificial Green Man (Hyde 86, 88).

Through such emblematic representation, masochism is recovered from associations with the sexually unnatural; it is also given the high moral seriousness of ancient religious ritual. Yet, as it is practiced by Gerald, masochism seems to be condemned, not just by Birkin but by the narrative itself, since the extremity of Gerald's masochism could be said to bring about his death. However, the Mother/Nature Goddess trope also provides another way to understand the fatal flaw that kills Gerald. Within the symbology relating to the vision of women as fertility goddesses, Gerald can be seen as the sacrificial self, or double, of Birkin. Gerald becomes the blood sacrifice not because he is masochistic—both men are that—but because he is worldly and earthy in contrast to Birkin's ethereal spirituality and because he challenges woman physically where he might better speak to her. Faced with the problem of reconciling an egalitarian ethos ("star equilibrium") with a concept of women as unconquerable goddesses and men as most naturally their abject worshippers, the novel divides the masculine into absolute, sacrificial masochism and a sort of priestly service of woman, which includes occasional verbal self-assertion. But, it would be a mistake to think the two modes represent separable courses of action; the narrative structure of the book emphasizes their inseparability with its inter-

weaving of the two heavily mythologized stories. In order for Birkin
to successfully mate with the benevolent aspect of the Great Mother
figured by the "good" sister Ursula, Gerald as his other half must
be sacrificed to the destructive aspect of the Great Mother in the
person of Gudrun.

The narrative logic demands that Gerald be sacrificed because,
like Max in *The Night Porter*, Gerald appears as a criminal against
life itself. In retrospective, we learn how Gerald's attitude toward
the devastation of nature caused by his family's coal mines changed
from horror and denial to complicity and finally pride as he began
to continue his father's work. At last, he surpasses his father in re-
pudiating nature and celebrates himself as "the God of the machine" (223). Thus, as in Max's case, the sacrifice of the man is presented to the audience as morally right. Rather than making us
observe an alien or repulsive ritual, the plot instead draws us in to
desire it, to experience it as what must and should be. These sacrifices
function for the audience in two ways. First they satisfy our sense
of justice, and second they appease our sense of guilt at our own
complicity and compromise with social evils. Like classic tragedies,
these dramas of male sacrifice are cathartic.[27]

It is the idea of such catharsis that Iris Murdoch parodies in novels such as *A Severed Head* that explicitly portray ritualized masochistic sexual behavior. *A Severed Head* focuses on an adulterous husband entrapped in the farcically entangled web of crossed desires
and sexual connections of a large group of strange acquaintances.
Unlike Murdoch's later novels, which allude to rather than depict
sadomasochistic dramas and only obliquely discuss the characters'
perverse desires, *A Severed Head* explicitly explores the experiences
of the masochist hero. It is also more self-consciously primitivist
than Murdoch's later novels in its evocation of the forces that oppose rationalistic approaches to life and in its apparent endorsement
of a sort of mystic fatalism.[28] Psychoanalysis is targeted as the main
mode of rationalism that limits the character's thoughts.

When the story opens, Martin Lynch-Gibbon, the protagonist
and narrator, is struggling to hold onto his maternal older wife, Antonia, who wants to divorce him to marry her analyst, Palmer An-
derson. Martin's mistress, Georgie Hands, a junior lecturer at the
London School of Economics, also threatens to escape his control.

Throughout the story Palmer seems to play the role of antagonist
by moving powerfully into the breach whenever Martin suffers any
reversal. However, the story progressively reveals Palmer's half-sis-
ter, Honor Klein, as Martin's true adversary. An anthropologist who
studies "savage tribes," she is dark, "animal-like and repellent," an-
drogynous, not in the usual sense of resembling an adolescent boy,
but "like some insolent and powerful captain."[29] She is an expert
with samurai swords and voices a brutal philosophy according to
which violence redeems. Honor is love object as opponent.

For Martin, part of the process of learning the difference between the dangers posed by Honor's philosophy and Palmer's (psychoanalytic theory) entails learning about difference itself. Palmer
tries to infantilize Martin by enclosing him into his own affair with
Antonia, saying, "We shall hold onto you, we shall look after you"
(35). As a couple, Palmer and Antonia rapidly "come into existence
as a sort of institution with its own palpable strength, atmosphere,
and even traditions" (37). Dealing with life on the terms dictated
by this institution would keep Martin within the comedy of man-
ners to which the story initially seems to belong. But Honor forces
Martin out of the family drama into a less fixed relation to the
world, into the terrifying openness of possibilities not bounded by
forms learned in childhood.

The primal scene is reenacted for Martin in the form of Antonia
and Palmer in bed together civilizedly chatting with him about
wine. During this humiliating ordeal, his knowledge of Oedipus
Complex theory (and Palmer's investment in it) leaves him little
space to express to them the rage he feels, unless he wants to indulge
in a childish tantrum. As he puts it, "the stage was set for my regression to the situation of a child" (139). In contrast, the act of
incest between Palmer and Honor that Martin witnesses resists containment by a theory that would predetermine a "mature," "sane"
response.

Pertinent to Murdoch's depiction of Martin's reaction to this
scene is Jane Gallop's claim that brother-sister incest differs from
cross-generational incest in that it "plays out, in a purified form, the
question of sexual difference. Both partners are of the same generation and origin, so they can paradigmatically be thought to differ
only by sex."[30] By foregrounding and affirming difference, such a

representation of sexuality smashes beyond Oedipal uncertainties and anxieties. While Martin can and does retreat from his anger and fears about his wife into a comforting identification with Antonia, erasing her alterity in order to find her Palmer's parental golden double, or to assert, "I shall always be Antonia" (82), Honor's difference remains frighteningly, upsettingly ineradicable. Her unanticipated seductiveness demands more from him than his previous modes of thought can provide. In a comic attempt to solve the enigma of his attraction to her, he searches the library for information on incest, surprisingly concluding that "the psychological literature was scanty and unsatisfactory" (185). Mythology provides him more satisfying explanations, but he comments that the "lurid illumination I thus engendered served merely to display with a vividness which prostrated me the figure of Honor, aloof, frightening, sacred, and . . . taboo" (185).

Honor's image is that of the Medusa (188), but not exactly that figure described by Freud. To Freud the Medusa's head is a castration symbol which "isolates [the] horrifying effects [of the female genitalia] from the pleasure giving ones." The snakes that serve as Medusa's hair are phallic symbols whose presence confirms "the technical rule according to which a multiplication of penis symbols signifies castration."[31] But, we might ask, whose castration? Neil Hertz's discussion of "the interchangeability of the Phrygian cap and the head of Medusa" as signs of revolution suggests one answer.[32] Hertz points out a possible origin of this interchangeability in the myth of Attis, the Phrygian shepherd who castrated himself and died for love of the Great Mother and was reborn as a fertility god. The myth could be read to imply that man is always already castrated, not as Freud and Lacan would have it in relation to the phallic power of the Father, but in relation to the generative power of the Mother, and that it is only through a ritualized identification with her that he can attain approximate power. As Catherine Gallagher says, in response to Hertz, the Medusa's head as vaginal symbol need not signify woman's lack but may instead stand for the "reproductive power" of woman that can create "semiotic chaos" calling "men's authorship [and identity] into question," making evident masculine lack.[33]

Honor says of herself, "I am a severed head such as primitive

tribes and old alchemists used to use. . . . And who knows but that
long acquaintance with a severed head might not lead to strange
knowledge" (221). She is, in other words, made greater and more
valuable by the very difference detaching her from the phallocentric
domestic sphere she terms "ordinary life," and what she has to offer
has at least as much to do with knowledge as with sexual pleasure.
In some ways Murdoch's rendering of Honor through Martin's eyes
anticipates Hélène Cixous's celebration of the monstrous (because
demonized) and powerful feminine in "The Laugh of the Medusa."
From the moment she appears in the novel, like an embodiment of
Murdoch's own propensity for manipulating the plot and characters
into the most unlikely configurations possible and then knocking
them apart, Honor busies herself "dislocating things and values,
breaking them all up, emptying structures, and turning proprieties
upside-down."[34] Like Cixous's Medusa, Honor derives her power
from her subversive skepticism about the system that would deny
the value of her difference and can only see it as the horrifying signifier of lack. In this way, Honor also resembles the Victorian Medusa, described by Richard Dellamora as an avenger of crimes
against women. This Medusa's power increases through some men's
sympathy with her opposition to the patriarchal society that also
oppresses them.[35] Cixous says, "You have only to look at the Medusa
straight on to see her and she's not deadly. She's beautiful and she's
laughing" (342). Thus we are shown Honor at the last, still absolutely, darkly different but beautiful and "compelling [Martin] with
her smile" (248).

However, the celebratory quality of Martin's discovery of
Honor's difference often partakes more of that festive cruelty that
Nietzsche noted in human rituals than of the pure joyousness of
Cixous's account of the Medusa. *A Severed Head* often reads like a
masochist's "coming-out" story. At the beginning of the story,
Martin talks of his need for a master/mistress and his "sense of not
having suffered enough" (13). He is "the knight of infinite humiliation"; he gives in to the power of "a monstrous love" with a sense
that he has at last come into his own; he waits for Honor "as one
awaits . . . the searing presence of a god," and prostrates himself
before her (133, 153, 198). Martin's excessiveness combined with
Honor's apparently deliberate excision of all the attributes com-

monly associated with femininity from her appearance and behavior add comic touches to all his gestures of submission. Yet the idea of male submission to female power is romanticized rather than mocked.

As in the dominatrix pornography that Thaïs Morgan has illuminatingly discussed, phallic power is the target of the mockery.[36] Morgan argues that both the masquerade of the dominatrix and the mask of Medusa "use the signs of masculinity to mock masculinity" (125); "the dominatrix [resplendent in her fetishes] shows up the 'phallic woman' and the 'Phallic Mother' for frauds based on the even greater fraud of the Phallus-as-Power" (131). Likewise, when Honor enthralls Martin with her sword play, the sword, which makes "a sound like a whip moving," is so much the phallic symbol as to be ridiculous. Her display of phallic power is both so theatrically false and so extreme as to foreclose any possibility of Martin's patriarchal mastery based on his possession of a penis. Looking at her posed with the sword resting on her lap like an "executioner," he realizes that "it was the new Year" (118). What is executed, or rather what Martin offers up as sacrifice is his concept of himself as a natural possessor of women, the controller of their respective values. By the novel's conclusion he has renounced his privileged position as master of a mistress and a wife and is ecstatic just to be accepted as an equal by Honor.

Still the tension between them persists and is marked more strongly than that between the surviving lover-combatants at the end of *Women in Love*. The cathartic sacrifice of the demonic double in Lawrence's novel apparently does away with the possibility of the sort of union between men that enables the oppression of women. *Women in Love* ends with Birkin weakened by the loss of Gerald, feeling incomplete but unable to express in anything but negative terms his need for a separate world of male interdependence and love. When Ursula authoritatively tells him that, in essence, the male sphere as a locus of love and value is "a theory, a perversity" and "false, impossible," he can only answer "I don't believe that" (481). Whatever Birkin believes, we have been shown that all he can rely on is his relation to Ursula, in whose presence he feels "like a beggar," but without whom he feels certain he could not survive (408). Conversely, *A Severed Head* ends with Martin's insolent response to

Honor's pronouncement that he must take the chance of being
destroyed by the passion between them, "So must you, my dear!"
(248). This riposte reminds us that the will to power over woman
that seems dead in Martin can be resurrected.

Murdoch treats the same theme more subtly but more violently
in a later novel, *The Sacred and Profane Love Machine*. In this text
the philandering husband, Blaise Gavender, is himself a psychologist. His wife, Harriet, is an idealized (and idealistic) golden goddess
of domestic harmony and decorum like Antonia, but his mistress,
Emily, is his "priestess-like" partner in sadomasochistic rituals.[37]
Embroiled in power struggles with each other and a large cast of
other more or less sadomasochistically inclined characters, this triad
seems destined for a resolution out of classic mythology when, near
the end of the novel, Blaise is attacked by the pack of half-wild dogs
his wife has taken in. But instead, Harriet herself becomes the blood
sacrifice, killed by terrorists in an airport where she had been awaiting escape from her unravelling marriage. If a golden age of confidence about what love is and brings, what is now touted as "family
values," dies with Harriet, transgressive love is equally unable to sus-
tain itself within a world that offers no space for open sexual expression outside the ever constricting family circle. Hurriedly married to Blaise, Emily gives up their special rituals and becomes "an
ordinary married woman" a house/wife who, like her murdered
predecessor, believes she "contains" her already bored husband
(344–45).

The Sacred and Profane Love Machine moves beyond the sort of
representation of the sacrifice of male power that concludes the
other texts I have discussed here and suggests the ultimate political
uselessness of such sacrifices that are also erotic consummations.
Blaise has bowed down to Emily, given himself over to her "Absolutely. For ever," as his "queen" (221). But what can she command
him to do except put "the longed-for wedding ring on to her finger"
(360) and give her his own name as that which can only belong to
the sacred love? The social machine grinds on and all their dramatic
soul-searching and rending of flesh only brings the characters back
to the self-deceiving, empty conventionality with which they began
and to which they cling all the more desperately for having almost
lost it. The paternalistic cruelty that supports Emily and Blaise's

bourgeois complacency is emphasized by the exclusion from their house of their illegitimate son, Luca, who is put in an institution and replaced by a new, legitimate pregnancy. In their newly reconfigured household, the name of the father rules and orders all.

The novel might be read as condemning male masochism as nothing more than a ruse for concealing male power were it not for the inclusion of a minor character, Edgar, whose masochism is associated with almost saintlike self-effacement. Edgar embodies an essentially "masochistic notion of goodness," which Murdoch often suggests "comes through allowing or even promoting destruction of oneself in order to prevent oneself from destroying others."[38] The other characters treat him contemptuously, while he glories in being used by them. Edgar is no simple "moral masochist," however. We are told that he is intensely sexually perverse. "It was no accident that he was unmarried and alone, that his love for women was unrequited, and his love for men undeclared." At the periods in his life when he has acted on his desires, sickening "catastrophe[s]" resulted. He perceives himself as accompanied always by "his demons," but "needed no analyst," and instead, in saintly fashion, finds help through prayer (354).

In the last section of the novel, as Edgar relives the "exquisite sweet pain" that the events of the story have given him, he has an important vision. He sees a cherry tree covered with white blossoms and first believes that it is unseasonably in flower (it is midsummer) and then realizes that it is filled with a climbing rose. Later, having achieved a difficult resignation to the frustration of all his desires, he takes out of his pocket a bundle of old love letters he had sent to a woman, now dead, who long ago rejected him, and as "a shower of white rose petals suddenly [flies] about him. . . . Edgar look[s] down at the strewn whiteness, like little messages" (365). In their revitalizing effect on him, the petals, more than the old letters, seem messages of love, at once sacred and profane, signifying the simultaneous triumph and defeat based on the deliberate, determined misrecognition of pain for pleasure.

For if, as Benjamin would have it, masochism is about the need for recognition, it is also about the need for misrecognition. First, as Reik says, pain is disabled as an instrument for enforcing the law by the masochist who misrecognizes punishment as erotic reward.

But even more subversively, the male masochist, rather than recognizing the man as the ultimate power that he must be by definition in a patriarchal culture, misrecognizes the woman as the most powerful one. Consequently the ancient primacy of the mother, ordinarily so obvious in the experience of infants but so rigidly denied by modern cultures, is reaffirmed. In literary texts like the ones I have discussed here, such misrecognition works not, as Benjamin claims, to make mutual recognition impossible by reifying the polar opposition between the dominator and the dominated but to free men and women from restricting binary concepts of the gendering of power. Woman worship, because it goes against the grain of the social structures containing the rebellious devotees, does not simply substitute one dominator for another—it calls the phallocentric basis of such structures into question. Even when male power is only unsettled for a moment, as in *The Night Porter* or *The Sacred and Profane Love Machine*, before the rule of the fathers is restored, the myth of their omnipotence is exposed as a lie. A gap opens in patriarchy through which desires can flow elsewhere.

The cover of Benjamin's *Bonds of Love* shows a reproduction of Edward Burne-Jones's *The Baleful Head*. Perseus and Andromeda lean over a well whose surface, between their faces, reflects the head of Medusa that he holds aloft. Benjamin could hardly have chosen a more appropriate image for the romance of male power. Perseus wears heavy medieval armor and looks fierce. While his and Medusa's faces are partially obscured by each other and, in the reflection, by the edges of the well, Andromeda's full smiling face glows in the water. Perseus's hand, in the foreground, encircles her bare wrist while her hand rests, almost out of the viewer's sight, on his mailed wrist. Her apparent pleasure seems to come out of her contact with his power. But because, above the well, we can see only the side of her face, with the mouth's corner downturned, her pleasure is visually represented as an illusion. Perhaps, as Benjamin argues, this is the sort of pleasure most available to women in our culture, which Benjamin sees as deeply sadomasochistic in its concept of love, but it is not the only sort of pleasure that textual representations of masochism describe. Texts like those discussed above maintain a tradition that celebrates the sacrifice of man to woman as the vehicle of poetic justice.

Still, changing the sacrificial victim's gender from female to male does not provide a politically satisfying vision. Texts that insist that a man be willing to die as a sacrifice to woman in the name of love are disturbing for feminist as well as generally humanitarian reasons. Such thinking has always fed misogyny, providing a rationalization for controlling women's sexuality. However, this line of reasoning also usefully reveals the price of male power to be the renunciation of the possibility of love. René Girard claims, "sacrifice is the most crucial and fundamental of rites," and "also the most common-place."[39] Looking at the dismal history of the relations between dominant and subordinate groups, one might be inclined to agree. If so, the feminist reader in particular might want to consider the different purposes gender-specific sacrifices are represented as having and to distinguish between the one in which the sacrifice of woman allows the full, deconstructive force of love to be resisted and the other, the sacrifice of man that allows love some play. Both types of sacrifice are terrible nightmarish responses to a cruel world, but man's willing sacrifice of himself has the additional aspect of a mysterious purity in that it is far less obviously self-interested than his sacrifice of woman.

4

UNVEILING WOMAN'S MOST UNSPEAKABLE DESIRE

Glimpses of the Mistress of the Game

> Veiling and unveiling: isn't that what interests them? What keeps them busy? Always repeating the same operation every time. On every woman.
>
> Luce Irigaray, *This Sex Which Is Not One*, trans. Catherine Porter with Carolyn Burke

> Men are forced to admire us, love us, and be desirous of us; insomuch that rather than not have and enjoy us, they will deliver to our disposals their power, persons, and lives, enslaving themselves to our will and pleasures; also, we are their saints, whom they adore and worship; and what can we desire more than to be men's tyrants, destinies, and goddesses?
>
> Margaret Cavendish, *Female Orations*

T HESE TWO EPIGRAPHS might be considered, more than any others in this book, to be dialogically related, for if Cavendish's orator poses a question about how much and what sort of power might be claimed by women within a patriarchal society that deifies us as well as demonizing us, we might read in Irigaray's text a shocking answer. Veiling the woman is not only a way of silencing her and rendering her mysterious, it is also inescapably a way of giving her significative power. Feminine power, like the phallus, in Lacan's famous observation, "can play its role only when veiled." In fact, according to some of Lacan's interpreters the woman "is" the phallus,[1] a reading of femininity that makes sense if we think of woman as the eternal object of desire, the object which, if she could be possessed, would do away with lack, and so signifies the mastery, the accession to fatherly power of her possessor. But what if the feminist, rather than ripping away her veils and insisting on emerging from them as a subject, castrated in relation to the concept of absolute power as all subjects must be,[2] instead refuses the everlasting strip show in an/other fashion? What if woman, rather than passively waiting to be veiled as powerful fetish object and unveiled into powerless subjectivity, claims her own unreadability by manipulating her own veils and through her play with them speaks her desires? To think of woman in this way is to imagine an oracle who glories in her role rather than lamenting it, a triumphant demoness who secretively owns herself in order to publicly own man.

The psychic location of this woman might be understood as Alice Jardine does Derrida's description in *Glas* of the femininity of the text ("the text veils itself by itself unveiling itself") as "a realm of sexual undecidability," where there is neither castration nor "uncastration."[3] But the crucial difference would be that rather than considering resistance to interpretation and disruption of phallocentric meaning inevitable to femininity and, hence, attributes of woman, we might think of each woman's potential femininity as a performance, and the dominant woman's as a veiling she deliberately assumes in order to do her Salomelike dance, in which she paradoxically hides through an overdramatized disclosure of her presence-to-herself.[4] Through this sort of reading one could escape the reinscription of "metaphysical boundaries" between masculine and feminine that Jardine rightly points out occurs in Derrida's "genderization of writing as 'feminine operation' " and renders problematic for feminists his valorization of authorial gestures toward "becoming woman."[5] We could also avoid the patronizing assumption that all women internalize patriarchal values. If we avoid that assumption, we will no longer be trapped in a paradigm that predetermines an inability to recognize women as speakers or actors in cultural narratives.

It is often difficult to read female characters as empowered speakers and actors because, although literary and film narratives contain many would-be dominant women, they are ordinarily contextualized in ways that reveal what acute anxiety they cause both men and women. This anxiety registers strongly in feminist debate, where dominant heterosexual women virtually disappear. While feminists have argued vehemently for over fifteen years about S/M sexual game playing's compatibility with feminist goals, the players in the game almost always figure either as lesbians or as a dominant man and a submissive woman. Female domination of males has generally been the empty space at the center of the discussion, a topic rarely touched upon.

Although the well-known *Against Sadomasochism: A Radical Feminist Analysis* focuses on lesbian S/M, most of the essays included also discuss male domination of women extensively but remain silent on the topic of male masochism. In the few exceptions, the authors quickly dismiss female dominance of men as insignificant. For example, Diana Russell condemns as "contra-feminist," "sex role reversals with women playing the traditional male role and men the traditional female role, *or* women playing the sadistic role and men the masochistic role," because, as her language here suggests, she understands masochism as traditionally and inextricably connected to the position of women in society. John Stoltenberg makes the rather amazing claim: "True masochism is relatively rare in genital males." He seems unaware that men ever act out masochistic fantasies except with hired sex workers, and so claims that what seems to be masochism in men is "a variant of normal phallocentric domination or economic control."[6] A more recent and interesting example of feminist theorists' lack of attention to women's sexual domination of men is Julia Creet's essay "Daughter of the Movement," which focuses on representation of and debate over S/M encounters between women. Creet also includes commentary on women's (written) fantasies of being dominated by men. She begins by asking, "What happens . . . when a girl becomes a woman who positions herself not as an object of male desire, but as a subject who desires another woman." But Creet's answer that "her desire is almost *unimaginable* within [the] framework" of feminist/Lacanian accounts of the acquisition of subjectivity, suggests by omission that the *entirely* unimaginable figure is the girl for whom sexual maturation entails desiring a man as a subject desires an object.[7]

When this scandalous person is not ignored altogether by feminist theory, she is often lost in logically circular maneuvers like Jessica Benjamin's. Benjamin, first, bases her reading of masochistic relationships almost entirely on *The Story of O*, then mentions almost as an afterthought that "the roles of master and slave are not intrinsically or exclusively male and female respectively; as the original 'masochist' of *Venus in Furs* reminds us, the opposite is often true." Lest this reminder influence us too much, she quickly goes on to assert, with no support from literary texts or case studies, that "even when men and women reverse their roles, as they often do, the sense of 'playing the other' is never lost." We are left wondering why the dominant and submissive roles that are assigned so differently by Sacher-Masoch have suddenly (and retrospectively) become so deeply gendered that the men and women who play them can only seek in vain to "lose" their connections to masculinity and femininity. As Benjamin shows, her reading of female desire is consonant with "the well-known difference between male and female sexual pleasure."[8] Because what is "well known" about female desire seems to be all we know, we cannot recognize a female pleasure not fundamentally different from (masculine) aggression, one that does not confirm the currently dominant visions of both gender and sexual difference.

Of course, such feminist commentaries on women's sexuality are not meant to be prescriptive, nor to foreclose possibilities of pleasure. They emerge from important work done to protect women from the very real dangers of a misogynistic world in which men hold most of the power. It is realistic and right to think first of women's victimization when we think about sexualized violence and cruelty. However, it becomes problematic when we cannot think of women any other way than as victims or survivors of someone else's aggression.

We can see a good example of the way this sort of thinking can interfere with otherwise strong feminist work in Michelle Massé's analysis of female masochism in relation to gothic narratives. On the one hand, she insightfully explains the pleasure women derive from masochism as an adaptive strategy dictated by culture. But on the other, note, in the following statement, how apparent female sadism falls back into masochism and the possibility of a different sort of response to the dominant sex vanishes: "The masochist seeks affirmation of her existence whether through taking up the cross of martyrdom and assuring that others respond to her passivity and pain, through implicit accusation of her victimizer, or through re-enactment of sadism." Sacher-Masoch's Wanda similarly disappears into a discussion of *The Story of O.* Massé says, "O's name follows the nomenclature of many of the Gothic's nameless protagonists; it signifies nothing, a cipher . . . while having no value in itself. Her name suggests what Wanda . . . asserts: '*Woman's character is characterlessness.*' "[9] Wanda's name, not commented on, suggests not nothingness but authority. And the context of the quote from *Venus in Furs* deals not with women's lack of decided characteristics, but with their lack of character in the sense of the moralistic principles that Wanda claims restrict men's behavior. Wanda argues that Severin should beware arousing her sadism because women have no stake in obeying the social contract and so may indulge their cruelest impulses without internal restraint.[10] Wanda's philosophizing is heavily historicized within the text by references to women's place in civilized societies throughout time, and the text itself is part of the history of literary depiction of female sadists. So by equating Wanda and O, Massé accomplishes a feminist foregrounding of ways female characters voice misogynist views of woman, but she also obscures both part of the history of literary representation of female cruelty and some of the cultural conditions that determine its form.

In studies of female dominance by nonfeminist researchers, the prevalent focus on prostitutes guarantees the conclusion that a woman will assume a dominant position in relation to one man not because of any desire of her own but only in order to please another man. For example, in *Pain and Pleasure: A Psychoanalyst Explores the World of S&M*, the "world" that Robert Stoller explores turns out to be not that of S/M social clubs, where one might expect to find women attempting to act out their desires as free agents, but the world of S/M prostitution rings, "clubs" in which clients, almost always male, arrange for paid sessions.[11] Stoller most often interviews these prostitutes in the presence of their procurers.

The few texts that discuss female dominant sadomasochism typically treat this topic by looking, as I have in the preceding chapter, at the desires of the man involved and positing a woman who, at her most active, simply performs in the script he dictates. Reading masochism in this way accords with the cultural feminist position that women are naturally nonviolent and opposed to hierarchies, but such readings also betray a sort of hostility to sexual aggression that could be considered subversive of feminist goals.[12] If the essence of femaleness is imagined as the absence of aggression, then women are indeed always already marked as passive or receptive objects.

This sort of thinking is obviously responsible for such classifications as Freud's designating erotic masochism as feminine masochism. It also, perhaps somewhat less obviously, depends on both a totalization of heterosexuality as inescapably patriarchal and on the belief that the terms feminine and masculine signify a fixed and coherent group of characteristics. Recently feminist theorists and queer theorists have done much to deconstruct Freud's accounts of gender formation. Particularly apropos is Judith Butler's examination of melancholy's function in constructing both sexuality and gender. Arguing that "the melancholic answer to the loss of the same-sexed object is to incorporate and, indeed, *to become* that object through the construction of the ego ideal," she claims that "if melancholia operates through incorporation, then the disavowed homosexual love is preserved through the cultivation of an oppositionally defined gender identity" (63, 69). For a man this means the feminine must become "the unthinkable, the unnameable," but an unnameable made concrete as a prohibited "cultural possibility," within culture as much as "excluded from *dominant* culture" (77). While Butler's analysis of the genealogy of gender formation is focused here (and elsewhere) on object choice, we may conduct a similar analysis of the gendering of modes of expressing desire.

Jonathan Dollimore reminds us that the word *perversion* was associated with "the wayward, assertive woman, the woman on top" long before it acquired its association with homosexuality. As he argues, the social is sexualized just as surely as the sexual is socialized, and genders are constructed to serve political as well as familial interests.[13] There seems no reason to assume that taboos that serve to continue the family, such as those against incest or female object choice for girls, should be any stronger or any more implicated in gender formation than those serving the patriarchal state, such as the prohibition of sexual aggression in women.

When women may not express sexual desire as an urge to control another through physical manipulation and restraint, that mode of expression must be maintained as a choice demonstrably present but outside the pale of the dominant culture. Where feminine can only mean passive/receptive and heterosexual can only mean male-dominant, female dominance must be both culturally represented and read as feminization of man. Thus the term "feminine masochism" effectively erases the woman's desire in the S/M scenario because the man occupies the feminine place.[14] However, where culture writes gender otherwise, desires will be differently gendered and the dominant woman will reappear as an actor in the performance of gender and in the text.

One of the most marked recent instances of female desire being erased in the act of reading from a text ostensibly depicting female dominance can be seen in the relationship of Gilles Deleuze's commentary on Leopold von Sacher-Masoch's *Venus in Furs* to the novel itself. In 1967 Deleuze published, in one volume, a French translation of *Venus in Furs* along with a 109-page commentary on it, called *Le froid et le cruel*. This book was translated into English in 1971, as *Masochism: an Interpretation of Coldness and Cruelty*, and reissued in 1989. At that point the commentary seems to have utterly subsumed the novel, as many libraries now catalog the book solely under Deleuze's name. One explanation of the vast appeal of Deleuze's commentary on *Venus in Furs* might be that although he presents his theory as the basis of a radical new understanding of sexual perversity, he fills the book with comfortingly familiar ideas. While Deleuze says his reading of masochism is meant to replace Freud's, as I argue above, the Deleuze of *Coldness and Cruelty* is not the vehemently anti-Freudian Deleuze of *Anti-Oedipus* or *A Thousand Plateaux*. In fact, in interpreting *Venus in Furs*, Deleuze relies heavily on Freudian terminology and such figures from the Oedipus Complex theory as the Oedipal mother and the oral mother.

Deleuze's reading of masochism does update Freud's in one respect, but here it also goes some distance towards reconciling the figure of the male masochist with that of the culturally valued "real man." Like contemporary psychoanalytic theorists and sociologists who have studied members of sadomasochistic subcultures, Deleuze finds that the self-styled masochist actually frequently dominates his sexual encounters with a partner whom he has designated dominant, by setting limits for her and dictating the rituals through which he will receive supposed punishments. Consequently, the Freudian view of the masochist as an unhappy, ineffectual victim of a repressive society and his own thwarted, inward turned drives is problematized, and like many later professional observers, Deleuze claims that sexual masochism can best be understood as an indirect means to power over others. The main difference Deleuze sees between the sadist and the masochist is that the former dominates in order to destroy while the latter dominates in order "to educate, persuade, and conclude an alliance with the torturer."[15] While Deleuze points out the contractual and dialectical aspects of masochism, he also stresses that they convey a deceptive sense of reciprocity belied by the masochist's command of the educator's role, which is so complete that the masochist not only "forms" his mistress but "speaks through [her] mouth" (21). However, Deleuze's theory probably has been so influential not only because of its conventional relegation of woman to a subordinate role in the drama of sexuality, but for some feminist reasons, as well.

Deleuze's theory can attract a feminist reader because he envisions the body of the male masochist as the site of *both* the subversion of patriarchal law and its confirmation. For Deleuze male masochism allows man to express his need for a self-image opposed to that of the father and allied with the image of the mother, but in which triumph over the father's law is achieved at the expense of an actual female partner, through the appropriation of her voice and desires. Consequently, Deleuze's paradigm of masochism's pedagogy accounts for the curious situation so apparent to feminist observers of the rituals of romantic love: that male gestures of abject submission seldom work to the advantage of the women they ostensibly address. However, although Deleuze's theory conveniently explains away what might otherwise be called the paradox of male masochism—its failure to undermine men's power—his vision of the masochistic puppet master and his doll-like torturer presents problems when we try to apply it to specific literary texts. When it comes to describing what happens within literary texts, Deleuze's theory falls short to say the least, as becomes evident when we attempt to understand how it can describe narratives that represent men as achieving masochistic satisfaction within a reciprocal love relationship.

Deleuze sees Wanda, in *Venus in Furs,* through Severin's perspective and so declares her devoid of subjectivity, simply the incarnation of "the element of 'inflicting pain' " (38).[16] But in numerous speeches where Wanda warns Severin of her autonomous desires and cautions him against assuming that what satisfies him will also satisfy her, Sacher-Masoch's novel suggests a possibility never realized within the story: that the lovers could recognize each other as desiring subjects and use the forms of masochistic ritual to negotiate a relationship pleasing to them both. This possibility, rather than representing an idealization or, as critics like Kaja Silverman would have it, a utopian vision of masochism, is simply the informing principle of a great number of courtship narratives.

In contrast to uneasy, ambivalent narratives of female dominance that reassure sexual conservatives by insisting on the impossibility of integrating such behavior into a social life, texts otherwise as diverse as *Moll Flanders, Pride and Prejudice,* and the film *Something Wild* draw on another tradition that represents courtship as a female-dominant sadomasochistic encounter, which redresses the social inequality of the sexes through a complex educative interchange enough to allow both partners to believe in the authenticity of the woman's love. In these slippery stories, masochistic enactments of role-reversal confuse the flows of power so that the separation of master/mistress and slave cannot be maintained. Roles no longer function to mask the speaking subject and his silenced love object, but instead provide speaking positions for both partners, and dialectic gives way to dialogue.

One might certainly make a case that the eponymous heroine of *Moll Flanders* is depicted as a dominant woman, basing the reading on her cold, calculating treatment of most of her husbands, her successful cross-dressing, and her general aggressiveness. However, the text provides amply for other readings, not least in its accounts of her abject response to her first seducer, her compulsive seemingly self-destructive criminality, and her religious conversion. Living in a society that commodifies women, Moll seems to accept her object status, conducting herself as one who literally cannot afford desires of her own beyond insisting on being sold at the highest possible price despite an adverse market. (One of the first lessons in gender relations she receives is that "the Market is against our Sex just

now.")[17] I will focus here on one section of *Moll Flanders* that out-
lines a female strategy to gain dominance, a strategy often represented positively in the literature of courtship.

This section of *Moll Flanders* begins just after Moll, abandoned
by her charming but improvident linen-draper husband, assumes the
name Mrs. Flanders. Moll first takes up residence in the Mint among
financially ruined men. She notes that they show no restraint in their
debauchery, but always experience pleasure mixed with pain so that
"Sighs . . . interrupt their Songs," and in the midst of paying for "a
lewd Treat, or a wicked Embrace," they "cry *what a Dog am I!* (109–
10). She then moves on to a nautical community. As potential husbands, the captains are divided by Moll into two groups. The first
group consists of men who own good ships and are "resolv'd not
to Marry but with Advantage, that is, with a good Fortune." The
second consists of "Such as being out of Employ, want[ ] a Wife to
help them to a Ship" (111). In other words, Moll learns that all in-
dustrious respectable men expect their marriages to improve their
material circumstances, "and that LOVE had no Share, or but very
little in the Matter" (112).

Among the bankrupts in the Mint, men far outnumber women
and so must not only pay them but flatter and defer to them, but
among the respectable, Moll discovers that, "as the market run[s]
very Unhappily on the Mens side. . . . Women had lost the Privilege
of saying No . . . [and] if the Man was by great chance refus'd at
one House, he was sure to be receiv'd at the next" (112). A curious
picture emerges of the difference between debauchery and respect-
ability. The dissolute rakes of the Mint court women whose volition
they must recognize; their poor degraded mistresses may be secretly
despised, but they retain the power to say no. In contrast, respectable women desired as the matrimonial objects of good men are in
a position analogous to that of rape victims; whatever their desires
may be they cannot say no.

This disagreeable state of affairs brings low one of Moll's neigh-
bors, a young lady with the temerity to ask her suitor's acquaintances about his character and fortune. He is so insulted that he
rudely announces that his courtship of her is over, and begins court-
ing another woman. Moll brings her superior knowledge and energy
to bear on the case, telling the young lady that "a Woman can never

want an Opportunity to be Reveng'd of a Man that has us'd her ill, and that there [are] ways enough to humble such a Fellow as that" (113-14). The implementation of Moll's stratagem provides one of the novel's several moments of romantic relief from what would otherwise be an overwhelmingly cynical vision. And if marriage is to be presented by the novel as an institution worth saving, or love as an emotion that is ever relevant to human existence on earth, the novel must include such moments. Such narrative moves exemplify how representations of women's desire to dominate function as a necessary part of the story of love, rather than as a rupture in it. They point to a long tradition of literature naturalizing women's cruelty not in order to justify misogyny but in order to imagine that women might choose to be kind.

Moll and the young lady begin their campaign against the haughty suitor by spreading gossip that he is a boasting misogynist, "Debauch'd in his Morals"—in fact a polygamist—and on the verge of financial ruin (114-15). His new sweetheart's family rejects him, and he is turned away by all the other marriageable women in the area. Then, with the help of a male relative, the young woman lets it be known that she is being courted by a rich gentleman. The devastated former suitor writes "the most passionate Letters to her in the World, excusing his former Rashness" (116). When she finally allows him to appear before her, it is in the position of a defendant at the bar, and she fires off her trumped-up charges against him with such force that "He was so confounded at her Discourse that he could not answer a word" (117). After experiencing this public shaming and silencing, after being stripped of his identity and redefined by the young lady, the suitor becomes at once "the most modest, and the most importunate Man alive in his Courtship" (117), or in our terms, he demonstrates a masochist's ardent desire to submit to his beloved. Some more "turning the Tables upon him" follows in which all their former exchanges are reenacted with their roles reversed (118). And even when she consents to marry him, she holds back a large part of her money, giving what she does "as a mighty Favour." All of this high-handed treatment renders him "much the more obliging Husband to her when he [has] her" (119).

Throughout this episode and in the extended moralizing on the value of female self-respect that follows it, Moll stresses women's pleasure in cruelty and the excitement it arouses in men. The juxta-position of this adventure to the account of Moll's life in the Mint reminds us that the behavior of the prudent captains opposes that of men who love pleasure. Moll also tells us explicitly that the mari-ners' courtship habits are not "what I had found in the Country" (112). Through this contextualization, Moll's young neighbor's dominance of "her" captain not only during the courtship but after their marriage is naturalized and eroticized. While we might read Moll as a mouthpiece for Defoe, still the little morality play in which this puppet performs urges female aggression and male masochism as the natural and pleasurable means by which marriage can become more than a mere financial arrangement, can involve passion as well as prudence and yielding on both sides without self-sacrifice.

Pride and Prejudice dramatizes a similar moral through the ro-mance of Elizabeth Bennet and Fitzwilliam Darcy. From the first chapter of the novel we view a situation almost identical to that among *Moll*'s captains except that in *Pride and Prejudice* most of the men have no financial motives to marry. Marriageable women so far outnumber eligible single men that the bachelors tease the maidens and hold themselves aloof while the women agonize and plot. Darcy in particular takes advantage of the situation, sneering at the local belles and especially Elizabeth, whom he refuses to part-ner at a ball. Although he is captivated shortly afterward by Eliza-beth's aggressiveness and "independence of mind," he courts her in a style that she deems "all pride and insolence."[18]

His initial failure to win her love is foreshadowed in their first conversation when she reproaches him for despising his friend Bin-gley's submissiveness. She remarks, "To yield readily—easily—to the *persuasion* of a friend is no merit for you," and then goes on to explain that she thinks he undervalues "the influence of affection" (34). We could read this speech as advocating affectionate flexibility in both sexes, if Elizabeth's manner of delivering it and the rest of her conversation were not so aggressive as to suggest that the only yielding she has in mind is his. Clearly, her banter is meant to teach him that she regards submission as the sign of male love. "Despise me if you dare," she challenges him, and he, "so bewitched" as he had never been before, responds, "Indeed, I do not dare" (35). But when he replies to her rejection of his marriage proposal, she is disgusted to see that "his style was not penitent, but haughty" (141). This unsuccessful attempt at courtship is followed by a long period in which her prejudice against him dissolves as he performs difficult, humiliating tasks to win her.

During their climactic love scene, Elizabeth's speeches reveal the spontaneity with which she had hurt Darcy. As she says, she "had not the smallest idea of [her criticisms of him] being ever felt in such a way" (253). Here, unlike the corrupted, commercialized world of the captains, women are in an innocently cruel state of nature and need no instruction in humiliating men. All the instruction is for the male lover. Darcy declaring, "by you, I was properly humbled," both affirms the appropriateness of her treatment of him and stresses its necessity to the development of his love for her (254–55). Throughout the chapter, Elizabeth dominates the encounter. While Darcy asks questions, attempts to explain himself, and describes the agonies he has experienced because of her disapproval, she responds with one command after another: "We will not quarrel," "Do not repeat what I then said," "The letter shall certainly be burnt," "You must learn some of my philosophy." From the scene's repeated references to learning and teaching, such as Darcy's "You taught me a lesson, hard indeed at first, but advantageous" and from Elizabeth's concluding resolve to teach Darcy "to be laughed at," emerges a pedagogy of masochism that reverses Deleuze's paradigm, one in which a woman uses traditional courtship rituals to gain the power that her social situation threatens to undermine and punishes her lover in a way beneficial to them both.

My final example of romantic narratives in this tradition, Jonathan Demme's 1986 film, *Something Wild*, provides a surprisingly similar vision of courtship as a space filled most satisfyingly for both partners by female aggression and male submission. The similarity may be surprising because, as Jane Shattuc points out, both those critics who attack postmodernist film as representing a movement away from historicization, including "clear historical depiction of gender roles," and feminist film critics who celebrate postmodern film's departure from "the threateningly strict gender codes of reproduction" have seen films like *Something Wild* in terms of a rupture in traditional representations of gender relations.[19] But if we concentrate on this film's representation, including its romanticization, of relations between men and women during courtship, we will see the ways that it continues a tradition.

The love story enacted by Charley (Jeff Daniels) and Lulu (Melanie Griffith) does initially seem set in a world of gender relations very different from those of Moll Flanders and Elizabeth Bennet. Although Charley exploits his ancient privileges as a white male by walking out on his check in a restaurant and leaving the waitress to pay, he is quickly captured and enthralled by Lulu. Her name's association with Louise Brooks's character in *Pandora's Box*, whose hairdo she also copies, suggests her capacity for sexual cruelty. And while her voodoo accessories are sometimes comic, they are also sinister, implying the anger beneath her sexy playfulness, especially when they borrow from the style of Frida Kahlo. Unlike Darcy or the Captain in *Moll Flanders*, Charley does not have to be taught to respond with guilt when confronted with a woman's rage. Nor does he resist her forceful lovemaking in any overt way. He squirms with pleasure when she handcuffs him to the bed.

However, as the film progresses, we learn that he is lying to make her believe he is still married, when actually his wife has deserted him. The lie protects him from having to pass beyond improvised performances with Lulu into a more permanent relationship. The wistful longing for nurturing and comfort that underlie Lulu's toughness also gradually emerge, so that her visually suggested identification with Kahlo becomes more and more comprehensible. Under the eyes of conventionally feminine women like the old ladies who run a thrift shop, her mother, Peaches, and her high school classmates at their reunion, the dark Lulu reverts to her former identity as Audrey, a delicate blonde whom everyone assumes can only attain status and power through her man. Once again, it seems, we look at a premarital game in which choice belongs only to the man and desperation to the woman.

This conventional relationship between men and women is insistently coded not only as oppressive but as darkly evil. Against Charley's blissful, sexual enslavement in the first daylight half of the film is set the nightworld of male dominance and female acceptance of pain, comically suggested by Charley's story of his wife running away with the dentist and frighteningly dramatized in Lulu's agreement to go away with her criminal estranged husband, Ray. But even in the latter case, the film hints that male love tends toward the masochistic. Played by Ray Liotta, Ray is agonized by his love for Lulu/Audrey. He is meltingly admiring of her strength. He tells Charley, "She looks like she could fuck you in half." Finding the handcuffs in her purse he dreamily remarks, "Old habits die hard." At his most violently aggressive, he still pleads, "Why are you doing this to me? Why can't you just give me a chance?" Possessive and selfish as the cruel infant in Melanie Klein's psychoanalytic theory, Ray represents the dark side of male perversity complementary to Charley's clowningly pliant lover not only in his viciousness but also in his tormented sincerity.

The film's strange climax in a glaringly white suburban bathroom, where Ray and Charley lock into such a visually confusing death embrace that they seem to merge in the mirror, contextualizes the subsequent scenes of Charley's transformation. As if he had absorbed Ray, he becomes a mate for both Lulu and Audrey. His potential to run back into the safety of ordinary henpecked husbandhood (or to lie his way out of it) seems derailed by the charge of Ray's electrical presence as a passionate sacrificial victim.

The final scene moves toward resolution through a series of ambiguous gestures. Once again, Charley eats in the little café where he had run out on the check, but now leaves a five-dollar bill on the table, which Audrey, unseen by him, picks up. He is pursued by the waitress, played by reggae singer Sister Carol East, who berates him in the street demanding, "Do you expect to eat and not pay?" Audrey appears suddenly, dressed in a costume, a polka-dotted dress and picture hat, in the style then associated in the popular press with Diana, the Princess of Wales. It might not be reaching too much to interject at this point that "English" has long been used in "personals" advertisements as a euphemism for sadomasochistic play in which a man is beaten by a woman. After paying his bill, she leads him to an old-fashioned station wagon, but when she starts toward the driver's seat, he takes her arm and guides her to the passenger side just as, on the soundtrack, Sister Carol goes into the opening of her scolding version of "Wild Thing," with a harshly growled, "Oh, oh, riiight." As we might expect in a late 1980s courtship narrative, the conclusion of *Something Wild* does not suggest the same degree of confidence in marriage as a medium for resolving gender inequality that the courtship narratives from 1722 and 1813 do. Skepticism about marriage informs almost every one of the film's references to it. Still, in keeping with its romantic tone, the film suggests that the pleasure available in sexual encounters between men and women may last for a while at least if they can overturn the usual structure of dominance and submission.

Considered together, such narratives indicate that what is now called masochism has been represented, throughout history, even if inconsistently, as an attitude and set of behaviors that, when taught to men by women, can make possible a mutually satisfying marriage; this masochism can, in essence, transform the male body from an instrument of punishment for women into a medium through which women can generate pleasure for both themselves and their partners. It has also been a means of writing woman back into the discourse of desire as more than an object. This move would seem necessary to eroticism, for, as Jane Gallop says, "In order to be erotic, the object must depend on the viewer, on the aroused one, on our fantasies, our imagination, our constructs, our framing, and yet, the object must also remain independent, still real, still other."[20]

Lillian Faderman's writings on butch and femme role-playing among lesbians offers another model for understanding the way recognition of women's aggressive and dominating impulses operates to reeroticize relations between partners, to turn a socially linked pair into lovers. Working with numerous interviews in addition to texts, Faderman explains how feminist (over)reaction against rigid sexual roles resulted in a prohibition of sexual aggression among women that was in turn replaced by "the return of butch and femme" with a difference. "The roles are often charged in a way that would have been unthinkable in the sexually tame 1970s," because "the actors who indulge in these roles, femme as well as butch, are now frequently cognizant of the feminist image of the strong woman. The femme fantasy ideal may now be a lesbian Carmen rather than a Camille," in other words, femininity may be interpreted as aggressive.[21] One can see in traditional narrative representations of courtship that, among heterosexuals just as among lesbians, maintaining erotic tension often involves imagining the feminine as powerful and dominant, rather than as a blank space occupied by a sexual aggressor.

However, as Faderman's historically situated analysis shows, erotics change through time, causing corresponding changes in the performance of genders. Perhaps nowhere in the last few years has this been more evident than in the translation of Choderlos de Laclos's 1782 novel *Les liaisons dangereuses* into the popular 1990 film *Dangerous Liaisons*. Looking at a project like this, that stretches the same story across two centuries, helps show what can change and what must remain the same in textual representation of female sadism.

Stirring up a flurry of poststructuralist questions about authorship and identity, John Malkovich purrs to Glenn Close, "I often wonder how you managed to invent yourself." And she, her magnificent head lifted proudly, replies, "I had no choice did I? I'm a woman. . . . And I've succeeded because I've always known I was born to dominate your sex and avenge my own." Many associations place this scene from the film *Dangerous Liaisons* in the late 1980s. The characterizations seem to have grown naturally out of the actors' previous roles, especially Malkovich's as woman's subordinate dream man in *Making Mr. Right* (1987) and *Places in the Heart* (1984) and Close's as man's vengeful nightmare woman in *Fatal Attraction* (1987) and *The World According to Garp* (1982). Their pairing had the late 1980s' trendy topic of female-dominant sadomasochism written into it.[22]

The director, Stephen Frears, seems to have reached this theme through a logical progression from male brutality's defeat by the feminine in *The Hit* (1984) and the aggressive male's guilty submission to a feminized partner in *My Beautiful Laundrette* (1985) and *Prick Up Your Ears* (1987), to the son's rejection of the bloodstained patriarch in favor of bitchy, capricious woman in *Sammy and Rosie Get Laid* (1987). Only the film's technical conservatism works against the sense that it could not have been made any earlier than it was. Yet, it translates not only from another language but from another historically determined tradition of representing the erotic. If ever a film compelled its educated viewers to think about problems of translation, *Dangerous Liaisons* does. Laclos's *Les liaisons dangereuses* has undergone numerous renarrations, the most well known of which are probably Richard Aldington's translation of the novel into English, Roger Vadim's fluffy, jazzy *Les liaisons dangereuses*

1960, Hampton's play that was further adapted to make Frears's film, and Milos Forman's less commercially and artistically successful film, *Valmont*. The Frears/Hampton translation is successful not simply in terms of the film's popularity but, more importantly, in its preservation of the novel's peculiar tone and energy, which seem to emanate from an erotics of evil.

Not all the sexual misbehavior in the novel can be understood in this way. *Les liaisons dangereuses* often indulges in what seems to be merely a sophisticated naughtiness, as when the Marquise de Merteuil describes the "adventure with Prévan."[23] But the most powerfully charged erotic exchanges, those that make us understand Baudelaire's fascination with the novel, occur within its central games: the Vicomte de Valmont's seduction of Cécile de Volanges and the Présidente de Tourvel and the Marquise's manipulation of Valmont. And it is also here that the most formidable problem of translation appears, because concepts of attractive sexual evil have changed considerably since the eighteenth century. For this reason, any attempt to describe the erotics of the film must begin with some attention to the erotics of its source.

Both film and novel concern themselves with sadism and masochism, but very differently, in ways that seem determined by era and medium. When Laclos wrote his novel, masochism had not yet been given a name, nor had the masochist been created in the Foucauldian sense, by the intersection of the discourses of Sacher-Masoch, Krafft-Ebing, Havelock Ellis, and Freud. Positions we now associate with masochism are assumed as disguises by Valmont who, like the Captain in *Moll Flanders* and Darcy in *Pride and Prejudice*, sees them simply as signifiers of romantic love. That he expects women to interpret his submissive gestures this way is demonstrated by his conventional references to himself as the "slave" of both Tourvel and Merteuil whenever he wishes to wheedle some concession out of either one of them. The perversity of the pleasure he takes in his comically exaggerated charade of self-abasement is suggested by Merteuil's contemptuous remark that in his letters "the author lashes his sides to warm himself up, and the reader remains cold" (79, *33*). The novel predetermines this alienated response to Valmont's letters by continually exposing his falseness and apparent emotional confusion. Since we have no way of distinguishing be-

tween what he feels and what he pretends to feel, we can feel nothing
with him.

Unlike narratives of successful courtship, *Les liaisons dangereuses*
deals with deception rather than instruction and the realization of
evil rather than the attainment of good. Consequently, the novel's
main source of erotic energy comes not from its masochism but
from a sadism closely following Sade's in spirit, if not in practice, in
that it is constituted largely in response to orthodox religious ideology.[24] In 1782, sadism, too, was still nameless, but Sade was
Laclos's contemporary and, if the authors do not define themselves
similarly in relation to theology, their cruelest protagonists do. In
such texts as Sade's *Justine* and *Juliette*, God appears as a representation of the father in his most irrationally punitive aspect, not as
superego but as destroyer, paradoxically authorizing opposition to
him by smiting whoever upholds his laws. Thus, violent erotic impulses are liberated, not because their expression is not clearly prohibited, but because such expression seems to allow man to appropriate divine power. In short, sadism is defined, by Sade, in deliberately
blasphemous terms, as the ultimate male maturity and empowerment. *Les liaisons dangereuses* engages with religion somewhat more
conventionally. At the conclusion, vice receives a perfunctory punishment and the dull, good Mme. de Rosemonde holds all the cards
(and letters). Still, the excitement of the dramas enacted in the letters comes from their presentation as deliberate campaigns against
heaven.

Merteuil means her manipulation of Cécile and Danceny to dem-
onstrate, among other things, the worthlessness of Cécile's "clois-
tered education" and his religious vows. When Merteuil's plot cul-
minates in both young people hollowly professing religious vocation
as their last resort in a world in which they are too weak and foolish
to survive otherwise, Merteuil has succeeded even beyond her intention to expose the inapplicability of the doctrine of her time to
heroic souls like herself. Valmont's sacrilegious intentions seem, on
the surface, more ambitious. Merteuil seeks to evade religious law,
while Valmont would rewrite it. Like Satan, he sets out to rival God.
Tourvel's religious faith is her greatest charm, in his eyes, because
of his desire to become "the God she has preferred" (34,6). Of her
prayers he boasts, "What God did she dare to invoke? . . . It is I who

control her fate" (64, *23*). To redirect her prayers to himself, Valmont even uses a priest, Father Anselme. However, it is finally Merteuil who usurps divine prerogatives. In the model letter Merteuil writes to structure Valmont's rejection of Tourvel, she is addressed consistently as "my angel" (325, *141*). Merteuil causes Tourvel, the apostate angel, to be cast out of her unlawful heaven of love. Then, she demotes Valmont from devil to dupe and shows him that death is the price he has paid for his Faustian moment of omnipotence.

We might see Merteuil intertextually as the satanic figure of the traditional pact-with-the-devil tale, who exercises his power only to reaffirm God's, or, in Freudian terms, as the phallic mother in the masochist's fantasy whose cruelty always implicitly serves a phallocentric concept of gender difference.[25] While she states her sadistic credo in anti-male language, Merteuil's sadistic desires realize themselves exclusively through masculine sexuality, which founds her power. She uses men like surrogate penises to sexually torture her enemies. In all her fierce resistance to male and divine power, she affirms both and suggests their oppositional interdependence. The attractiveness of the character depends on her figuration of male power as satanic. She mirrors man back to himself as a sexy devil.

Through the characters' role reversals, the novel's erotics teasingly oppose their era's sexual and religious ideologies, but these reversals do not deconstruct the patriarchal ideology that prescribes dominant-submissive gender roles as ordained by God. In fact, since a large part of the novel's humor comes from Merteuil and Valmont's mistake in believing that they can reverse the religious, social, and familial hierarchies on which cultural concepts of identity depend, it is doubtful that we are seeing any moments at all of what Barbara Babcock calls "symbolic inversion and cultural inversion."[26] While we may admire Merteuil and Valmont's attempts to subvert a code that defines desire as weakness and sin, we may also find comic the abundant evidence that they have internalized that code.

The change of medium from novel to film brings a change in probable audience response. It is one thing for us, as readers, to enjoy the dual pleasures of identification with rebellion and detachment from its doomed excesses while both are safely contained within a novelistic "world" historicized for us by references to contemporary events and allusions to contemporary literature. Such a world is always elsewhere. It is another thing entirely for us, as audience, to smile at sadistic games played out on a screen in front of us by actors who are our contemporaries. Here images continually intrude from films set in eras other than the one in which the story ostensibly takes place.

As a primarily visual medium, film generally presents images into which possible narratives are intertextually coded. With increasing frequency, male (hetero)sexual cruelty appears in images that predict the punishment on behalf of woman that will follow. The torture, murder, or rape of an attractive woman, usually by a sneering sadist, at the beginning of the "action" film is as much a convention as the car chase near the end. In the last ten years, cinematic representation of heterosexual male sadism more and more often entails contextualization within feminist or pseudofeminist sensationalist narratives in which it functions as the catalyst for a woman's "consciousness raising" and results in drawn-out acts of revenge. Some popular films in this genre are *Extremities, Shame, The Accused, Sleeping with the Enemy,* and *Thelma and Louise.*[27] Conversely, in films released since 1980, female enactment of a sadistic role is more often represented not only, in the tradition of ridiculous reversal, as belonging to the comic mode but also as a wholesome or at least sensible response to a difficult world, as in *Eating Raoul, After Hours, Woman in Flames, Something Wild, Personal Services, Track 29,* and *Batman Returns.* Consequently, for the frequent moviegoer, the image of a dominatrix is likely to be associated with characters that invite identification and the image of a male sadist is likely to be associated with past evocations of anger.

In addition, the politically sophisticated audience at which Frears aims his films has been conditioned by a great many arthouse favorites to associate period costuming and sets with a condemnatory treatment of currently repudiated social mores, perhaps especially those governing gender roles and behavior. Such films project onto an exoticized past, shown to be markedly other than the world the audience inhabits, the conflict between the individual libido and exterior authority, a conflict that psychoanalysis posits as eternal and ordinary observation tells us is ongoing. To recapture the disturbing eroticism of *Les liaisons dangereuses,* Frears works both within and subversively against these conventions.[28]

The admirer of Laclos's novel may see the characters in Frears's *Dangerous Liaisons* in something like the form of nesting Russian dolls, each shaped and painted by a text or an intersection of texts. The outermost dolls are composed by Frears's direction, Hampton's screenplay, and the actors' interpretation. More central dolls are made by Laclos's published text(s). But where can we find the last doll? In prior texts? In the antifeminist cinematic theater of cruelty where crimes against women are enacted as farce, or the cinema of normative retribution in which Black Widows and Lady Eves turn to women in flames? In the text of society itself? If we think—even for a moment—about the source of the gorgeously compelling figures passing before our eyes, we may find ourselves looking into the dizzying mystery of identity. And it is exactly this antiessentialist vertigo that Frears evokes in the first images of the construction of those performers on the social stage, Merteuil and Valmont. Consequently, the fetishization of Close/Merteuil in star images such as her golden descent from a carriage in front of Rosemonde's chateau, is problematized. Like the self she invents in her letters in the novel, the film's Merteuil is a self-representation, her own gaze in the mirror having endowed her with signifying power before ours can.

However, the film's Merteuil does not robe herself in the same satanic guise as the novel's Merteuil. How could she when satanic sacrilege in films mostly means slitting chickens' throats and wearing bright yellow contact lenses? Almost from the beginning in film, blasphemy and satanism have been relegated to the horror genre, where they function not to shock religious sensibilities but as motivational devices. In *Dangerous Liaisons*, the religious subtext almost disappears; Danceny is no longer a Knight of Malta and neither he nor Cécile dedicate their lives to the church. Tourvel's faith, which in the novel defines her seduction as blasphemy, appears in the film only visually and in highly compromised forms. We see her taking communion but with her attention on Valmont, underscored by the camera's shift to her point of view just as the wafer dissolves in her sensual mouth, and, later, by the closeup of her face directing amorous glances at him during mass. Even more suggestive of her hypocrisy is that before her seduction Tourvel (Michelle Pfeiffer) always wears dresses with transparent panels imperfectly closed over the tops of her breasts and a cross conspicuously gleaming at the top of her cleavage. One can hardly help associating her with Belinda in Pope's "The Rape of the Lock." Under these circumstances it would be comic for Valmont to aspire to replace God in her affections or to substitute his billet-doux for her bibles, and indeed, the scene in which he explains his intentions to Merteuil revises the original text to translate both his character and Merteuil's to accord with late twentieth-century concepts of sexy evil.

A series of rapid cuts, from the delicately pretty face and graceful stemlike form of Cécile (Uma Thurman) behind the grill of the cloister, to Merteuil describing her as "a rosebud" and Valmont protesting "she'd be on her back before you'd unwrapped the first bunch of flowers," to Tourvel picking roses in the Rosemonde garden, visually and verbally establishes the connection between roses and sweet, pure women as one that facilitates their commodification. The lovely images tell us that, like roses, such women are raised and cared for in special, protected enclosures until they are claimed by men. The untouched rosebud opens into a rose, which exists only to be picked and enjoyed. Buy a bunch of roses, Valmont tells us, and you have bought a girl.

In the contrasting scene, Merteuil appears unconsumable. A bow on her gown has risen up to conceal her breasts. The camera, like Valmont, leans toward her face, and her expression is cryptic and smug. Everything about her speaks self-containment. He tells her that he wants "the excitement of watching [Tourvel] betray" her own values, remarking, "Surely you understand that. I thought betrayal was your favorite word." She replies, "No, no, cruelty: I always think that has a nobler ring to it." This exchange, not in the novel,[29] offers an interpretation of Merteuil's character. She is a sadist. It also anticipates the much later revelation, which *is* in the novel, that Valmont is Merteuil's real quarry, not Cécile or Tourvel. For how can a rose betray itself or be abused? Cécile and Tourvel have been introduced as already objectified and appropriated. The viewer can be expected to understand this because films generally treat the sexual seduction of pretty women as inconsequential or comic, as if always implicitly accomplished. Valmont clearly does not understand that his plot is meaningless, because he is distracted by the erotic value of Merteuil's self-revelation. At her words, the camera shows us his face suffused with adoration and for the rest of their scene he appears mesmerized by his desire for her. For the viewer, the film's plot receives meaning from Valmont's intensely dramatized masochism.

What follows, within the same scene, is an amazingly condensed version of the offering and acceptance of the contract between Merteuil and Valmont, which in the novel is not completed until letter fifty-seven. In the novel, as Peggy Kamuf points out, Valmont misreads Merteuil's dual intentions in offering the contract, both to set a limit to his affair with Tourvel and to defer forever his possession of herself, since her "project" is always to possess men "outside of an exchange in the public or symbolic register," which would define her as defeated.[30] According to this reading, the contract would work as Deleuze claims masochists' contracts always do: to parody through reversal and "an excess of zeal" the contractual relations of patriarchal law in which "woman typically figures as an object" (Deleuze 80). Kamuf differs from Deleuze, however, by attributing agency to the woman. She is not a character in a joke the male masochist tells to amuse and reassure himself but a participant in a ritual she initiates, the writer of the contract rather than simply "the party with whom the contract is entered into" (Deleuze 80). The film suggests that Valmont misreads the contract because of his preoccupation with his erotic subjection to Merteuil.[31] Through the circumstances of this misreading Valmont is translated from an eighteenth-century sadist into a modern masochist, a translation that offers a corrective to the standard psychoanalytic reading of the male masochist as a solitary dreamer dreaming (absent) woman's power.

By making Valmont's misreading crucial to the unfolding of the plot, the film reverses the sexual politics of the novel to the extent that it, as Nancy Miller argues, presumes a female reader "expected to identify with the site/sight, topographical and visual, of her figured complicity . . . within the dominant order" and so, like the women readers within the story, is "doubled into" a position like that of the prostitute Emilie "by the act of reading itself."[32] The film foregrounds Valmont's role as (mis)reader and Merteuil's as producer of texts. Whereas one might say that in the novel he writes the plot while she reads and responds (although actually the first

letter between them comes from her), in the film she definitely
authors the contract that he must decode to determine his fate.

Valmont seems to understand his contract much as Deleuze understands Sacher-Masoch's, as a means of implying "not only the
necessity of the victim's consent, but his ability to persuade, and his
pedagogical and judicial efforts to train his torturer" (Deleuze 66).
In his view, the contract creates the illusion that the man serves the
woman, who now embodies law, while actually it exists only to authorize his desires. We see Valmont enjoying the complex irony of
indulging himself bŷ command, when, appearing to be almost overcome with love, he rolls Tourvel on top of him in bed and startlingly
asks, "When will you start writing to me again?" (The letters are to
be passed on to Merteuil.) And again when, in an ecstasy of erotic
misery, he beats and insults Tourvel, claiming to do so at the insistence of "a woman I adore." The Aldington translation correctly
renders the "refrain" of this renunciation scene, "*Ce n'est pas ma
faute,*" as "it is not my fault" (325, *141*). The novel defines his cruelty
in terms of morality. The irony comes from the reader's understanding that, as Merteuil insists, Valmont's sadism is the fatal fault
that makes it impossible for him to be genuinely either "a woman's
lover or her friend, but always her tyrant or her slave" (324, *141*). It
clearly is his fault that he is Merteuil's slave and Tourvel's tyrant.
But in the film, the words he reiterates are, "It's beyond my control." This reference to the controlling contract suggests ironies,
some obvious within the narrative, others playing on the social context of its translation.

The most obvious irony is that, at least superficially, Valmont has
exercised far more control than he acknowledges. In the novel during a renegotiation of the contract, Merteuil insists on the "sacrifice" of Tourvel and provides Valmont with a model rejection letter,
which he "simply" copies and sends (326, *142*). In the film, Valmont
deliberately tempts Merteuil "to impose some new condition" and,
when she obliges, he invents the vicious wording of the rejection
himself. Other readily apparent but dissonant ironies involve his belief that he can control his emotions, Merteuil, and their game. As
Bill Overton points out, the phrase "also refers to what Valmont can
recognize only later, that in betraying Tourvel he has surrendered
control to Merteuil."[33] However, the film's most interesting ironies

are generated not by Valmont's misunderstandings but by the confrontation the film stages between different visions of sexual evil. These visions are historically determined.

As E. Ann Kaplan has asserted, "Psychoanalysis and cinema are inextricably linked both to each other and to capitalism, because both are products of a particular stage of capitalist society."[34] In this sense, *Dangerous Liaisons* is self-referential. Paralleling Merteuil's repeated comparisons in the novel of herself to an author or playwright, the film defines her as a director, most explicitly in her use of theatrical performances as backgrounds for manipulations of the other characters. The opening and concluding images of her looking into a mirror and creating herself as both the object of the gaze and its source seem constructed to subvert the usual relationship of female film characters to director and audience. The film presents its knowing treatment of psychoanalytic and Marxist theory as if from within Merteuil's consciousness. This is brought to the film's surface when, seeming to speak from outside the character and historical setting, Merteuil gives a conventional modern interpretation of Valmont's obsession with sexual pursuit, calling it "immaturity."

The film's construction of masochism is informed by psychoanalysis. That Valmont's attraction to Merteuil comes from an unresolved Oedipus Complex is suggested by his obsessive rivalry with the childlike Danceny (Keanu Reeves) and his reference to sex with Merteuil as "coming home." The film's insistent visual association of mirrors with Merteuil suggests her role as narcissistic mother and also, because Valmont is seen receiving only fragmented images of himself in her realm, her blockage of his individuation. But the film's representation of masochism owes much more to sociology than to psychoanalysis. We are shown symbolic practices and objects that continually return us to questions about objectification and commodification, that is, questions about masochism's relation to capitalism, which in turn, seem related to Merteuil's enormously attractive resistance to being consumed.

Throughout the film, flesh means vulnerability to commodification. First, the nakedness of Tourvel's maid, Julie, allows Valmont to buy her when he surprises her in bed with his servant. Then Emilie's nakedness is the sign of her prostitution and objectification, as Val-

mont names her his "desk." This scene and a later one, in which
Cécile takes dictation on Valmont's bare back, are equally tainted
with implications of masochistic subjection, both because they
comically reify cultural inscription on the body as sex play and because they suggest the physical marking so important to sadomasochistic ritual. The early objectifying images we have of Cécile and
Tourvel also suggest their status as victims within a sadomasochistic
drama. Cécile appears behind bars in the gothic setting of the con-
vent; Tourvel bends across a cane.

If the bodies of other characters come to signify their enslavement, Merteuil's provides a space to display fetishes of her dominance. When she arrives to instruct Cécile in the harsh facts of sexual life, her black leather gloves stand out with almost surreal
intensity against her bright gold traveling suit. When Valmont, trying the same trick he used on Julie, surprises Merteuil in bed with
Danceny, they are both neatly clothed, as if to emphasize the protection that she extends even beyond the boundaries of her person.
The film's association of her fetishistic displays with her sexual
knowingness and control works against the sort of aestheticization
of woman that Rita Felski sees in heroines of decadence like Wanda.
According to Felski, in *fin de siècle* narratives featuring aesthete heroes, "the threat of the natural is negated by being turned into art;
the female body is transformed into a visually pleasing play of sur-
faces and textures under the scrutiny of the male gaze," while
"women themselves lack the ironic self-consciousness that their presence inspires in others."[35] Almost the opposite might be said of
Merteuil. Her body is deployed as an object in her war; it consistently expresses her self-conscious, powerful control. But, through
this usage, Merteuil's body also becomes the site of a powerful vali-
dation of capitalist consumerism. She buys her own physical integ-
rity in the form of objects that cover the body, onto which its in-
cipient objectification is displaced.

Dangerous Liaisons is by no means unique in linking sadism and
consumerism. Beyond the fact that both are more available to the
affluent, sadism has an intrinsic affinity with purchasing goods. The
ritual sadomasochistic drama offers what may be the most "commercial form of sex," because its enactment depends on the use of
costumes and equipment not generally available free and also be-

cause its articulation as fantasy "contains its own narrative" and so lends itself particularly well to commercial publication. As fiction and metafiction, as telling and as selling, as a highly commercially appealing vision of sadomasochistic drama and as a self-referential commentary on its own erotics, *Dangerous Liaisons* shows us that "from a strictly capitalistic viewpoint, [sadomasochism] is the ideal sexual practice."[36]

Walter Benn Michaels argues that, far from parodying the dominant culture's contractual relations as Deleuze claims, all masochists' contracts express a capitalist desire for ownership; the masochist "wants to own the right to sell himself."[37] Valmont seems to understand his contract as possessing this sort of power. By the end of the film, Valmont twice conflates offering documents to support his upholding of the contract with offering up himself: once when he brings Tourvel's letter to Merteuil's bedroom and again when, having impaled himself on Danceny's sword, he gives the youth his confession and Merteuil's letters. But Merteuil miraculously seems to own herself without having to sell herself, because she successfully passes off a disguise as herself. Fools like Belleroche and Danceny who fall into love with her mask of kindness are given a costume to make love to. Valmont falls in love with her cruelty, but her sadomasochism is a closed system. She sticks a fork into her hand under the table and smiles. There is no place for him within such a system. So she denies the contract that he would have authorize the fulfillment of his desires and paradoxically, through his subjugation, creates him as a subject. Where he wants affirmation of his right to own under the law, she exposes law as a fiction meant to contain desire and laughs at the very idea. And, within a capitalist system, what could be more nefarious?

Perhaps to liberal audiences Merteuil's greatest evil is rejecting the last two decades' liberal erotics. In some ways, she begins well. In an exemplary feminist style, she attacks the "rose world" where, according to Rosemonde's doctrine of sexual relations, male desire is always primary: "Men enjoy the happiness they feel; we can only enjoy the happiness we give." Like the heroines of classic Hollywood comedy, as Naomi Scheman persuasively describes them,[38] Cécile and Tourvel are good Freudian daughters whose desire exists only in response to a man's. In a late 1980s film by a director known for his critiques of gender politics, the downfall of Freudian daughters must have a didactic overtone. However, after Merteuil accelerates their romances to their inevitably tragic conclusions, she then rejects the properly modern substitute for traditional romance—monogamous egalitarian love. In its place she demands inequal relations with a weaker, subservient partner. And unlike her literary model, she eliminates her self-proclaimed mate, refuses to be limited even by her own writing of herself, and returns to the mirror to create herself anew. The final image urges us to see her, not as she has invented herself previously, but as she sees herself now.

In this last scene the film breaks decisively from the novel. In the novel, Merteuil is not only rejected by society (hissed by her fellow audience members at the opera), she is afflicted by God with disfiguring disease and loses her wealth. The film ends with her retreat from the censorious opera crowd to her home where she: "sits at her dressing-table, alone, removing her make-up. As it comes off, a new MERTEUIL seems for the first time revealed, weary, fragile, vulnerable almost. She looks at her reflection with the anxiety someone feels in the presence of their only friend."³⁹ The camera moves in lovingly close to her face as she strips away her make-up mask and a new face emerges, vulnerable and appealing as Hampton describes it in the above quote, but also troubling in its appeal for empathy because she has been, after all, the death of her lover. This new conclusion raises the question of how we are to think of such a figure.

Both traditionally and according to cultural feminism, she must be read as male-identified and wrongly so, an evil woman who reverses and so reinscribes all the horrors of patriarchy.⁴⁰ Naomi Greene's interpretation, based on Deleuze's commentary on *Venus in Furs*, of another deadly dominant woman, Death (Maria Casares) in Cocteau's *Orphée*, exemplifies such a reading. While Greene goes beyond Deleuze in attributing agency to the male masochist's woman partner, she stigmatizes the dominant woman's feeling for Orpheus as inferior to that of "warm" characters like the film's petite-bourgeoise Eurydice. Though Cocteau emphasizes that Death forsakes her status and identity to possess Orpheus for a few moments, she is described by Greene as only "professing" love, exhibiting only "a cold and cruel sentimentality." Recognizing that Coc-

teau presents "his" Death differently, in fact, as a figure who, once
touched, "renders real life unbearable," Greene must condemn his
vision as "a disavowal or 'neutralization' of reality."[41] One might
compare this to Adrienne Rich's response to the film in her poem
"I Dream I'm the Death of Orpheus." In the figure of the poet's
Death, the narrator recognizes herself, a woman "with certain powers" operating under prohibitions, pledged to the rational (to "lu-
cidity") but compelled onward by desire that will not "leave her in-
tact."[42] Here not only masochism, as Leo Bersani would have it,[43]
but also its complementary sexual cruelty shatters logic and the coherent self it allows, shatters gender and the law that has made it,
kills the poet not out of the real world (whatever that may be) but
into life "on the wrong side of the mirror," beyond the duality of
an image of presence and its reversed reflection. Both Cocteau's
Death and Frears's Merteuil go through mirrors, pulling their lovers
after them.

Through Merteuil's and Valmont's sexual transgressions, both
the novel and the film eroticize resistance to the moral discourses
that empower society. Both locate that resistance within a contract.
However, while *Les liaisons dangereuses* finds the contract itself excitingly evil, *Dangerous Liaisons'* greatest charge of excitement comes
from the violation of the contract. Around this central and profound difference in erotics, the film's narrative builds what often
seems to be a faithful translation. And despite its many departures
and changes from the original text, the translation is faithful, in
that, like its original, it allows us the subversive pleasure of a thorough enjoyment of what our society calls evil and what, from within
the strictures of rationality, we hardly know how to call otherwise.
In the shining moment in which Merteuil appears before us straight
from hell and trailing veils of glory, we see not an evil Eve, lost, and
fallen away from "the" feminine ideal, but an outlawed woman with
undeniable power. Suddenly the question of choice in women's lives
seems real and pressing, not simply a politically expedient fiction of
the late twentieth century.

When we can distinguish the figure of the desiring dominant
woman, veiled as she is, from the ground of her man's and her culture's desires, we can achieve a new vision of female subjectivity. It
becomes possible to imagine a sexuality not always already com-

pletely determined but one that permits agency and that allows for resistance. Whether she is lauded as the loving instructor of her romantic mate or demonized as her competitive lover's destroyer, she is also an actor in the performance of identity. To rediscover this figure as she has been traditionally represented in tales of female will and power is to rediscover the world lost to purely patriarchal narrative, to reenvision woman's entry into language not as a disruptive and incoherent interruption of symbolism and order, but as an articulated part of the cultural stories that work overtly to inform our sense of what love is.

5

RE-VIEWING THE BLOOD ORGASM
When the Postmodern Woman Takes Back
Her Knight

> Break out of the circles; don't remain within the psychoanalytic
> closure. Take a look around, then cut through!
>> Hélène Cixous, "The Laugh of the Medusa" (trans. Keith Cohen
>> and Paula Cohen)

AFTER LOOKING AT the many diverse literary traditions of representing behavior that might currently be called female dominant sadomasochism, we can achieve a different reading of textual
erotics than psychoanalytic approaches allow. Past modes of figur-
ing the dominant woman and the submissive man can be seen as
reflecting societal changes affecting relations between the sexes.
And in one text's revisions of prior texts' renderings of the erotics
of the situation between yielding man and his chosen mistress, we
can read a history of the struggle to express a vision of love's disruptive power. This struggle gains a certain intensity in the literature and film produced in the period when a great increase in
women's power as actors in the world promises to extend the nego-
tiations between men and women beyond courtship, to negate clo-
sures, letting both partners renew the contract endlessly. When marriage does not require woman to relinquish her own name and give
up her freedom, when instead of entrapping her, it depends on her
continuing consent, female power stops being merely a fantasy or a
metaphor.

The texts produced by our contemporaries sometimes dramatize
what could result. When we move from automatically assigning psychoanalytic meanings to the roles the characters assume in these

dramas, we may discover things outside "the psychoanalytic enclosure" that pertain to the new feelings and practices possible in a different world not only of gender relations, but of gender identities.
Woman, man, heterosexuality, and love can be defined anew. More
than two decades of academic investigation into the construction
of sexuality and gender should have taught us that erotics undergo
continual revision. If we have not learned that lesson in cultural
framing then we are doomed endlessly to inflict on each other all
the horrors of coercion and condemnation that arise from belief in
a "natural," universal, and absolute sexuality.

Yet it is difficult to write on sexuality without rewriting sexual
norms. This difficulty has been nowhere more evident than in discussions of male masochism informed by psychoanalytic theory.
When it has already been decided that we are looking at disavowal
of "the reality of sexual difference," appropriate reactions are
largely predetermined. Historically, psychoanalysts have been willing
to tolerate as natural some expression of masochistic desires by
women, and some feminist critics have worked within this absence
of official condemnation to legitimate women's enactment of masochistic rituals as a subversive strategy.[1] But men's masochism and
our vision of it generally remain constrained by the tenets of psychoanalysis. Freeing our understanding from psychoanalytic paradigms means detaching masochism from femininity.

Essential to most psychoanalytic theories of both sexuality and
identity are two separable and definable groups of attributes: the
masculine and the feminine. Psychoanalytic literary theorists often
insist that the masculine and the feminine are not to be confused
with man and woman, but, instead, are subject positions occupied
through complicated and shifting identifications. The claim that it
is significant that the masculine and the feminine are associated both
popularly and by analysts with differently sexed bodies is frequently
treated as a quibble. And, although I am, of course, quibbling on
the modern and archaic meanings of the word quibble when I say
this, psychoanalytic theorists often seem to object to quibbles for
the same reasons that Samuel Johnson does when he claims that:

A quibble is to Shakespeare what luminous vapours are to the trav-
eller; he follows it at all adventures; it is sure to lead him out of his

way and sure to engulf him in the mire. It has some malignant power over his mind, and its fascinations are irresistible. . . . A quibble, poor and barren as it is, gave him such delight that he was content to purchase it by the sacrifice of reason, propriety, and truth. A quibble was to him the fatal Cleopatra for which he lost the world and was content to lose it.[2]

First, such a quibble is seen as intellectually unsophisticated; it suggests old-fashioned, unprofessional feminism in which rather than carefully analyzing Freud and Lacan, one simply reacts angrily against their misogynistic theories and remarks and so dismisses all they say as what Woolf styled "cock-a-doodle-dum."[3] Like Shakespeare lost in the trivial (in Johnson's view), one neglects what is important. Second, such a quibble is wrong or even in a sense immoral because it represents "the sacrifice of reason, propriety, and truth" to the pursuit of delight at the expense of loss of worldly reality. To reject "masculine" and "feminine" as terms useful to cultural analysis may seem like wallowing in the mires of liberation fantasy, like giving ourselves up to the joy of imagining that we might have within us some flow of desire that could not be neatly charted in relation to images of the eternal two, mother and father. Or it may resemble the madness of daring to dream that our enactments of self might take place outside what Deleuze and Guattari call the "intimate theater," a restrictive internal space produced by the Oedipus Complex theory's "familialist reduction" and conventionalizing containment of desire.[4] Yet, I must insist that quibbling in this way is necessary to understanding the development of the modern concept of masochism. Jane Gallop says at the end of her study of recent feminisms,

> I am beginning to realize that feminists need to stop reading everything through the family romance. If we are going to understand our relation to the academic institution [and I would add to other social institutions] within which we think and teach and speak, we need to recognize its specific dynamics which are obscured in the recourse to familial metaphor.[5]

I must quibble with masculine and feminine as useful descriptive terms because masculinity and femininity cannot refer to stable groups of attributes and attitudes at any point in time, let alone transhistorically.[6] No age has *one* femininity or masculinity. Every place and time, like each human being, has many conflicting versions of each. While ideologies may work to bring these masculinities and femininities into coherence, they cannot succeed any more than individual subjects can. This can be illustrated by a brief look at two attitudes that dominant cultures of the Western world frequently prescribe as appropriate to the reception of punishment by a male.

Consider the admonition to "take it like a man."[7] It is commonly interpreted as meaning to accept physical and/or emotional pain silently and unflinchingly, that is, without protest. Still, this apparently passive concept of masculinity does not always rule out retaliation, which, in fact, the equally popular recommendation that a male not "take it lying down" demands. Following the latter maxim, we might argue that a man who receives a blow from a woman should hit her back. But yet another concept of masculinity conflicts with this one and, for at least the last two centuries, has posed a threat to its coherence: the concept of the gentleman.

In the gentleman, a sense of gender superiority and of class superiority blend. The presence of one suggests the other, so that to act as a superior member of one's gender (which comes from secure recognition of the superiority of one's gender and one's class) confers status indistinguishable from class status. Charles Dickens's *Great Expectations* provides a classic account of the convoluted nature of gentlemanhood, but more on this later. Predicated on *noblesse oblige*, the key component of gentlemanly behavior is deference to women. Consequently, a man following this model must accept pain from a woman without protest, but he can never retaliate.

To review, according to one model of masculinity, superiority should be asserted, while in the other any demonstration of a need to assert superiority would suggest its lack. One masculinity says, in effect, I dominate because my body is stronger; what you think punishes me I receive as nothing, while you will be hurt by the punishment I inflict on you. This seems an exemplary masculinity if masculinity is equated with physical prowess; still the emotionality suggested by the apparent compulsion to respond can be read as effeminate. Gentlemanly masculinity implies, by contrast, that I dominate because you are incapable of influencing my behavior, which reflects my superior intellect and morality without reference to your feeble displays of will. The latter is certainly more enviable because it seems to replicate the relation between adult and infant or human and object. However, it can be deemed effeminate, since it is passive. But it is important to remember that both of these masculinities are postures always exposed as inadequate by any effective resistance. Consequently, from some vantage point, a masculinity can always be proven to be femininity in disguise; masculinity cannot be located anywhere; and taking it like a man always means responding to punishment by hitting back and by not hitting back. All of this quibbling leads me to the question, since masculinity is so mutable—as it varies situationally and is established in one place only to begin immediately dissolving through its failures and contradictions—what sense can it make to analyze gender relations by foreclosing the issue of the gendering of masochism as is done when we adopt Freud's vision of the male masochist as "feminine masochist"?

It has been my purpose throughout the preceding chapters to show how literature and film have provided an escape from psychoanalytic narratives of the gender identity development and the binarism at the core of these narratives by maintaining earlier traditions of viewing and representing the attitudes and behaviors that we now call male masochism. However, the course of literary tradition does not run smooth, and, as we have seen, one text's engagement with a prior text's representation of eroticism generally concerns itself more with responding to previous erotics than with transmitting them faithfully. But by following the convoluted path of such revisionary responses, we may at last reach a perspective from which we can look back, otherwise than psychoanalysis dictates, over the dynamics of power between men and women.

We might begin by considering the following passage from Edgar Allan Poe:

> There came from some far, far distant and unknown land, into the gay court of the king I served, a maiden to whose beauty my whole recreant heart yielded at once—at whose footstool I bowed down without a struggle, in the most ardent, in the most abject worship of love.[8]

Now one could hardly repeat the narrator's words without some sort of distancing ironic or parodic tone, and in this response to the passage, we can read some of the changes that have taken place in the way we usually interpret past rhetorics of love. Here Poe seems to draw as confidently on romanticized medieval imagery as he does on the emblematic personified heart for representations of the lover's passion. Gradually in the passage of time from his age to ours, the signifying power of the knight has shifted. While our hearts still "know," "speak," and "bleed," in response to love, the knight who displays his love wounds like medals and kneels to receive more no longer stimulates sympathy and reader identification. Rather, in our era of the egalitarian love ethic, he is read as repellently exhibitionistic and masochistic.

It is not, however, simply a belief in wholesome sexual mutuality that informs the current readings of past (or archaic) representations of desire. Our readings are also determined by cultural constructions of gender difference that declare both male masochism and male sexual display abnormal. In the late 1980s controversy over whether the NEA and NEH should fund artistic projects and exhibits that some Americans find morally offensive, would-be censors often equated the exposure of male sexuality with (sado)masochism. For example, when Hilton Kramer wanted to give the impression that he did not criticize Robert Mapplethorpe on homophobic grounds, he went so far as to claim that whenever the display of male sexuality seems to be the point of a work then that work becomes repugnantly sadomasochistic.[9] While Kramer's view might be dismissed as atypical because of its conservatism, if we believe the testimony provided by contemporary sexologists, feminist antipornography groups like Women against Pornography (WAP), and residential communities throughout America (as represented in their legislation on pornography), male sexual display seems to arouse more hostility than sexual excitement in women and heterosexual men. Even if, as Walter Kendrick suggests in *The Secret Museum*, it has not always been the case that the phallus "can play its role only when veiled," Lacan's claim seems true enough now.[10] In a culture in which male power is built upon mystification of sexuality and gender, the man who makes a public show of his sexuality is always tainted with implicit masochism.

Because male sexual display necessarily reveals the lack of an empirical basis for the privilege that accompanies biological difference, the male masochist strips off the (symbolic) phallus as he publicly bares himself for the blow. When he compounds this crime against the fathers by delightedly embracing the victim's role, he would seem to place himself outside the pale, happily free to undermine society's standards. The man who could be king but "would prefer not to," is potentially powerfully disruptive. Critics who conceive of their own role oppositionally and work to disempower hegemonic ideologies might look to the figure of the male masochist as a model of transgression, whose willing inversion of patriarchal values, including a jubilant offering up of self, could unsettle the dominant discourse on masculinity. However, before elevating him as the new hero, we must pause to consider that the literary figure of the male masochist comes to us through the Victorian novel and the language of Freudianism, which have worked together to contain his rebellion within a conservative power structure.

In order to establish a literary vantage point from which to view this difficult figure, I will look at reinscriptions of gender hierarchy in the dramatizations of male masochistic pleasure in two consistently popular and influential Victorian novels, *Great Expectations* and *Wuthering Heights*, and examine the ways such representations provided a context for Freud's theory of feminine masochism, before passing on to a discussion of ways that two of our contemporaries' revisionary responses to these texts challenge currently popular ways of thinking about masochism.

Because of its paradoxical familiarity and weirdness, *Great Expectations* is an ideal reference point to begin an intertextual exploration of the dialogues male masochism has held with patriarchal culture. In apparent defiance of general values, this novel continues to be one of Dickens's most popular, despite featuring a protagonist, Pip, who invites us to come watch him bleed. Or to put it in his own words, after declaring his absolute subjection to Estella, Pip tells us: "In what ecstasy of unhappiness I got these broken words out of myself, I don't know. The rhapsody welled up within me, like blood from an inward wound, and gushed out." Self, Other, pain, pleasure, authenticity, and the literary, all flow together for Pip, who tells Estella, "You are part of my existence, part of myself. You have been in every line I have ever read, since I first came here, the rough common boy whose poor heart you wounded even then." And under the influence of his goddess's disdain, these confluent forces produce an "ecstasy of unhappiness," a rhapsody of anguish, a heart-rending orgasm of blood.[11]

It is probably correct, as both sexologists and psychoanalytic theorists have claimed, that sublimated sadomasochism is a basic ingredient of much art. Theodor Reik used Dickens's novels to support his theory that the development of masochistic fantasies into art involves repression of their eroticism. A long critical tradition determines current readings of Pip's narrative as exemplary of what Freud termed moral masochism, that is, a guilty pursuit of social suffering not eroticized in any conscious or obvious way. Yet in *Great Expectations*, and a number of other Victorian novels, masochistic content is often explicit, confessionally foregrounded rather than sublimated. In their treatment of masochism, these novels illustrate Foucault's claim that during this period, "Sex was driven out of hiding and constrained to lead a discursive existence."[12] And within this discourse, rigidly maintained lines separate male and female roles. From the moment in chapter 8 when Estella glides majestically onto the scene, female domination and punishment of males is eroticized. Moreover, Pip's displaying of his love wounds is not gender-neutral, as moral masochism seems to be.[13]

As Kaja Silverman has observed, in the accounts offered by patients of their fantasies and sexual behavior on which Reik and Krafft-Ebing as well as Freud and Gilles Deleuze base their influential theories of masochism, the male masochist consistently differs from the female masochist in showing an openness verging on exhibitionism. "He acts out in an insistent and exaggerated way the basic conditions of cultural subjectivity, conditions that are normally disavowed; he loudly proclaims that his meaning comes to him from the Other, prostrates himself before the Gaze even as he solicits it, exhibits his castration for all to see, and revels in the sacrificial basis of the social contract."[14]

What are we to feel, faced with such a shameless display? That critics have almost universally preferred the bleak, original ending of *Great Expectations* to the happier conclusion published first, may owe as much to conventional morality as to aesthetics. The extravagant humiliations and physical tortures Dickens heaps onto Pip in the last chapters of the book do double-duty as punishments for his deviant as well as his selfish desires. Moral closure is provided by the removal of Estella from Pip's life, and with her all possibility of renewing the masochistic carryings-on. Perhaps, as the anxious inheritors of the Victorians, we are more comfortable seeing Pip receive undesired punishment than we are with the published ending's sly suggestion, through the beloved's return, that masochistic pleasures can pulse in and out of a man's life forever.

The original ending's mood also fits our sense of what Victorian morality demanded. However, it does not so neatly fit the conventions of other famous Victorian stories of transgressive desire such as *Wuthering Heights*, *Jane Eyre*, "Goblin Market," and *Middlemarch*, all of which end not with punishment but with reward. Part of the modern project of reconstructing the Victorians seems to be repressing their ambiguity about sexuality, which is reflected in their willingness to tolerate inconsistency in sexual morality tales.[15] By ending the narrator's storytelling and his romantic agonies at the same point, *Great Expectations*'s original conclusion suggests what Susan Sontag calls "the modern contribution" to the cult of love, the conflation of artistic creation and romantic love as "the two most exquisite sources of suffering."[16] Pip's narration dissolves into the resolution of his love problem. The end of his suffering in love signifies the end of his suffering for art, his artist role. And this we seem to prefer to an ending that denies the possibility of resolving Pip's aestheticized desire to suffer and display his suffering.

But different traditions would dictate different responses. C. S. Lewis begins his famous study of medieval literature, *The Allegory of Love*, with the regretful observation that because his readers typically consider male domination of women the only natural form of eroticism, they are likely to be "repelled" by "these medieval lovers—'servants' or 'prisoners' they call themselves—who seem to be always weeping and always on their knees before ladies of inflexible cruelty."[17] Lewis's words recall D. H. Lawrence's earlier complaint that the representative hero and heroine of popular love stories are a "Sheik with a whip up his sleeve, and a heroine with weals on her back." To a large extent, as I discuss in chapter 3, Lawrence maintains his affiliation with another tradition by identifying male masochistic rituals with wholesome sexuality, thus positioning his writing against Freudianism to recall a vast intertext of normative representations of male masochistic display.[18]

Within this tradition, men's ritualistic acts of self-abasement are usually metonyms of passionate love for an exalted lady. That religious iconography influenced representations of erotic love is obvious. However, the early Christian church did not create a connection between passion and pain any more than philosophical writings from Plato's to Lacan's called into being a connection between desire and lack. Aside from any of its other functions, masochistic display provides an exteriorized and displaced dramatization of emotional suffering. Showing a cold disregard for political realities, literature has always found, in the condition of the slave, the captive, and the victim of torture, an objective correlative for the experience of desire for a specific person. And the poet coyly disclosing his agonized subjection is a familiar figure. The distinguishing features of what we might call, without restrictively historicizing it, the courtly love display is its focus on the divine lady, whom no one else can replace, and its combined eroticization and spiritualization of the ordeals undergone in her name.

Many critics have argued that courtly idealization of woman is just another face of misogyny, not in any sense a strategy of resistance to it. For example, R. Howard Bloch sees the courtly love ethic's insistence on the unattainability of the lady as complicitous with the early church fathers' poetics of virginity, which suggest that feminine purity can only be preserved and perfected by death. To Bloch all the male masochism central to Western eroticism seems to mask a sadism that compels the forced possession of woman through the very act of speaking her praise. However, in his apparent equation of virginity and unattainability (and the pen, the penis, and the gaze), Bloch ignores the possibility that unattainability need not invariably be understood as sexual coldness. His interpretation of male masochism's discourse leaves out the female love object's potential to become a subject and, by speaking, possess not just herself but the male poet. Not only was this potential realized in the work of the female troubadours, awareness of it informs hundreds of years of what Bloch dismisses as unsophisticated readings of

courtly love as an attitude friendly to feminism.[19] If the question is
how male masochism has been constructed throughout literary history, it does not seem useful to dismiss as naïve these centuries of reinscription of courtly love as an idealization of antipatriarchal pleasure in the service of a female subject.

However, male masochism has often appeared textually bound in
other tropes. In some texts the woman's cruelty is presented as the
essence of her attraction. One can trace, through history, style
changes in literary masochism and sadism, although Mario Praz
seems to be oversimplifying trends in Romantic and Victorian literature when he divides the nineteenth century into the era of "the
Fatal Man (the Byronic hero)" and that of the "Fatal Woman."[20]
Nonetheless, Victorian literature characteristically depicts masochists in what seems to be a gender-related mode: for the most part,
only low, "unnatural," or evil female characters seek abuse in love,
while male masochists are otherwise surprisingly ordinary young
gentlemen. This phenomenon may occur because legitimate Victorian literature developed, as Steven Marcus makes abundantly clear
in *The Other Victorians*, in the shadow presence of a large literature
of flagellation.[21] In these highly formulaic texts, the most popular
protagonists are a submissive young male and a dominant woman.

In the pornography of the Victorian period (and much of our
own), the discourse of male masochism shifts its focus from emotions about idealized women to sexualized activities with debased,
prostituted women. Values that the courtly tradition attached to
male masochistic acts and longings are reversed in Victorian pornography and in the high cultural products with which it sometimes
overlaps.[22] In these writings, male masochism promises degradation
rather than transcendence. Troubadour poetry valorizes the volun-
tary sufferings of men in love as the most "meritorious" experience
humanly attainable.[23] This idea has never completely vanished from
literature. But in the world inhabited by Victorian writers, where
intentionally erotic beatings were readily available as a commodity,
the woman who actually or symbolically dispensed them was unlikely to be seen as a spiritual guide. Dickens uses a conventional
simile from courtly poetry to describe Estella approaching Pip, on
his first day at Satis House; "Her light came along the dark passage

like a star" (89). The effect is parodic because we have already seen
that this unpossessable lady is more likely to light the way to hell
than heaven.

The revisionary radicalism of Dickens's characterization of
Estella is apparent if we compare her to the eponymous female figure in Dante Gabriel Rossetti's "Blesséd Damozel." While Rossetti's poem transgressively posits a heaven of sexual longing, it is
conventional enough in its depiction of the superior woman in
whose presence man knows his lack. Through contemplating *her*
sweetly endured suffering, the masculine narrator suffers voluptuous
pangs. And if his thoughts are sexually tantalizing as he imagines
"the gold bar of heaven" warming under her breasts, they are also
transported upward to questions about the spiritual. *Great Expectations*, by contrast, shows us a world in which, although the lady's
starlike ascendancy over her knight can no longer bode well, it remains pleasurable.

Dickens's texts balance celebration and condemnation of the
same forbidden behaviors, making delinquency itself a strand in the
web that holds the individual subject to official power. Thus, we can
understand the elusive mood in which Pip reveals (and is revealed
revealing) his sexual masochism. The erotically charged encounters
between Pip and Estella always seem to refer the sophisticated reader
outside the text to a sexual subculture that cannot be discussed.
D. A. Miller has shown this sort of coding in *David Copperfield*,
especially in the evasively narrated account of the friendship that
develops at night between handsome Steerforth and admiring David
in their boarding-school bedroom.[24] Dickens's reference to what
Miller calls an "open secret" in the cultural context is even more
obvious in the interchanges between Bill Sikes and Nancy in *Oliver
Twist*. While no child can learn about prostitution from the text,
few if any adults fail to receive a strong impression that Nancy is a
prostitute and Bill her pimp. However, what the intersection of the
written text and the reading of culture that we bring to it actually
tells us is that to be a thief working for Fagin and bullied by Sikes
is *like* being a prostitute. Similarly, the narration of the love story
of Pip and Estella interacts metonymically with common knowledge
about masochistic ritual, suggesting not only something still more
perverse and forbidden, but also the implicit similarity between the

romantic idealization of women that Victorian society fosters and the patronage of prostitute-dominatrixes, which the same society officially forbids.

Estella has many of the attributes one would expect to find in a prostitute-dominatrix. The sources of her power are the house where she is confined, the older woman who rules it, and her own emotional remoteness. She maintains the dignity of a "queen" while stooping to perform unladylike violent actions (86). The attentions that arouse Pip's passion also belong to the scripts of masochistic fantasy and practice. She feeds him from a dish on the ground "like a dog," slaps his face as hard as she can, contemptuously doles out physical favors as a means of exchange, uses him as her "page," and consistently refuses to take him seriously as a man (92, 111, 123, 260, 288). This display brings to mind the one we cannot be shown—the one that can never be integrated into a properly patriarchal Victorian marriage.

Pip learns at Joe's knee that, despite his society's sentimental idealization of the feminine sphere as a retreat from the violence of competition, it is either beat or be beaten in marriage. But events show him that society allows no choice of roles. When Joe refuses to control his wife's "rampages," preferring to admire and defer to her as "a master-mind," Orlick hammers her into slavish submission. Similarly, Magwitch's wild mistress is tamed into a docile servant by Jaggers. Estella gives herself to Bentley Drummle who beats the pride out of her. The masochistic pleasures available to Pip at Satis House must satisfy him because, the novel shows us, such irregular houses are the only outlets for them. The brutality of ordinary males forces women's submission everywhere else.

I am not arguing that *Great Expectations* should be considered an unusually sadomasochistic text. On the contrary, I agree with the general view that *Wuthering Heights* is the canonical Victorian novel most explicitly concerned with the representation of sadism and masochism. And as such, it is also extraordinarily concerned with their gendered containment. *Wuthering Heights* amply dramatizes male dominance in domestic violence: fathers and guardians beat children and husbands beat wives. But it is the reversal of customary patriarchal violence that energizes the narrative and motivates its climaxes when Catherine Earnshaw boxes Edgar Linton's ears dur-

ing their courtship and later invites Heathcliff to beat him. She exploits Heathcliff's love to treat him, by his own description, as a
"slave."[25] After her death, her ghostly presence brings him "both
pleasure and pain, in exquisite extremes" (261).

What seems singular about Heathcliff's behavior, in contrast to
the norm established by the other characters, is the rigidity with
which he separates his sadistic and masochistic roles. Throughout
the course of the novel, he "fiendishly" abuses his many enemies,
yet when Catherine challenges him to "take revenge" on her, he
meekly answers that, although she were "to torture [him] to death
for [her] amusement," he could never turn on her "in the same
style" (97). In Heathcliff-as-masochist we can see something of the
exhibitionistic male masochist Silverman describes. Nelly Dean's interpretation of his character is based on his desire to reveal the physical and psychic wounds he has received and cannot return. The two
epiphanies in Nelly's understanding of Heathcliff's true nature are
his threat to show Mr. Earnshaw the bruises Hindley has given him
and his "confession" of his painful and thrilling relationship to
Catherine's ghost.

The romance of Cathy Linton and Hareton Earnshaw restores
the social order that predated Heathcliff's disruptive arrival, erasing
his concept of masochistic fealty as the mark of male love. The anguish of subjectivity that Heathcliff revealed, Hareton projects onto
Cathy Linton, and an uncomplicated illusion of man as triumphant
subject and woman as (lacking) object is reiterated. Cathy despises
Hareton until he gives "a manual check to her saucy tongue," breaking her lip (239). Soon after, Cathy apologizes profusely, wheedling,
and "smiling as sweet as honey, and creeping close up" to him (245–
49). Later still, Lockwood watches a reading lesson in which Cathy
pulls Hareton's hair and gives him "smart slap[s] on the cheek"
when his attention wanders (243). Male masochism is satisfied in a
secret little hearthside game, as silenced woman passes on to man
the power to decode/determine meaning. Unlike her mother,
Cathy cannot love two men simultaneously; her devotion always belongs to the one father whom, if he does not exist, she will create.
Cathy's "smiting beauty" is safely contained by her own idolization
of brute force and Hareton's willingness to use it on her. The antisocial passion of Catherine Earnshaw and her demonic slave Heath-

cliff that had threatened to tear the families apart ends at last in their peaceful, conventional consolidation, and the normal dominate the land, while the uncanny are exiled into the shadows.

Wuthering Heights first presents the man's declaration of his masochistic desires in the context of his perception that his object choice is inferior (Catherine because of her infidelity; Cathy because of her snobbishness), and the narrative's demonstration that he is working against social coherence (Heathcliff's separation of Linton and his sister, Hindley and his son; Hareton's attempted alienation of Cathy from her young husband). But the novel ends with a pseu-dodidactic vision of masochism satisfied within (and without troubling) the institution of marriage. In *Great Expectations*, although traditional marriage and masochistic desire spring away from each other like magnet poles, society continually shifts into new marital configurations that block male masochistic pleasure. Both novels naturalize male cruelty and female submissiveness as the background against which male masochistic displays are staged and into which the flaunting men ultimately recede.

Such repetitive normative attempts to distribute dominance and submission along gender lines provide a context for Freud's terming "feminine masochism" an inclination he and most theorists have found and studied chiefly in male patients. When the social contract demanded that women be considered childlike, the male masochist's desire "to be treated like a small and helpless . . . naughty child" could be considered a desire to be feminized.[26] In addition, as long as it was considered natural and inevitable for all societies to subordinate women to men, the state of being dominated by the opposite sex could be considered feminine. By this logic, a man's desire for control by a woman masks a desire to be feminine, that is, to be a woman. Consequently, male heterosexual masochism becomes a contradiction in terms. To see woman as powerful and rightfully dominant is to disavow the "reality" of her castration, her lack. So the man who wants to bow down to woman would seem to be denying his own gender and perversely locating elsewhere the phallic power to which his gender should entitle him to aspire. Still this Freudian account is based on repressing all other masculine-feminine oppositions that dissonantly suggest alternative power relations.

Despite Ian Gibson's attempts to explain Victorian sexual ideology coherently, his polemical history of corporal punishment in England, *The English Vice*, repeatedly reveals the dissonance surrounding masochism in the Victorian years. On the one hand, respected sexologists like William Acton deplored corporal punishment of boys because they believed it would lead to premature interest in sex and on to masturbation and all its attendant diseases and subversive attitudes. Yet, on the other hand, most Victorians apparently believed that the sort of manly self-restraint and moral rectitude that Acton recommended could only be taught and enforced through corporal punishment, so ritualized beating was an important part of discipline in many British institutions, including most homes, schools, and the armed forces. While girls experienced little physical punishment, it was the rare boy who grew to adulthood without enduring numerous beatings.[27]

Being beaten might, therefore, seem to to belong to the masculine condition, an idea reinforced in boys' stories, which insistently portrayed right-thinking boys responding with affection and gratitude to those who beat them (82–84). Because of its association with upper-class socialization and with military training, being beaten related to male maturation, to being made into a man; but because it was also considered erotic, being beaten had associations with dangerous romantic submission to women. That beating was fairly generally thought of as pertaining to sexuality is clear in the considerable slippage between serious discussions of flagellation in "the respectable press," accounts of it in "scandal papers," and depictions of it in pornography (Gibson 194). As Gibson's many examples show, it is often impossible to distinguish one type of text from the others without knowing the larger context. The instability of the boundary between erotic and socializing beatings blurred the distinction between manly restraint and unmanly, that is, immoral, but still masculine release.

This area of instability in masculinity overlapped another in the representation of woman, which, as Mary Poovey shows, was "a site of cultural contestation during the middle of the nineteenth century," as the old image of woman as sexually voracious and cruel disrupted the new depictions of the maternal, morally superior guardian of the home.[28] Fictions of the Victorian dominatrix make some attempt to reconcile these conflicting messages about gender.

She is sadistic and immoral, but loving. "The principal fantasy of Victorian flagellant pornography is that women positively revel in administering the birch," but "the typical flagellant lady is hardly terrible. . . . Her relationship with the person being beaten is a loving one, a sexual one, as is evidenced by the pleasure both parties take in the flogging" (Gibson 277, 281). If the Victorian male masochist saw himself as unnatural in refusing his manly right to dominate, he could claim to be emphatically natural in choosing to please women sexually. Still, when masculinity means transcending the natural by disciplining one's instinctual impulses, such natural surrender must be resisted.

Freud displays his own anxieties about masochism's unsettling relationship to fixed definitions of masculinity and femininity in his essay "A Child Is Being Beaten." Masochism in women would not be hard to explain, since "[i]nstincts with a passive aim must be taken for granted as existing, especially among women,"[29] except for the troubling fact that the passivity of his "masochistic" female patients is only manifested in fantasies of watching boys being beaten. Although he posits a fantasy in which the girl herself is being beaten by her father, "[i]t is never remembered, it has never succeeded in becoming conscious. It is a construction of analysis" (185). Moreover, the male patients, according to his theory, should energetically repress their divergence from the only norm of masculinity that Freud recognizes—active dominance. Instead they revel in fantasies of submission to women and stubbornly remain "unconscious" of the erotic fantasies about powerful fathers that Freud attributes to them (197–98). These recalcitrant patients likewise apparently refuse to conform to gender norms; "it is precisely in unmanly boys and unwomanly girls that these beating-phantasies appeared" (202). Rather than question the standards by which (or the prior texts according to which) he interprets these apparently sadistic women and masochistic men as gender failures, Freud decides that "in the last resort we can only see that both in male and in female individuals masculine as well as feminine impulses are found and that each can equally undergo repression and so become unconscious" (202). As Sherwood Williams says, "The byzantine complexity of psychoanalytic procedure masks the monotonous certainty of its predetermined result." Williams points out that Freud's reasoning in the Dora case typifies "the strategies of sexological interpretations in general" in that the analyst reads the patient's rejection of psychoanalytic doctrine as affirming it.[30] By this same reasoning, rejecting fixed and complementary patriarchal gender roles affirms their reality, and their appropriateness to the affect of adult men and women.

In the contradictory identifications of men's masochistic fantasies, Freud might have read an attempt to negotiate with the equally contradictory self-mythologizing of a culture whose high art simultaneously urged the release and the imprisonment of men's masochistic desires. Instead, he peremptorily resolved the conflict by suppressing male masochism's relevance to real acts performed by actual human beings in favor of a theory of fantasies that refer only to unconscious guilt. In Parveen Adams's words, "something of reality . . . is missing from the Freudian theory of masochism."[31] By erroneously conflating femininity and passivity/receptivity in the masochistic fantasy, Freud misses what seems to be one of male masochism's greatest sources of pleasure: a temporary release from society's coercive descriptions of gender roles that enables a relaxation of the moral and physical tension of sexual responsibility. He also ignores a long literary tradition that represents men's showy self-abasement as natural behavior intrinsic to passionate love and courtship. In its epistemological dependence on a particular, anti-courtly concept of gender difference, Freud's theorizing about male masochism is a product of Victorian literature. Its language predetermines the aim of treatment: to reduce the male patient's masochism so that he can (re)gain his masculinity.

One of the textual locations where the subversive potential of male masochism seems most released from its long linguistic and narrative entrapment is within feminist revisionary responses to earlier narratives.[32] Kathy Acker and Angela Carter have both achieved considerable recognition for writing postmodern feminist fiction concerned with sadomasochism. Even a brief comparison of their writings shows in what dramatically different ways such release can be realized. Although postmodernist feminist writers' interest in sadomasochism can easily be attributed to both the growing visibility of ritualized sadomasochistic activity in our times and to the central role the debate on sadomasochism has played in feminist politics in the last decade, Acker and Carter direct our attention more strongly toward prior texts than toward current events. Both writers could be grouped with the feminist postmodernists that Donna Haraway calls "Cyborg writers," whose "writing is about the power to survive . . . on the basis of seizing the tools to mark the world that marked them as other," whose "tools are often stories, retold stories, versions that reverse and displace the hierarchical dualisms of naturalized identities."[33] Allusions, which are frequently parodic, appear on nearly every page of their narratives. Large sections of Acker's novels and stories can be best described as pastiche, and her writing is often announced as plagiarism; she is the author of books entitled *Hello, I'm Erica Jong*, *Don Quixote*, and *Great Expectations*, and a short story, "Wuthering Heights."

Acker's aggressive appropriations always involve feminist revision to emphasize the horror of a masochism which is forceably introjected in those who resist the deadening of emotion that Acker believes our phallocentric, materialistic society demands. Her *Great Expectations* typifies her method: an obsessive and starkly antierotic dwelling on what is usually suppressed in artistic depictions of sadomasochism—physical realities like infected sores and psychic realities like the despair accompanying the certainty that "there's no possibility that anyone'll love you anymore or that love matters. . . . there's no hope of realizing what you want."[34] When Acker's narrator speaks both as a woman and as Pip (or as Pasolini or Rimbaud) gender is not so much shifted as redefined. At the same time that the masochistic content of prior texts is foregrounded, it is also detached from traditional concepts of gender, rewriting the masochistic hero as s/he who is locked in passionate battle with the phallic oppressor.

Thus the parental figures of Dickens's novel dwindle into a stereotypically absent/ineffectual father who fails to prepare the protagonist for the horrors of life ("I expected my father to be a strong totally sexually magnetic daredevil, macho as they come, but he was kind and gentle," [208]) and a mother who "committed suicide in a hotel room because she was lonely and there was no one else in the world but her" (242). Circling continually back to these lost, broken figures, as if to understand them would be to understand oneself, and in fact ending with the salutation "Dear Mother," the

text is intersected and interrupted just as continually by references
to "real" powers in the form of political leaders and famous authors.
The phallocentrism of power is always emphasized. The family romance explodes as Acker evokes the pressures of society, just as the
romanticism of texts like *Great Expectations* and Keats's "Eve of St.
Agnes," which Acker quotes extensively, is torn apart by their contact with bloodied chunks of *The Story of O*. It is as impossible for
the protagonist to locate him- or herself in relation to imagoes of
the parents as it is to reconcile texts of romantic love to texts of
desire as murderous madness. The predetermined social and textual
contexts of the protagonist's thoughts render his or her experience
of desire literally self-destructive. "Desire makes the whole body-
mind turn on itself and hate itself" (211).

Acker's protagonist is aligned with Virginia Woolf's Orlando,
finding situational gender identities. The novel begins with the
opening of Dickens's *Great Expectations*, but also contains the beginning of *Orlando* in which the narrator tells us "there can be no
doubt of his sex" as a prelude to a story that will continually raise
doubts about it (206). Acker's protagonist is the artist's female audience as "allower of exhibited pain so that he [can] keep going." But
as the defiantly masochistic "author of the work you are now reading," the narrator becomes a man (211).

While figures like the artist of *Great Expectations* or the female
knight in Acker's *Don Quixote* seem initially gendered, and, indeed,
gender role reversal seems crucial to the text's meaning, masculinity
and femininity are deconstructed through some of Acker's descriptions of sadomasochistic rituals. In the section of the latter novel
entitled "Heterosexuality," an S/M encounter between a self-styled
masculine woman and a man masquerading as a young girl is first
narrated (by Don Quixote's companion, lover, and dog who speaks
both parts) with pronouns that reflect the man's and his partner's
concept of his own genders' division into the real (the femininity
with which he identifies) and the apparent (the masculinity, always
represented parenthetically, that corresponds to his genitalia). But
as she whips him, the female (depicted sometimes as a dog and
sometimes as a woman) realizes: "This man had no intention of
taking responsibility, for he hated and feared his masculinity as much
as I did. By making all this pain clear, both he and I for the first

time accepted that sex."[35] And at the same time the feminine pronouns disappear. As David Brande argues, "This diversion from semiotic play is not a retreat to biological sexual difference as ground
for gender differences but an implied assertion that the characters'
shared practices have, at least temporarily, 'denatured' biological difference to the degree that wordplay with gendered pronouns is re-
dundant."[36] When masculinity is recognized not as an invariable and
coherent set of attributes naturally belonging to the one to whom
the penis is attached but as a group of conflicting (and afflicting)
constructs that hurt both the partners, "that sex" can be moved
from the position of repression (within parentheses) to that of acknowledged enemy.

However, Acker seldom allows her characters such moments of
freedom. Even this scene is contained at its beginning by the bitch/
woman's announcement, "If you want to stay the night here, you
do as I want. That's a contract" (138). And its end is sealed by "the
man or fake man or whoever he was" saying, "since you've given
your life to punishing me, if you ever deviate, falter, or alter in the
slightest way, I will turn on you and treat you in a manner so hor-
rendous you will wish you had never, in the beginning, turned to
women for happiness" (141). Gender, twisting voluptuously in its
chains and turning on itself and the Other so that the lovers would
seem to be moving to someplace beyond, turns at last again into
what culture and society make it—a system that endlessly entraps
and controls biological women. Masochism is ultimately depicted as
no effective means of resistance but as a symptom of the illness of
socialization and acculturation.

The way that masochism works in these novels differs substan-
tially from its functions in Victorian novels. If both recontain the
male masochist into the narrative of gender hierarchy, there is no
sense in which this can be read as good in Acker's texts. Masochism
is doomed from the beginning as a method of resistance, and because it has opened an aperture that makes another possibility visible, even momentarily palpable, when gender roles close back in,
the recoil in revulsion from the world is intensified. "Don Quixote
was disgusted that human heterosexuality had come to such an extreme end" (141). In their attitude toward liberatory strategies in
general and masochism in particular, Acker's novels belong to the

punk movement's "angry reaction against the elation of so much 1960s art (with its intoxicated dreams of social change, peace, aesthetic renewals, new possibilities)" and instead offer "a parodic and deeply disturbing image of victimization, alienation, and hopelessness."[37] Her response to past visions of courtly love is both mocking and mourning.

Like Acker, Angela Carter often rewrites masochism as unsettling to the concept of biologically determined gender differences. Carter, however, does not depict masochistic ritual as the compulsive expression of an illness constructed by cultural cruelty that blocks more direct means of experiencing sexual pleasure. Instead, for many of her characters masochistic activity directly expresses intense love and desire. Though indulging in this activity has dangerous repercussions for the female characters because of their relative powerlessness within society, Carter's male characters often seem jubilantly masochistic. Carter's revisions of past narratives about male masochism recapture something of the celebratory mood of their originals. But unlike the most famous Victorian novelists, Carter does not recover legitimacy by veering away from celebration into condemnation. Instead she revises Freud and the Victorians to retrieve the male masochist as the New Woman's knight and his own savior in the battle against patriarchy.

From what angle can we view these revisions, scandalous because of their own apparently friendly rewriting of the masochistic script? Although one might think that such revisionary responses would be well received by feminist critics, Carter has actually been harshly criticized for her treatment of sadomasochism. The romantic lushness of Carter's revisions raises problems for some politically engaged critics to whom the swooning masochism of her fictional characters "verges dangerously close to pornography."[38] Andrea Dworkin and Susanne Kappeler condemn Carter's *Sadeian Woman* on similar grounds, believing that it simply romantically reinscribes the poetics of sexual cruelty that Kappeler, at least, believes Carter set out to deconstruct.[39] These critics seem right to suspect that Carter's texts glorify sexual cruelty, but to conclude that they do so in the service of patriarchal values is to imagine that the only possible opposing values are those of nineteenth-century femininity:

gentleness and nurturance. Carter envisions a woman-centered world of love and ritual otherwise.

Female attempts to evade the equation of femininity and masochism were characteristically represented as unnatural in the very nineteenth-century novels that most fervently disclosed the pleasures of male masochism. It is here that respectable fiction is most easily distinguishable from sadomasochistic pornography. For instance, Miss Havisham is designated monstrous partly because she tries to ungender masochism. In a masochistic manifesto, she tells Pip "what real love is. It is blind devotion, unquestioning self-humiliation, utter submission, trust and belief against the whole world, giving up your whole heart and soul to the smiter—as I did" (261). That she can see no reason that Pip's maleness should make any difference in his experience of this strange ecstasy is depicted as another indication of Miss Havisham's "dreadful" hunger for unnatural experiences. Her enjoyment of Pip's masochistic sufferings is contextualized by evocations of her ghoulishness; she makes her speech as a "figure of the grave" animated by a terrifyingly "ravenous" passion (260–61). Carter follows this literary precedent to the extent that she begins with female monsters when she elaborates, in theory and narrative, on male masochism's power to act as its own cure by annihilating the Victorian marriage economy that has kept closing on it.

In *The Sadeian Woman*, Carter's study of the implications for feminism of the Marquis de Sade's texts, some hints about forbidden female pleasures slip into her discussion of that fiendish dominatrix, Juliette. Carter's recognition that Sade allows sexual pleasure only to those who repudiate the mother and her power moves her to speculate about freedom not "defined by tyranny." She wonders whether, if one were not forced to affirm the father's power, a different confrontation with the mother's power would be possible. And would sex need the rules that contain alterity always within a male-dominated hierarchy? For Carter, eliminating the father from the masochistic scenario does not signify simply a subversion of "the Law," but a possibility of escape from legislated sexualities.[40]

Carter is not alone in considering the masochist best understood in relation to female power. Parveen Adams follows Deleuze in rejecting Freud's hypothesis that the father always symbolically occupies the dominant role. They see the mother as the true object choice in the masochistic drama. However, both Adams and Deleuze emphasize the metaphysical or unconscious universal construction of this mother figure. To Adams, she is the phallic mother, to Deleuze the oral mother, both seemingly inescapably predetermined inhabitants of the human psyche.[41] Carter suggests that masochists' "mothers" have far more specificity, that they are consciously constructed from whatever concrete and experiential materials are at hand, under the control of whatever laws are physically enforced.

Carter's vision of masochism's possibilities demonstrates its pragmatism in her response to the four cross-dress weddings at the climax of *Juliette*. In Sade's novel, Juliette and her patron, Noirceuil, first dress as brides and marry members of their own sex who are costumed as bridegrooms. Then, in the second ceremony, Juliette and Noirceuil both take the male role in marriages to members of their own sex, dressed as brides. Carter dreams of the one inversion that Sade avoids—an exchange of clothes and roles between the man and woman. Implicit in Carter's belief that, were Noirceuil willing to relinquish his power, Juliette could have access to her own outside of identification with him, is a disbelief that power exists only in relation to phallic maleness. To Carter, the placement of woman in the power position in the masochistic drama need not be a displacement, it can be a *re*placement. The free circulation of socially gendered objects, like clothes, can "truly suggest an anarchy of the sexes" (99). Carter reaches at least the border of such anarchy in the revision of the Sadeian wedding at the center of her novel, *The Passion of New Eve*.

The representation of male masochism in this novel suggests but does not follow through on calling into question conventional concepts of gender difference. The narrator, a young man named Evelyn, undergoes a forced sex-change operation to become Eve, woman as "the *Playboy* centerfold," with a transvestite's bearing, "a little too emphatically feminine."[42] Since childhood he has adored Tristessa, Hollywood's emblematic female masochist, whose films reduce *Wuthering Heights* and *Great Expectations* (among other stories) to spectacles of gorgeous feminine suffering. When at last

they meet, Tristessa has aged into a strong resemblance to Miss Havisham. "She lived in her own wedding cake, had burrowed deeply
into its interior" (112). The consummation of Eve's desire is pre-
cipitated by his discovering that Tristessa, *himself*, is a transvestite.
Forced by a bullying man into a drag wedding, Eve, "a boy disguised as girl and now disguised as a boy again" marries Tristessa,
the feminine aspect of man (132). Susan Suleiman praises this scene
and the scene of lovemaking that follows it for "going beyond the
old dichotomies" to show us love and desire unfixed from gender
but, as Ricarda Schmidt has observed, Eve's language upholds patriarchal values since s/he continues to describe femininity as masochistic submission.[43]

While the two scenes do insist on the constructed, antinatural
quality of gender, they do not release passion from determination
by the concept of femininity as the binary opposite of masculinity,
or from the association of masochism with femininity. Conventional
gender difference is maintained nowhere more rigidly than by Eve's
rhetorical question of Tristessa, "How could a real woman ever have
been so much a woman as you?" (129). The rhetoric of such questioning of the male masochist (fantasy) comes from and remains
within Freud's and his literary precursors' designation of masochism
as connected to that mystical something that separates the female
psyche from the normal/male psyche. If femininity becomes nothing more than enacting a role and putting on a set of clothing, the
lifting of the mask/masque reveals nothing but the male desire that
the feminine exist so that masochism can be connected to an Other.

In *Nights at the Circus*, Carter gives us woman as someone other
than Other, someone not defined by and absorbed into the patriarchal power structure. The novel's line of narrative almost disappears
under flurries of sly references to literary and theoretical texts. In
what Pauline Palmer calls a Bakhtinian "medley" of allusions to
texts by "Shakespeare, Milton, Poe, Ibsen, and Joyce" (Palmer
197)—as well as Dickens, Goethe, Dostoyevsky, Marx, Freud, Foucault, Lévi-Strauss, Irigaray, Kristeva, Alban Berg, Jack London,
Robert Walser, and Bakhtin himself—the authority of any one language or vision is undermined. Each moment in the narrative is
framed to remind us that we are seeing through language.

Fevvers, the aerialist heroine of *Nights at the Circus*, is a different sort of monster from Eve: not constructed or born but hatched, in defiance of biological genre, with both arms and wings. Fevvers is more than a parodic literalization of Apollinaire's admiring description of Sade's Juliette, "a figure of whom minds have as yet no conception, who is arising out of mankind, who shall have wings, and who shall renew the world."[44] Tania Modleski observes: "To fall in love with a trapeze artist comes as close as possible to falling in love with a disembodied woman, one whose body, at any rate, appears to defy the physical laws which tie us to earth and wed us to mortality."[45] But Fevvers is an earthy and decidedly mortal new woman. Compared by the newspaper to an angel, "there was, off-stage, not much of the divine about her unless there were gin palaces in Heaven where she might preside behind the bar."[46] In *The Sadeian Woman*, Carter complains about the modern period's "downgrading of the physical value of the imperiously attractive woman" so that female secondary sexual characteristics have "become the signs of a denaturised being. . . . As if they were as surprising and unusual physical appurtenances to find on a woman as fins or wings" (68). Placed at the turn of the century, on the brink of this colossal error, *Nights at the Circus* seems to be reaching back to recapture what might have been, had the female body spoken itself as uncontainable power and had the female object of man's most rebellious desire not been defined as an "idol of perversity."[47] In Fevvers we see physical difference with a vengeance, but the revelation of her glorious difference would hardly cause any man anxiety about becoming similar. It simply cannot be read as diminishment.

The novel begins and ends with the newspaper correspondent, Jack Walser, interviewing Fevvers. He is violently attracted to her superior size and strength and her crude aggressiveness, but tells himself that he is following her in order to classify her, ideally as an ordinary woman in fancy dress. However, the text denies him the power of the pen. Fevvers narrates large sections of the book; his perceptions only occasionally appear in the third-person chapters.[48] But when his perception fuses with the narrator's, Fevvers as dominatrix becomes not the figure for the phallic mother, but a self-revisionary voice and indescribable body always escaping containment in Victorian/Freudian language. As in the scene in which she puts him between her knees and takes off his " 'silly kid' " clown

makeup, the woman he would like to cast in the role of a combination tigress and nurse continually unmasks them both with a sweep
of her big hand (143). And what is revealed is another sort of masochistic drama entirely than the one he would script.

In *The Passion of New Eve*, Tristessa's house is composed of the
artificial tears he has made. It is the same sort of glorious monument
to male suffering as *Great Expectations* and *Wuthering Heights*, a
structure in which Estella and Catherine Earnshaw, the love objects
of male masochism, fade into shadows. The true beauty, to which
our attention is always diverted, flows from the man's pain. His or-
gasmic blood and tears write the novel. She shines through his tears.
Her brilliance only reflects his ardent anguish, just as the prostitute
dominatrix's supposed desires are only a complementary reflection
of her client's always-primary ones.

In *Nights at the Circus*, the characters are unhoused twice over.
A major concern of the plot is the process by which Fevvers is freed
from her entrapment in the role of spectacle. In the beginning of
the story, "Fevvers inhabits those marginal institutions of society—
the whorehouse, the freak show, and the circus—which safely contain those elements which threaten to disrupt the orderly and legitimate exercise of power," but Fevvers's excessive difference bursts all
its containers.[49] Having traveled to a wild and primitive Russia—the
setting of Sacher-Masoch's fantasies—Fevvers rising "big enough to
crack the roof of the god-hut" (290) and Walser rapturously submitting to her power are not refugees from "the reality of sexual
difference" but from a specific, domestic definition of it.

Before Fevvers's and Walser's release from sexualities structured
by society, their desires are released from containment within any
one discourse. Carter's dramatization of Fevvers and Walser's passionate movement into "the 'woman on top' " position is so heavily
and contradictorily intertextualized that none of the meanings past
discourses have attached to the display of man's submission to
woman can adhere (292). "Feminine" masochism falls away, along
with the vision of a single, transcendently significant sexual difference, the disavowal of which leads to madness. In the absence of
recognizable boundaries, concepts of transgression and reversal are
rendered nonsensical. All that remains visible are the diverse cultural
discourses that construct masochism's many opposed and harmo-

nizing representations—and the final vision of Fevvers and Walser glorying in the boundless pleasure his unlimited acceptance of her subjecthood and her unlimited assumption of power have released: "The spiraling tornado of Fevvers's laughter began to twist and shudder across the entire globe, as if a spontaneous response to the giant comedy that endlessly unfolded beneath it, until everything that lived and breathed, everywhere was laughing" (295). When Walser joins in unreservedly, although aware that "he might be the butt of the joke," we are reminded of what has been obscured by the last century of literary normalization of masochistic ritual to fit gender roles, that the first line masochism always threatens is the one drawn between pain and laughter.

CONCLUSION

JULIET:
  'Tis almost morning, I would have ye gone—
  And yet no farther than a wanton's bird,
  That lets it hop a little from his hand,
  Like a poor prisoner in his twisted gyves,
  And with a silken thread plucks it back again,
  So loving-jealous of his liberty.

ROMEO:
  I would I were thy bird.

  William Shakespeare, *Romeo and Juliet*

THE MARQUIS DE Sade may have been thinking of this moment in Shakespeare's play when he named the vicious, eponymous protagonist of *Juliette*, but we have no other record of Shakespeare's Juliet being understood in this way: as monstrous because she fears that, in the intensity of her love, she will indulge her power to destroy Romeo. Neither has he been despised, throughout the ages, for his swooning abandon to passion and to his beloved mistress. Despite all that critics have written on the play's misogyny, for centuries it has been alluded to in other literary texts as a model of romantic feeling. Yet now that model seems distant, as if it belonged irretrievably to another age or to an unattainable state of mind, or even to false consciousness.[1]

A vision of love and romance more in harmony with those of most educated people in our era is provided in Jeanette Winterson's novel *Oranges Are Not the Only Fruit*:

> I want someone who will destroy and be destroyed by me. There are many forms of love and affection, some people can spend their whole lives together without knowing each other's names. Naming is a difficult and time consuming process; it concerns essences, and it means power. But on the wild nights who can call you home? Only the one who knows your name. Romantic love has been diluted into paperback form and has sold thousands and millions of

copies. Somewhere it is still in the original written on tablets of stone. I would cross seas and suffer sunstroke and give away all I have, but not for a man, because they want to be the destroyer and never the destroyed. That is why they are unfit for romantic love. There are exceptions and I hope they are happy.[2]

Romantic love remains a value here, but men's and heterosexual women's ability to experience it appears only within contradiction. It is impossible. No, on second thought it is possible—"there are exceptions"—but not probable. Ultimately it is again deemed unlikely and not even desirable, through the sarcastic expression of the "hope." The protagonist Jeanette is depicted throughout the novel as a misfit, just as we could expect that an honest lesbian with a good sense of humor would be perceived by the ignorant villagers and religious fanatics that form the community around her. But transported into dialogue with her feminist readers, Jeanette could expect much more agreement. Not only is her contempt for the paperback version of romantic love the norm among us, but also her view of men as almost without exception unable to give themselves up to love, to experience the shattering destruction of the self that love brings.

Given the evidence all around us of women's oppression under patriarchy, it does not appear that most men are trying to relinquish their status as subjects. Although women seem to be on the verge of power now that we have achieved a few basic rights and some voice in government, most of us are still in danger of violence from men, whether we are in our homes or out in the world. One study after another documents our dismal plight as recipients of prejudice and hostility. Probably it is safest for us not to forget that many men seem to wish to use heterosexuality as a way to block women's empowerment. However, I also think it is well worth considering that the exceptional cases whom Jeanette postulates would now be named masochists. And naming does mean power.

Coppélia Kahn's discussion of "what's in a name" for Romeo sheds some light on what has been at stake for men in naming. "In patriarchal Verona," as she points out, "men bear names and stand to fight for them." But Romeo does not confer his name on Juliet, he gives it up into her keeping so that his identity is bound to hers.

And although he temporarily renounces his "identity as Juliet's husband" when he fights Tybalt, his true name is hers and as her love she calls him home. When he lies down to die beside her, he dramatizes "his refusal to follow the code of his fathers."[3]

One of the ways that the naming of the masochist has worked is to make it more difficult to "call home" the rare man who wishes to relinquish some of his power. Such men would not be called into death, as Romeo is, for we do not inhabit a patriarchy as omnipotent as Shakespeare's imagined Verona, but they would have to experience the terror and excitement of the self's destruction. If they could lose their identification with the unified masculine self posited (but never allowed) by patriarchy without "becoming woman" by erasing actual women, they might reach the conscious distribution of identifications over a range of subject positions praised by many feminist theorists. They might perform gender with the freedom of those who experience a sort of negative capability in reference to identity. But our era seems to have little interest in such men if they dare to use sexual rituals as a way to break themselves free. In psychoanalytic theory and in much feminist theory, we have so strongly naturalized male dominance that the submissive male has an aura of the uncanny about him, so much so that perhaps we no longer want to call him home.

There is no one so uncanny as the double, so one reason that we might want to distance the figure of the male masochist is that if he is read as one who wretchedly and compulsively obeys life's demands that we suffer, we might all see in him a reflection of our own abjection in culture, society, and even our own bodies. Still it is politically useful to distinguish between what is forced against the conscious will of the "individual" and what is consciously perceived as a choice. Before we describe all so-called masochistic behavior as "compulsive," we might remember how many other sexualities have been understood in exactly the same way by previous generations. Men and women who made socially forbidden object or frequency choices were regularly considered the victims of compulsions and so were "helped" by psychology or medicine. Of course, people not conforming to societal expectations will sometimes be unhappy. But is all behavior followed by unhappiness necessarily "compulsive" and in need of a cure? How much more useful to recognize a spectrum of "choices" or choices (however our own politics causes us to see them), allowing us to see some difference between obeying a coercive cultural dictum and choosing to give ourselves intense pleasure by performing acts that might have unpleasant later consequences. It is important to keep in mind the laughter and ecstasy of "the masochist."

Terms of criticism belonging to different ideologies can only be understood in terms of those ideologies—for example, terms for criticizing potential insiders whose behavior may place them outside the pale. In the last decade, the word liberals prefer for such behavior is "inappropriate." This term implies relative judgments. Behaviors become "wrong" in relation to context. The absolute moralism that would make a conservative call the same behavior "immoral" is rejected, because it implies fixed concepts of good and evil that classify behaviors. The term that was until recently used by radicals for self-criticism, "politically incorrect" (despite its appropriation by conservatives to vilify anything even mildly liberal), implies an even greater latitude of tolerated behaviors in that it presumes judgments of behavior will be made in accordance with what helps attain a particular political goal. If one strives toward a particular goal, clearly, some choices will be incorrect because they are not helpful, although they need not be deemed wrong in a moral sense. The use of "politically" as a modifier intensifies the focus on context, stresses that the action is being judged not absolutely wrong but wrong in relation to one's professed politics. Thus "politically incorrect" constituted to radicals a politicizing of the judgment that a behavior was "inappropriate," with a further elaboration on why and in what specific circumstances it was inappropriate. In this spirit, one might ask if it is politically incorrect for feminists to use the psychoanalytic term *masochist* in referring to men who eroticize female dominance. For those whose political goal is to free women and men from repressively structured concepts of sex and gender, the answer should probably be yes, but such an answer would be utopian in the way that all calls to reform the political problems of language are utopian.

We are even less likely to get rid of the term *masochist* than we are to get neutral pronouns to replace the masculine and feminine singular pronouns. Still, w might politically correctly, in the best original sense, treat the word *masochist* as skeptically and use it as carefully as we do the masculine pronoun. For it is definitely useful to recognize, within the group of behaviors and attitudes now totalized as masochism, a multiplicity of masculinities and both elaborate upholdings of and resistances to what is imagined variously as "the" masculine and as patriarchal power. Through doing so we can better understand not only mainstream constructions of gender but also the gender identifications that have taken form on the peripheries and how these other constructions have been possible.[4]

If we want a feminist criticism to interact with feminist politics and enable change rather than create a sense of despair, we need to account for more than women's victimization and its acceptance. We also need to recognize and account for those who escape, even if only partially. If we wish to imagine how heterosexuality could ever be compatible with feminist goals, it may help to distinguish, as do so many of the writers I have discussed, between the behaviors that psychoanalytic theory would group together under the categorization of masochism, and to place them in relation to past and present modes of expressing love. Just as it has been very useful for literary critics to expose the ways literature has colluded with the dominant power structures and spoken the dominant discourses, it is also useful now to look at the ways literature—and even authors themselves—have resisted and have written dreams of resistance.

Although patriarchy persists and the love of men continues to do the majority of women little apparent good, all the gestures of resistance to patriarchy made through literature and in the name of love are not meaningless. Stories of heterosexual love do more than delineate the monumental wall between the two enforced genders; they also record how the wall was constructed and account for the yearning of men, as well as women, for a contact that will break them through. It should give us hope that so many on either side of the wall have been able to walk away in the company of their own, like Winterson's heroine, refusing to enact heterosexuality no matter what reprisals they face. And it should also give us hope that men have so persistently written erotic dreams of being ripped out of the grasp of the fathers and that women have so persistently written of love as the power to effect that change in allegiance. Love that reverses the hierarchies of misogyny is only a fantasy for most heterosexuals, but that it has been a fantasy not just for women but for men is an important part of that "cultural heritage" feminist critics often feel so ambivalent about preserving.[5]

While some of the texts and films I look at in this book clearly reveal why feminists have always had good reason to suspect the motives behind men's impulses to submit to women, all of the texts and films also suggest reasons that patriarchal powers are served by the demonization of men's submission to women. What is called masochism in men is always paradoxical, and what may be the strangest of all the paradoxes that its naming presents us with is that both the most traditional and the most subversive thing that we can do is to call it love.

NOTES

Introduction

1. Gilles Deleuze and Félix Guattari, *Anti-Oedipus: Capitalism and Schizophrenia*, trans. Robert Hurley, Mark Seem, and Helen R. Lane (Minneapolis: University of Minnesota Press, 1983), 33.

2. For useful overviews of the conflict about masochism among feminists within and outside the academic world, see B. Ruby Rich, "Feminism and Sexuality in the 1980s," *Feminist Studies* 12.3 (Fall 1986): 525–61; Susan Gubar, "Representing Pornography: Feminism, Criticism, and Depictions of Female Violation," *Critical Inquiry* 13 (1987): 712–41; and Mariana Valverde, "Beyond Gender Dangers and Private Pleasures: Theory and Ethics in the Sex Debates," *Feminist Studies* 15 (1989): 237–54.

3. Roland Barthes, *Sade/Fourier/Loyola*, trans. Richard Miller (New York: Hill and Wang, 1976), 140, 144, 151–52, 167.

4. Leo Bersani, *The Freudian Body* (New York: Columbia, 1986), 107. See also Leo Bersani, *Baudelaire and Freud* (Berkeley and Los Angeles: University of California Press, 1977); and Leo Bersani and Ulysse Dutoit, *The Forms of Violence: Narrative in Assyrian Art and Modern Culture* (New York: Schocken, 1985).

5. Linda R. Williams, "Reading and Submission: Feminine Masochism and Feminist Criticism," *New Formations* 7 (1989): 10, 18.

6. Laura Mulvey, "Visual Pleasure and Narrative Cinema," *Screen* 16 (1975): 6–18.

7. Gaylyn Studlar, *In the Realm of Pleasure* (Urbana: University of Illinois Press, 1988). It seems worth noting that Bersani announces at the end of *The Freudian Body* that he will forgo the pleasure of "proposing such an irritating label" as an aesthetics of masochism for what he appears to see as the fundamental inspiration of art.

8. Gayle Rubin, "Thinking Sex: Notes for a Radical Theory of the Politics of Sexuality," in *Pleasure and Danger: Exploring Female Sexuality*, ed. Carole S. Vance (Boston: Routledge and Kegan Paul, 1984), 280.

9. For case histories and surveys supporting the view that masochism is a choice that expresses a positive sense of self, see Andreas Spengler, "Manifest Sadomasochism of Males: Results of an Empirical Study," in *S and M: Studies in Sadomasochism*, ed. Thomas Weinberg and G. W. Levi Kamel (New York: Prometheus, 1983), 57–72; *Coming to Power: Writings and Graphics on Lesbian S/M*, ed. Samois (Boston: Alyson Publications, 1982); and Gini Graham Scott, *Erotic Power: An Exploration of Dominance and Submission* (Secaucus, N.J.: Citadel, 1983).

10. Sigmund Freud, "A Child Is Being Beaten," *The Standard Edition of the Complete Psychological Works of Sigmund Freud*, trans. James Strachey (London: Hogarth, 1953), vol. 17: 179–204 and "The Economic Problem of Masochism," *Standard Edition*, vol. 19: 159–70.

11. Gilles Deleuze, *Masochism: An Interpretation of Coldness and Cruelty*, trans. Jean McNeil (New York: Braziller, 1971), 42–60.

12. Gilles Deleuze and Félix Guattari, *A Thousand Plateaus: Capitalism and Schizophrenia*, trans. Brian Massumi (London: Athlone, 1988), 155–57.

13. Jessica Benjamin, *The Bonds of Love: Psychoanalysis, Feminism, and the Problem of Domination* (New York: Pantheon, 1988), 72–73, 219–20.

14. Pat Califia, "Feminism and Sadomasochism," *Co-Evolutionary Quarterly* 33 (1982): 37–38.

15. Mariana Valverde, *Sex, Power, and Pleasure* (Baltimore: New Society, 1987), 170–71. The five desires that are generally considered masochistic, according to Valverde, are: (1) the desire to be ravished by the passionate attention of the other, (2) the desire to be treated roughly during sexual activity, (3) the desire that pain be inflicted *as* a form of sexual activity, (4) the desire to be insulted and treated with contempt during sexual activity, (5) the desire to submit to a partner in a ritual scene (usually arranged and controlled by the submitting partner). Valverde objects to the classification of the first two types of desire as masochism and suggests that the behavior of those in the final group is better described as "S/M" (a term popular with organized groups who stage such scenes) than as masochism (172).

16. Jean Clavreul, "The Perverse Couple," in *Returning to Freud: Clinical Psychoanalysis in the School of Lacan*, trans. Stuart Schneiderman (New Haven: Yale University Press, 1980), 214, 216, 219, 221.

17. I am indebted to Winfried Schleiner for bringing the whole text of Dr. Meibom's letter to my attention and for allowing me to read his illuminating discussion of it in chapter 5 of his forthcoming book, Medicus prudens *or* medicus Christianus: *Perspectives on Medical Ethics in the Renaissance*. An English translation of Meibom's treatise, the title of which I quote, is in the Folger Library. For an English edition with modernized spelling, see John Henry Meibomius, *On the Use of Flogging in Venereal Affairs* (Chester, Penn.: Import Publishing, 1961). Ian Gibson discusses Meibom's letter in *The English Vice: Beating, Sex, and Shame in Victorian England and After* (London: Duckworth, 1978), but while recognizing that Meibom sees the sexual excitement resulting from flagellation as physiologically explainable and thus "a purely mechanical affair," Gibson still argues that Meibom treats such excitement as abnormal (1–5, 39–40). While Meibom's prescription for the impotent can certainly be seen as bordering on the frivolous, his diagnosis of flagellation's effects seems serious enough, and surely a physiological cure for impotence cannot be deemed abnormal or unnatural.

18. See Richard von Krafft-Ebing, *Psychopathia Sexualis: A Medico-Forensic Study*, trans. Harry Wedeck (1886; reprint, New York: Putnam's Sons, 1965).

19. Richard Brown, *James Joyce and Sexuality* (Cambridge: Cambridge University Press, 1985), 86.

20. R. Howard Bloch, "Chaucer's Maiden's Head, 'The Physician's Tale' and the Poetics of Virginity," *Representations* 28 (1989): 133-34.

21. For some concept of how much difference has been deliberately misread as sameness to produce this overview of premodern representation of love, see Joan Kelly's *Women, History, and Theory* (Chicago, University of Chicago Press, 1984). Kelly's discussions of various stages not only in the plots of romances but also in the ideology and symbology of courtly love make clear the cost of totalizing love traditions to create a fiction of "the literary past."

22. See Stephen Orgel, "Nobody's Perfect: Or Why Did the English Stage Take Boys for Women?" *The South Atlantic Quarterly* 88:1 (Winter 1989): 14-15, 26.

23. William Shakespeare, *A Midsummer Night's Dream* 2.1.210; Charles Dickens, *Great Expectations* (1861; reprint, Harmondsworth: Penguin, 1965), 92.

24. See Canto V of Dante's *Inferno*. I agree with John Ciardi's reading of this as "the tenderest and most sympathetic treatment accorded any of the sinners in Hell" (63). According to Francesca's account, Paolo was inspired to erotic action (and she inclined to receive it) by reading the story of Lancelot. Literature provides a context in which Paolo, through his unlawful but natural yielding to love, can be equated with a famous hero. It is also interesting to note how Ciardi's translation, with its emphasized "black whips," heightens our impression of sadomasochistic passion for both partners (Dante Alighieri, *The Inferno*, trans. John Ciardi [New York: Mentor-NAL, 1954], 61-64).

25. See Ellen Carol Dubois's Introduction to *Feminist Theorists: Three Centuries of Key Women Thinkers*, ed. Dale Spender (New York: Pantheon, 1983), xii, for a succinct discussion of the difference between this and other eras in the history of feminism.

26. In *City of Dreadful Delight: Narratives of Sexual Danger in Late-Victorian London* (Chicago: University of Chicago Press, 1992), Judith Walkowitz discusses at considerable length the political power women gained in English society in the late 1800s. See especially 61-80.

27. For a good discussion of the impact of the women's rights movement in Victorian England on men's concepts of female power, see Judith Lowder Newton's introduction to *Women, Power, and Subversion: Social Strategies in British Fiction 1778-1860* (Athens: University of Georgia Press, 1981). Newton comments on the perceived conflict between female empowerment and the maintaining of "chivalry" and on the anxiety surrounding woman's role as social conscience. One might also consider the argument persuasively advanced by Elizabeth Langland, in "Nobody's Angels: Domestic Ideology and Middle-Class Women in the Victorian Novel," that women's access to power did not come solely through feminist opposition to the extant power structure, but also through active participation in its revision to meet the demands of a changing economic and class system (*PMLA* 107 [March 1992]: 290-304). Working with Mary Poovey's and Nancy Armstrong's theories about the development of Victorian ideology, Langland shows that nineteenth-century "discursive practices . . . gave women unprecedented political power," as key figures in the maintenance of "middle-class hegemony" (291-92).

28. Joan Kelly, *Women, History, and Theory*, 25.
29. Robert J. Corber, "Representing the 'Unspeakable': William Godwin and the Politics of Homophobia," *Journal of the History of Sexuality* 1 (July 1990): 88.
30. Charlotte Perkins Gilman, *Herland* (1915; reprint, New York: Pantheon, 1979), 51, 86, 145.
31. Arthur Marotti, " 'Love Is Not Love': Elizabethan Sonnet Sequences and the Social Order," *ELH* 49 (Summer 1982): 398, 416.
32. Sigmund Freud, "The Economic Problem of Masochism," 161.
33. For a succinct summary of this position in literary criticism and theory, see Alice Jardine, *Gynesis: Configurations of Woman and Modernity* (Ithaca: Cornell University Press, 1985), 71–72, 99–100.
34. Jessica Benjamin, *The Bonds of Love*, 33.
35. As Roland Barthes shows, all modern discourses insist on opposing maturity/masculine presence and love, so that the man who would love is kept from the expression of his feeling by "a wall of language." (*A Lover's Discourse: Fragments*, trans. Richard Howard [New York: Hill and Wang, 1978], 211.) That the love constantly straining toward expression in *A Lover's Discourse* is homosexual can scarcely make it more "impossible" than the simple fact that it asks to speak itself as love and love itself has become unthinkable.
36. For a detailed exploration of Jude's entrapment and eventual destruction by conflicting "cultural paradigms of masculinity" brought into deadly play by his confused class identifications and by his culture's modernization of gender, see Elizabeth Langland, "Becoming a Man in *Jude the Obscure* in *The Sense of Sex: Feminist Perspectives on Hardy*, ed. Margaret Higonnet (Chicago: University of Illinois Press, 1993). She shows how Jude's tragedy is determined by his inability to relinquish the chivalric tradition of masculinity that became increasingly obsolete at the end of the nineteenth century.
37. Deleuze and Guattari, *Anti-Oedipus: Capitalism and Schizophrenia*, 2.

1. Mary Webb's Return of the Native Tess

1. See Andrea Dworkin, *Pornography: Men Possessing Women* (New York: Putnam's Sons, 1981) for what is probably the most extreme reading of male masochism as oppression of women. Of Sacher-Masoch she writes, "The nature of the act does not change the nature of the act; the male is the center of sensibility and power" (110). Note also that Dworkin later criticizes Theodor Reik for claiming (in *Of Love and Lust*) that "masochism in the male is a form of sadism," and attributes his interpretation to his need to maintain "the fictive dichotomy of absolute male and female sexual natures rooted in anatomical differences" (149–50).
2. For a full definition and explanation of the gynocritical approach see Elaine Showalter, "Toward a Feminist Poetics" in *Women's Writing and Writing About Women*, ed. Mary Jacobus (London: Croom Helm, 1979).
3. Lillian S. Robinson, "Treason Our Text: Feminist Challenges to the Literary Canon," *The New Feminist Criticism*, ed. Elaine Showalter (New York:

Pantheon, 1985), 118. Many of the (now more classic than "new") essays in this collection reflect concern with this issue.

4. For a discussion of such quasi-pornographic elements of Webb's fiction, see Michèle Barale, *Daughters and Lovers: The Life and Works of Mary Webb* (Middleton: Wesleyan University Press, 1986), 127–28.

5. Frantz Fanon, *Black Skin, White Masks*, trans. Charles Lam Markham (New York: Grove, 1965), 86. Cherríe Moraga also argues this point in "La Güera," in *This Bridge Called My Back: Writings of Radical Women of Color*, ed. Gloria Anzaldua and Cherríe Moraga (New York: Kitchen Table, Women of Color Press, 1982), 27–34. See also Judith Butler's discussion of the imperialist vision implicit in the ranking of oppressions (*Gender Trouble* [New York: Routledge, 1990]), 13.

6. Harriet Beecher Stowe, *Uncle Tom's Cabin* (1852; reprint, New York: Penguin, 1981), 471.

7. Kristin Herzog illuminatingly places Stowe's vision of the "childlike" virtues shared by women and blacks in a philosophical context in *Women, Ethnics, and Exotics* (Knoxville: University of Tennessee Press, 1983), 113–120.

8. Karen Sánchez-Eppler, "Bodily Bonds: The Intersecting Rhetorics of Feminism and Abolition," *Representations* 24 (Fall 1988): 32, 46. Lest a too attractive picture of the politics of these texts be created here, it should be noted that Sánchez-Eppler also shows how white, female abolitionists exploited images of slave women and how deeply marked with racism many of their writings are.

9. Trinh T. Minh-ha, *Woman, Native, Other: Writing Postcoloniality and Feminism* (Bloomington: Indiana University Press, 1989), 101.

10. Virginia Woolf, *A Room of One's Own* (1929; reprint, New York: Harbrace, 1957).

11. See Sandra Gilbert and Susan Gubar, *The Madwoman in the Attic* (New Haven: Yale University Press, 1979), 26.

12. Hélène Cixous, "The Laugh of the Medusa," 1975, trans. Keith Cohen and Paula Cohen in *Feminisms*, ed. Robyn R. Warhol and Diane Price Herndle (New Brunswick: Rutgers University Press, 1990), 349n.

13. Angela Carter, "Black Venus" In *Saints and Strangers* (New York: Penguin, 1987), 120. Ann Ardis, who discusses the quote from Waugh that I use as this chapter's epigraph in her *New Women, New Novels* (New Brunswick: Rutgers University Press, 1990), comments interestingly on the ways that late nineteenth-century and early Modernist constructions not just of masculinity but of the male artist figure demanded that woman, and especially the New Woman who was striving to speak of her own sexuality, be treated as "a territory to be colonized" (48, 90).

14. Gilles Deleuze, *Masochism: An Interpretation of Coldness and Cruelty*, trans. Jean McNeil (New York: Braziller, 1971), 21–22.

15. Gilles Deleuze's *Masochism: An Interpretation of Coldness and Cruelty* seems the most influential of these texts. Gaylyn Studlar provides what is to date the most extensively developed and applied discussion of masochism as a drive entirely separate from sadism in her study *In the Realm of Pleasure: Von Sternberg, Dietrich, and the Masochistic Aesthetic* (Urbana: University of Illinois Press, 1988).

16. Paul Robinson, *The Modernization of Sex* (New York: Harper Colophon, 1977), 26.

17. In *Civilization and Its Discontents*, Freud argues that humans' "instincts" result in their view of "their neighbor" as "someone who tempts them to satisfy their aggressiveness on him, to exploit his capacity for work without compensation, to use him sexually without his consent, to seize his possessions, to humiliate him, to cause him pain, to torture and kill him." Although here such behavior is attributed to generic rather than gendered "man," it should be apparent that culture and society have made it easier (and more acceptable under certain legitimating conditions such as acting in the interests of the state) for men than women to gratify these aggressive desires. While Freud deplores such "natural" behavior, he also warns that the restriction of outwardly directed aggression will turn it inward. (Trans. and ed. James Strachey [New York: Norton, 1961], 58).

18. Sigmund Freud, *Beyond the Pleasure Principle*, trans. and ed. James Strachey (New York: Norton, 1961), 49; *Civilization and Its Discontents*, trans. and ed. James Strachey (New York: Norton, 1961), 66; and "The Sexual Aberrations" in *Three Essays on the Theory of Sexuality*, trans. and ed. James Strachey (New York: Harper Colophon, 1962), 25.

19. See Robert L. Caserio's discussion of Freud's essay "The Economic Problem of Masochism" in "Mobility and Masochism: Christine Brooke-Rose and J. G. Ballard" *Novel* 21 (Winter/Spring 1988): 297–99.

20. Leo Bersani and Ulysse Dutoit, *The Forms of Violence* (New York: Schocken, 1985), 34. Leo Bersani, *Baudelaire and Freud* (Berkeley and Los Angeles: University of California Press, 1977), 77–82. What seems to be basically the same view of masochistic pleasure's tendency to dismantle the unified ego is reiterated in Leo Bersani's *The Freudian Body* (New York: Columbia University Press, 1986), 38–39.

21. Angela Carter, *The Sadeian Woman: And the Ideology of Pornography* (New York: Pantheon, 1978), 128–32.

22. Deleuze, 21, 78. Kaja Silverman rather dismissively terms Bersani's and Deleuze's interpretations of male masochism "utopian" ("Masochism and Male Subjectivity," *Camera Obscura* 17 [May 1988]: 56). Yet she grounds her own discussion in a sort of never-never land by treating culture and psychology as ahistorical absolutes. Although it may be true (especially in the case studies she discusses) that "the masochist only acts out in an exaggerated, anthropomorphic and hence disruptive way the process whereby subjects are spoken" (55), subjects are not always identically spoken by "their" cultures (or the various cultures through which they constitute themselves), which accounts in part for the revisionary quality of authors' responses to precursors. In fact, when Silverman discusses the political aspects of T. E. Lawrence's masochism, in "White Skin, Brown Masks: The Double Mimesis, or With Lawrence in Arabia," she closely examines the role "external images" derived from historical events play in constructing masochistic fantasies and also the "important historical consequences" of the acting out of such fantasies (*Differences* 1.3 [1989]: 48–49).

23. Edmund Bergler, *Curable and Incurable Neurotics: Problems of Incurable*

Neurotics: Problems of "Neurotic" versus "Malignant" Masochism (New York: Liveright, 1961), 277–78, 385; emphasis Bergler's.

24. Arnold M. Cooper, "Masochism as a Character Trait," keynote address, Masochism Symposium sponsored by the Psychiatric Services of Children's Hospital of San Francisco, October 25–26, 1986.

25. Michel Foucault, *The Use of Pleasure*, vol. 2 of *The History of Sexuality*, trans. Robert Hurley (New York: Vintage, 1986), 84–86, 72–74.

26. Francis Barker, *The Tremulous Private Body: Essays on Subjection* (London: Metheun, 1984), 88.

27. As a context for such a reading see Dale Bauer's discussion of the suicides of the female protagonists of *The House of Mirth*, *The Blithedale Romance*, and *The Awakening* in *Feminist Dialogics* (Albany, N.Y.: SUNY University Press, 1988), 4, 23, 30–1, 126–27, 154.

28. Gérard Genette, *Palimpsestes: La littérature au second degré* (Paris: Éditions du Seuil, 1982), 10. While I do not find Genette's method adequate to a full analysis of the ways intertextuality calls ideology into question, I will draw on his terminology to make distinctions between the types of textual connections, when such differentiation seems necessary.

29. A section from a poem written and recited by the main male character about the heroine exemplifies the subject matter and tone of *Seven for a Secret*:

"I, Robert Rideout, would cleave her soul asunder.
I'd take her in a net of love and make her suffer.
Never should she go flaunting in the plumage of her sisters
Out in the world where folks lose their souls.
I'd lief love her till she's blind and deaf to herself,
Until she canna-d-abear herself and is dead to herself.
And when she lies at my feet beseeching the cowman-shepherd for his love,
When her pretty hair is spread on the floor of our kitchen,
I'll speak unkind to her even a little longer. [New York: Dial-Virago, 1984], 80)

The song proves "prophetic." The love problems are resolved by "Gillian, the rich farmer's daughter, all bedraggled with tears, fumbling at his feet, kissing his socks" (281).

30. For a more detailed discussion of the correspondences between Hardy's major novels, including *Tess*, and traditional ballads, see Donald Davidson, "The Traditional Basis of Thomas Hardy's Fiction" in *Hardy: A Collection of Critical Essays*, ed. Albert J. Guerard (Englewood Cliffs, N.J.: Prentice-Hall, 1963), 12–17.

31. Mary Webb, *Gone to Earth* (1917; reprint, New York: Dial-Virago, 1979), 15. All further citations are included in parentheses in the text.

32. Thomas Hardy, *Tess of the d'Urbervilles* (1891; reprint, New York: Penguin, 1978), 270. All further citations are included in parentheses in the text.

33. See Kaja Silverman, "History, Figuration, and Female Subjectivity in *Tess of the d'Urbervilles*," *Novel* 18 (Fall 1984): 21–28, for a persuasive account of the many ways in which Hardy suggests that the male gaze is essential to artistic creation.

34. Elizabeth Langland points out a similar distinction in *Jude the Obscure* between a privileged, because middle-class, code of masculinity which demands chivalrous self-sacrifice and a despised (although sometimes compelling) "natural" maleness defined by overwhelming attraction to any available woman. As she shows, the pleasure in complying with the demands of either of these codes has to do with gaining gender identity. ("Becoming a Man in *Jude the Obscure*" in *The Sense of Sex: Feminist Perspectives on Hardy*, ed. Margaret Higonnet [Chicago: University of Illinois Press, 1993]). Both *Jude the Obscure* and *Gone to Earth* denaturalize the impulse to possess woman by exposing its complicity with the state.

35. Helena Michie's discussion of sisterhood in *Tess of the d'Urbervilles* as "a structure for the containment . . . of sexual differences among women" also seems apropos, especially in that, as Michie shows, 'Liza-Lu's replacement of Tess creates a sense of historicity at the expense of individuality recognition since the sisters are identified as interchangeable females, one marked for a fall and the other as her successor by biological forces unconnected to their choices. " 'There Is No Friend Like a Sister': Sisterhood as Sexual Difference," *ELH* 56.2 (Summer 1989): 405, 419–20.

36. Barbara Johnson, *A World of Difference* (Baltimore: The Johns Hopkins University Press, 1984), 130–31.

37. Gayatri Chakravorti Spivak, "Imperialism and Sexual Difference" in *Contemporary Literary Criticism: Literary and Cultural Studies*, ed. Robert Con Davis and Ronald Schleiffer (White Plains, N.Y.: Longman, 1989), 520–26.

38. Pascal Bruckner, *The Tears of the White Man: Compassion as Contempt*, trans. William R. Beer (New York: MacMillan, 1986), 116–32.

39. Renato Rosaldo, "Imperialist Nostalgia," *Representations* 26 (Spring 1989): 120–21.

40. John A. McClure, "Late Imperial Romance," *Raritan* 10, no. 4 (Spring 1991): 115, 129.

41. Donald Simpson, "Literary Critics and the Return to "History," *Critical Inquiry* 14.4 (Summer 1988): 729; Diana Fuss, *Essentially Speaking: Feminism, Nature, and Difference* (New York: Routledge, 1989), 16–18.

2. The Masochist as Exile between Two Goddesses

1. Sigmund Freud, " 'A Child Is Being Beaten': A Contribution to the Study of the Origin of Sexual Perversions," 1919, *The Standard Edition of the Complete Psychological Works of Sigmund Freud*, trans. James Strachey, vol. 17, (London: Hogarth, 1955): 198–99, emphasis Freud's.

2. Christopher Newfield, "The Politics of Male Suffering: Masochism and Hegemony in the American Renaissance," *Differences* 1.3 (Fall 1989): 75.

3. Gilles Deleuze, *Masochism: An Interpretation of Coldness and Cruelty*, trans. Jean McNeil (New York: George Braziller, 1971), 58. All further citations are included parenthetically in the text.

4. Frances L. Restuccia, *Joyce and the Law of the Father* (New Haven: Yale University Press, 1989), 9, 150, 143.

5. Thaïs E. Morgan, "A Whip of One's Own: Dominatrix Pornography

and the Construction of a Post-Modern (Female) Subjectivity," *The American Journal of Semiotics* 6.4 (1989): 112. I am indebted to Thaïs Morgan for showing me this essay in an early form as well as for generously discussing her research and ideas with me over a period of years.

6. Sandra Gilbert and Susan Gubar, *Sexchanges*, vol. 2 of *No Man's Land: The Place of the Woman Writer in the Twentieth Century* (New Haven: Yale University Press, 1989), 232–33, 261; Restuccia, *Joyce and the Law of the Father*, 155–56, 158–59, 176.

7. Ronald Bogue, *Deleuze and Guattari* (New York: Routledge, 1989), 54.

8. James Joyce, *Ulysses* (1914; reprint, New York: Random, 1961), 52–53. All further citations are included parenthetically in the text.

9. Sigmund Freud, "The Economic Problem of Masochism," 1924, *The Standard Edition of the Complete Psychological Works of Sigmund Freud*, vol. 19: 161–62.

10. William York Tindall, *A Reader's Guide to James Joyce* (New York: Farrar, Straus Giroux, 1959), 207–8. All further citations are included parenthetically in the text.

11. Stanley Sultan, *The Argument of Ulysses* (Columbus: Ohio State University Press, 1964), 310, 328. All further citations are included parenthetically in the text.

12. Hugh Kenner, *Ulysses* (London: George Allen Unwin, 1980), 118. All further citations are included parenthetically in the text.

13. Richard Brown, *James Joyce and Sexuality* (Cambridge: Cambridge University Press, 1985), 112. All further citations are included parenthetically in the text.

14. Sigmund Freud, *Three Essays on the Theory of Sexuality*, trans. James Strachey (New York: Basic Books, 1975), 23–24.

15. Leo Bersani, "Against *Ulysses*," *Raritan* 8.2 (Fall 1988): 21. All further citations are included parenthetically in the text.

16. Richard Ellmann, *James Joyce* (New York: Oxford University Press, 1982), 369–70. All further citations are included parenthetically in the text.

17. Leopold von Sacher-Masoch, *Venus in Furs*, trans. Aude Willm. In *Masochism: An Interpretation of Coldness and Cruelty*, 153. All further citations are included parenthetically in the text.

18. Henry Havelock Ellis, *Studies in the Psychology of Sex*, vol. 1 (1911; reprint, New York: Random, 1936), 128. All further citations are included parenthetically in the text.

19. Paul Robinson, *The Modernization of Sex* (New York: Harper Colophon, 1977), 25. Like Meibom, Ellis discusses male masochism as an aid to excitement in men who might not otherwise be able to reach orgasm through coition.

20. I am indebted to John Bishop for first and most persuasively presenting this view to me.

21. George Meredith, *The Ordeal of Richard Feverel*, (1859; reprint, New York: Modern Library, 1950), 500.

22. Stuart Gilbert, *James Joyce's Ulysses: A Study* (London: Faber, 1952), 322.

23. Theodore Reik, *Masochism in Sex and Society*, trans. Margaret H. Beigel and Gertrud M. Kurth (1941; reprint, New York: Grove, 1962), 145, 163.

24. The titles, alone, of some of Sacher-Masoch's other novels suggest his interest in parodying religious texts: *The Divorced Woman: The Calvary of an Idealist, The Fisher of Souls, The Mother of God.* For another view of the masochist's relation to the religious in Sacher-Masoch see Rita Felski, "The Counterdiscourse of the Feminine in Three Texts by Wilde, Huysmans, and Sacher-Masoch" *PMLA* 106.5 (October 1991):1102.

25. Fritz Senn, *Joyce's Dislocutions: Essays on Reading as Translation,* ed. John Paul Riquelme (Baltimore: Johns Hopkins University Press, 1984), 104–105. Ellmann, also, ridicules the idea that Joyce meant us to believe Bloom's virility was impaired because he cooked (*Ulysses on the Liffey* [New York: Oxford University Press, 1972], 161). All further citations of the latter work are included parenthetically in the text.

26. James Kincaid, *Child-Loving: The Erotic Child and Victorian Culture* (New York: Routledge, 1992), 257–59.

27. In "Against *Ulysses,*" Bersani argues that "Joyce exuberantly stages masochism with wild inventiveness, as if to insist on the profound difference between two kinds of masochism: the mysterious and monotonous repetition of a painful pleasure which Freud obscurely posits as the essence of human sexuality in the *Three Essays on the Theory of Sexuality,* and masochism as an occasion for extravagantly varied scenic effects" (18). I fully agree with Bersani that this Freudian view of sexuality is odd and offensive, but I do not see it expressed in *Ulysses*'s representations of masochism. Whether or not a given set of repetitions is monotonous seems a subjective judgment.

28. David Hayman, *Ulysses: The Mechanics of Meaning* (Englewood Cliffs, N.J.: Prentice-Hall, 1970), 45. All further citations are included parenthetically in the text.

29. Bloom's love for his children is essentially a conventional sentiment, but the intensity of his attachment to Rudy, who lived such a short time so long ago, and his recognition of Milly's sexual autonomy seem to diverge from more banally average parental feelings.

30. Charles Dickens, *David Copperfield* (1869; reprint, New York: Oxford, 1981), 569. It also seems relevant that David Copperfield initially hopes to educate Dora and train her to be an effective housewife but gives up that scheme in order to avoid destroying her as his mother was destroyed by her training at the hands of the sinister Mr. Murdstone. Dickens's novel reveals the way masculinity is normatively structured through identification with the father's parental power and (coercive) educative role, only to reject that normative masculinity as "degenerat[ion] into the spider" (568). But David, in renouncing his parental/teacher's role, in leaving off the "reasoning" with her that Dora perceives as torture, resorts to treating her as a delightful body and so unintentionally destroys her fragile being in that way.

31. Sedgwick discusses "homophobia as a mechanism for regulating the behavior of the many by the specific oppression of a few" throughout her study, but concentrates on the way this mechanism developed into its modern forms in the chapter "Toward the Gothic: Terrorism and Homosexual Panic" (*Between Men: English Literature and Male Homosocial Desire* [New York: Columbia University Press, 1985], 83–96).

3. Severed Heads and White Roses

1. The white rose has a particularly diverse emblematic history. It his been associated with both Aphrodite and the Virgin Mary. Once used in the language of flowers to represent sexual or ephemeral love, as opposed to the red rose's symbolic meaning of enduring passion, it also stands for virginity. Its reputed use as a symbol for the antifascist Resistance has been preserved in a number of films, including one titled *The White Rose.*

2. Jessica Benjamin, *The Bonds of Love: Psychoanalysis, Feminism, and the Problem of Domination* (New York: Pantheon, 1988), 141, 160, 219–20, 180. All further citations are included parenthetically in the text.

3. Gilles Deleuze and Félix Guattari, *Anti-Oedipus: Capitalism and Schizophrenia,* trans. Robert Hurley, Mark Seem, and Helen R. Lane (Minneapolis: University of Minnesota Press, 1983), 62; Gilles Deleuze and Félix Guattari, *A Thousand Plateaus: Capitalism and Schizophrenia,* trans. Brian Massumi (1987; reprint, London: Athlone, 1988), 155–56. All further citations of the former volume are included parenthetically in the text.

4. Sigmund Freud, "The Economic Problem of Masochism," 1924, *The Standard Edition of the Complete Psychological Works of Sigmund Freud,* trans. James Strachey, vol. 19 (London: Hogarth, 1955), 165; Theodor Reik, *Masochism in Sex and Society* (1941; reprint, New York: Grove, 1962), 277, 351.

5. Georges Bataille, *Eroticism: Death and Sensuality* (1957; reprint, San Francisco: City Lights Books, 1986), 16, 89–90, 18.

6. Gilles Deleuze and Félix Guattari, *Anti-Oedipus,* 51–112.

7. As R. M. Friedman, who clearly despises the film, points out, "nearly all the critics have made the mistake of identifying Lucia as a Jewess," a mistake that naturally intensifies the repugnance aroused by the plot and setting ("Exorcising the Past: Jewish Figures in Contemporary Films," *Journal of Contemporary History* 19 [July 1984]: 518). An interesting exception to the usual objections to the film is Mitro Golo Stone's "The Feminist Critic and Salomé: On Cavani's *The Night Porter*" in *Romance Languages Annual* 1989 (1990): 41–44. Stone suggests the the film's depiction of Lucia is illuminated by reading it through Jessica Benjamin's theory of women's masochism, but ultimately finds the film a "failure" because of its focus on Max and his guilt. She agrees with Peter Bondanella that the film is a "reaffirmation of what constitutes a traditional goal of Christian morality, consciousness of sin and guilt, expiation, and purification through punishment" (*Italian Cinema from Neorealism to the Present* [New York: Ungar, 1983], 52), but dismisses such themes as inherently opposed to feminist goals (44).

8. For a different reading of how *The Night Porter* resists Freudian interpretation, see Kaja Silverman, "Masochism and Subjectivity," *Framework* 12 (1980): 2–9. Silverman applies Lacanian theory to the film to support her contention that Freud fails to account fully for the role socialization plays in inculcating masochistic response. She claims that masochistic "pleasure issues from the compulsive repetition of those painful moments in which the subject is culturally mastered," not, as Freud would have it, from the subject's sense of painfully gained mastery of instinct (3, 5).

9. Laura Pietropaolo's reading of the film as a ritual of exorcism hints at its antipsychoanalytic subtext. As she notes, the trials are "an absurd form of pseudo-therapy," and one of the ex-Nazis is "a crafty psychiatrist who dismisses guilt as a mere disturbance of the psyche." ("Sexuality as Exorcism in Liliana Cavani's *Night Porter*," in *Donna: Women in Italian Culture*, ed. Ada Testaferri, University of Toronto Italian Series 7 [Toronto: Dovehouse Editions, 1989], 73, 78.)

10. Like Mirto Golo Stone ("The Feminist Critic and Salomé," 41, 43), I am skeptical about Teresa de Lauretis's claim that the film shows us "female experience" from within. (See Teresa de Lauretis, "Cavani's *Night Porter*: A Woman's Film?" *Film Quarterly* 30.2 [Winter 1976]: 35). Rampling is not very expressive in this film and often conveys nothing more than the blankness of a fashion model, while Dirk Bogarde is at the height of his powers. Moreover, as Stone points out, the film does little in the way of either point-of-view shots or narrative to present Lucia's interior life (43). As a result the emphasis must fall on his suffering in relation to her impassivity.

11. Raymond Durnat calls the film "Romeo and Juliet *but*," remarking, "The hostility of the Montagues and Capulets is replaced by far more daunting divides: Nazism and democracy, torturer and victim, art and masquerade and reality" ("Skin Games," *Film Comment* 17.6 (Nov./Dec. 1981): 31). I would add social and sexual masochism.

12. See Kaja Silverman, "Fassbinder and Lacan: A Reconsideration of Gaze, Look, and Image" *Camera Obscura* 19 (January 1989): 71–73.

13. Carol J. Clover, *Men, Women, and Chainsaws: Gender in the Modern Horror Film* (Princeton: Princeton University Press, 1992), 210 (emphasis is Clover's) and 226.

14. Susan Sontag, "Fascinating Fascism," *A Susan Sontag Reader* (1974; reprint, New York: Vintage-Random, 1983), 322.

15. See "Anti-Retro: Entretien avec Michel Foucault" by Pascal Bomitzer, *Cahiers du Cinéma* 251–52 (July–August 1974): 5–36.

16. Elaine Scarry, *The Body in Pain: The Making and Unmaking of the World* (New York: Oxford University Press, 1985), 56–57.

17. Gilles Deleuze, *Masochism: An Interpretation of Coldness and Cruelty* trans. Jean McNeil (New York: George Braziller, 1971), 39–43.

18. I argue otherwise in *Lawrence among the Women: Wavering Boundaries in Women's Literary Traditions* (Charlottesville: University Press of Virginia, 1991).

19. Sandra Gilbert, "Potent Griselda: "The Ladybird" and the Great Mother," *D. H. Lawrence: A Centenary Consideration*, ed. Peter Balbert and Philip L. Marcus (Ithaca: Cornell University Press, 1985), 141, 148–49, 145.

20. Two previous discussions of Lawrence that apply ideas from Deleuze, Emile Delavenay's "D. H. Lawrence and Sacher-Masoch," *The D. H. Lawrence Review* 6.2 (Summer 1973); 119–48, and Claude Sinzelle's "Skinning the Fox: A Masochist's Delight," in *D. H. Lawrence in the Modern World*, Peter Preston and Peter Hoare, eds. (Cambridge: Cambridge University Press, 1989), 161–79, emphasize the Freudian elements of *Présentation de Sacher-Masoch*. Both essays are much concerned with analyzing Lawrence. Sinzelle's essay ignores Deleuze and

Guattari's anti-Freudian writings and illustrates the sort of coercive logic that they attribute to psychoanalysis. Because, following Edmund Bergler, Sinzelle distinguishes between neurotic and perverse masochism on the basis of "pleasure being consciously felt" (167), he cannot allow for the possibility that Lawrence intentionally wrote about masochistic pleasure without labeling Lawrence perverse. Imagined as unconscious of his own desires and pleasures, Lawrence is firmly fixed in Sinzelle's text as a subject for Freudian interpretation rather than recognized as a respondent to Freud.

21. D. H. Lawrence, *Sons and Lovers: Text, Background and Criticism*, ed. Julian Moynahan (New York: Viking, 1968), 2–3. All further citations are included parenthetically in the text.

22. This is how Freud accounts for the son's transfer of loyalty in *The Future of an Illusion, The Standard Edition of the Complete Psychological Works*, trans. W. D. Robson-Scott (1927; reprint, New York: Anchor-Doubleday), 34.

23. That Lawrence had some knowledge of Freud's ideas and strongly disagreed with them at the time he was writing *Sons and Lovers* has been shown by Harry T. Moore, *The Priest of Love: A Life of D. H. Lawrence* (Harmondsworth: Penguin, 1974), 212–13.

24. D. H. Lawrence, *Women in Love*, eds. David Farmer, Lindeth Vasey, and John Worthen (1920; reprint, Cambridge: Cambridge University Press, 1987), 148. All further citations are included parenthetically in the text.

25. See Gerald Doherty, "The Greatest Show on Earth: D. H. Lawrence's *St. Mawr* and Antonin Artaud's Theatre of Cruelty," *The D. H. Lawrence Review* 22 (Spring 1990): 5–22, for a discussion of similarities between Artaud and Lawrence.

26. Virginia Hyde, "Architectural Monuments: Centers of Worship in *Women in Love*," *Mosaic* 17.4 (Fall 1984): 53–71. All further citations are included parenthetically in the text.

27. I agree with Pietropaolo that *The Night Porter* as a whole is "a formalized re-enactment with a cathartic purpose" (75–76), but would locate the moment of catharsis in the conclusion of the film when we see Max and the now clearly complicitous Lucia pay the price of the self-knowledge they have so horribly gained.

28. Other Murdoch novels that prominently feature characters who engage in or are attracted to masochistic sex play include *The Unicorn, The Nice and the Good*, and *The Sacred and Profane Love Machine*.

29. Iris Murdoch, *A Severed Head* (1961; reprint, New York: Viking-Compass, 1963), 64, 67. All further citations are included parenthetically in the text.

30. Jane Gallop, *Thinking Through the Body* (New York: Columbia University Press, 1988), 44.

31. Sigmund Freud, "Medusa's Head," trans. James Strachey, in *The Standard Edition of the Complete Psychological Works* vol. 18 (1922; reprint, London: Hogarth, 1964), 273–74.

32. Neil Hertz, "Medusa's Head: Male Hysteria Under Political Pressure" *Representations* 4 (Fall 1983): 50.

33. Gallagher, Fineman, Hertz, "More About 'Medusa's Head' " *Representations* 4 (Fall 1983): 55–56.

34. Hélène Cixous, "The Laugh of the Medusa" in *Feminisms: An Anthology of Literary Theory and Criticism*, ed. Robyn R. Warhol and Diane Price Herndl (New Brunswick: Rutgers University Press, 1991), 344.

35. Richard Dellamora, *Masculine Desire: The Sexual Politics of Victorian Aestheticism* (Chapel Hill: University of North Carolina Press, 1990), 136–42. While Dellamora focuses on the social prohibition of male-male desire as an oppression that men like Swinburne and Pater bitterly resented and sought to escape, at least within their texts, through "a rhetorical wish to be woman," he convincingly argues that "circa 1870, at a moment when "homosexual" and "heterosexual" are only beginning to be defined as terms of a fixed dyad, emphasis on male-male desire does not exclude the possibility of male-female desire" (130–31).

36. Thaïs Morgan, "A Whip of One's Own," *The American Journal of Semiotics* 6.4 (1989): 109–36. All further citations are included parenthetically in the text.

37. Iris Murdoch, *The Sacred and Profane Love Machine* (London: Penguin, 1974), 73. All further citations are included parenthetically in the text.

38. Dorothy A. Winsor, "Iris Murdoch's Conflicting Ethical Demands: Separation Versus Passivity in *The Sacred and Profane Love Machine*" *Modern Language Quarterly* 44 (1983): 396–409. Winsor interestingly points out ways Murdoch's novels contradict her philosophical writings, in which she explicitly condemns masochism.

39. René Girard, *Violence and the Sacred*, trans. Patrick Gregory (Baltimore: Johns Hopkins University Press, 1977), 300. My discussion of doubles and misrecognition in this text is, of course, in part a (dissenting) response to Girard's theory of the structure and function of sacrifice in religion and myth.

4. Unveiling Woman's Most Unspeakable Desire

1. Jacques Lacan, "The Signification of the Phallus," in *Ecrits: A Selection*, trans. Alan Sheridan (New York: Norton, 1977), 288. Also see Juliet Mitchell and Jacqueline Rose's discussion of the woman as phallus in "The Meaning of the Phallus" in *Feminine Sexuality: Jacques Lacan and the école freudienne* (New York: Norton, 1982), 82–84.

2. In considering the relation of subjectivity to power, I aim for a place between what I see as the two most extreme positions in this debate: that subjectivity equals power and that subjectivity can only mean forced submission to power. (For a powerful feminist argument in favor of the former position see Monique Wittig's "The Mark of Gender," *Feminist Studies* 5.2 [Fall 1985]: 63–73.) If we believe that perfectly coherent subjecthood is attainable, the first becomes possible; if we believe that power can be absolute, the latter must be imagined as our state. For a cautionary instance of the problems inherent in taking the latter position, one might note that Kaja Silverman's moving description of the "feminine subjectivity" of the masochistic protagonist in *Histoire d'O* ("It is the history of the female subject—of the territorialization and inscription of a body whose involuntary internalization of a corresponding set of desires facilitates its complex exploitation") could be as well applied to the figure of the

dominatrix, if power is totalized (Kaja Silverman "*Histoire d'O*: The Construction of a Female Subject" in *Pleasure and Danger: Exploring Female Sexuality*, ed. Carole S. Vance [Boston: Routledge and Kegan Paul, 1984], 346.) For if subjectivity always means powerlessness, how can we speak ourselves at all? Won't our mouths always only open like those of ventriloquists' dolls to give voice to a predetermined discourse?

3. Jacques Derrida, *Glas* (Paris: Galilée, 1974), 159. Trans. Jardine. Alice Jardine, *Gynesis: Configurations of Woman and Modernity* (Ithaca: Cornell University Press, 1985), 198.

4. See Judith Butler's influential argument for reading gender as performance, *Gender Trouble: Feminism and the Subversion of Identity* (New York: Routledge, 1990). All further citations are included parenthetically in the text. Thaïs Morgan discusses the dominatrix's performance of "gender as masquerade" illuminatingly in "A Whip of One's Own: Dominatrix Pornography and the Construction of a Post-modern (Female) Subjectivity," *The American Journal of Semiotics* 6.4 (1989): 127–31.

5. Jardine, 198–200.

6. Diana Russell, "Sadomasochism: A Contra-Feminist Activity," in *Against Sadomasochism: A Radical Feminist Analysis*, ed. Robin Ruth Linden, Darlene R. Pagano, Diana E. H. Russell, and Susan Leigh Star (East Palo Alto Calif.: Frog in the Well, 1982), 177. John Stoltenberg, "Sadomasochism: Eroticized Violence, Eroticized Powerlessness," in *Against Sadomasochism*, 126.

7. Julia Creet, "Daughter of the Movement: The Psychodynamics of Lesbian S/M Fantasy," *Differences* 5 (Summer 1991): 137.

8. Jessica Benjamin, *The Bonds of Love* (New York: Pantheon, 1988), 74, 82, 120.

9. Michelle A. Massé, *In the Name of Love: Women Masochism, and the Gothic* (Ithaca: Cornell University Press, 1992), 51, 118; emphasis Massé's.

10. Leopold von Sacher-Masoch, *Venus in Furs*, trans. Aude Willm. In *Masochism: An Interpretation of Coldness and Cruelty* (New York: George Braziller, 1971), 160.

11. Robert J. Stoller, *Pain and Pleasure: A Psychoanalyst Explores the World of S&M* (New York: Plenum, 1991). An entirely different world of S/M is revealed in Gini Graham Scott's *Erotic Power: An Exploration of Dominance and Submission*, based on interviews with members of S/M social clubs and organizations in New York and San Francisco. Although Scott does devote a section of the book to commercial sex arrangements, the majority of the material deals with behavior on dates and between established couples.

12. See Eve Kosofsky Sedgwick's *Epistemology of the Closet* (Berkeley and Los Angeles: University of California Press, 1990), 37–38, for a concise and uncompromising statement about the destructive impact "the anti-s/m, antipornography liberal-feminist move toward labeling and stigmatizing sexualities" had on public attitudes in the 1980s.

13. Jonathan Dollimore, "The Cultural Politics of Perversion: Augustine, Shakespeare, Freud, Foucault," *Genders* 8 (Summer 1990): 3.

14. For an interesting discussion of the inverse relationship between popular concepts of the gender roles in sadomasochistic ritual and present-day reality

see Linda Williams, "Power, Pleasure, and Perversion: Sadomasochistic Film Pornography," *Representations* 27 (Summer 1989): 46. I would add the speculation that the present situation of (mis)representative reversal is, in part, the product of Freud's translation and simplification of the masochistic eroticism typical in Victorian texts into psychoanalytic language and the subsequent further simplification that occurs in the popularization of Freudian theory.

15. Gilles Deleuze, *Coldness and Cruelty*, trans. Jean McNeil (New York: Georges Braziller, 1971), 19. All further citations are included parenthetically in the text.

16. In a discussion of Deleuze's theory, Maureen C. Turim makes the important point that while Severin fails to recognize Wanda's "psychological investment in the relationship because coldness and indifference are expressed," we "should not make the same assumption," but instead realize that "ritualized expression of indifference can be a form of abuse . . . well within the psychological playing out of sadism." (Review of Gaylyn Studlar's *In the Realm of Pleasure* in *Journal of the History of Sexuality* 1.4 [April 1991]: 716.) See also René Girard, *Deceit, Desire, and the Novel* (Baltimore: Johns Hopkins University Press, 1965) for a discussion of the role of "the indifferent person" in the sadomasochistic exchange (107).

17. Daniel Defoe, *Moll Flanders* (1722; reprint, New York: Penguin, 1989), 58. All further citations are included parenthetically in the text.

18. Jane Austen, *Pride and Prejudice* (1813; reprint, New York: Norton, 1966), 141. All further citations are included parenthetically in the text.

19. See Jane Shattuc, "Postmodern Misogyny in *Blue Velvet*" (*Genders* 13 [Spring 1992]: 76-77, 85-86) for a discussion of Fredric Jameson's criticism of postmodern film in "Nostalgia for the Present" (*The South Atlantic Quarterly* 88 [Spring 1989]: 47-67), and Barbara Creed's response in "From Here to Modernity: Feminism and Postmodernism" (*Screen* 28 [Spring 1987]: 517-37).

20. Jane Gallop, *Thinking Through the Body* (New York: Columbia University Press, 1988), 157).

21. Lillian Faderman, "The Return of Butch and Femme: A Phenomenon in Lesbian Sexuality of the 1980s and 1990s," *Journal of the History of Sexuality* 2.4 (April 1992): 595.

22. The play, by Christopher Hampton, which provides both the material for the screen play and some conditioned audience expectations, emphasizes the cruelty at the core of the story in a way one might expect from the author of *Total Eclipse*, a passionate reimagining of the mutual destructive attraction between Rimbaud and Verlaine.

23. Choderlos de Laclos, *Les liaisons dangereuses*, trans. Richard Aldington (New York: Signet-New American Library, 1981), 642, 113. All further citations are included parenthetically in the text and indicate both page number, in roman type, and letter number, in italic.

24. For an exhaustive discussion of the centrality of religious and biblical laws to Sade's literary texts see Janine Chasseguet-Smirgel *Creativity and Perversion* (New York: Norton, 1984), 6-23.

25. See Parveen Adams, "Of Female Bondage," in *Between Feminism and*

Psychoanalysis, ed. Teresa Brennan (New York: Routledge, 1989), 260–61, for an explanation along these lines of the phallic mother of the masochistic fantasy.

26. Barbara Babcock, *The Reversible World: Symbolic Inversion in Art and Society* (Ithaca: Cornell University Press, 1978), 14.

27. For an extensive discussion and analysis of the low-budget films that began this genre see chapter 3 of Carol Clover's *Men, Women, and Chainsaws: Gender in the Modern Horror Film* (Princeton: Princeton University Press, 1992).

28. Milos Forman's *Valmont* avoids the problem of translating the novel's erotics into modern terms by dismissing the question of evil entirely. The first scenes prepare us for the old revenge story of a woman scorned as Merteuil (Annette Bening) is depicted as sincerely—and pathetically, given his wooden unattractiveness—in love with Gercourt (Jeffry Jones), who rejects her in favor of marriage to Cécile (Fairuza Balk). The exposition suggests that Merteuil has been reduced by men's betrayals to a cackling hysteric. The victim of Valmont's violence in two scenes and the passive recipient of his declaration of war, she bears little resemblance to his demonic mistress in the novel. But Valmont (Colin Firth) seems more shallow and lazy than bad. He seduces Tourvel (Meg Tilly) with a minimum of effort (and screen time), and only briefly entertains the idea of falling in love with her. The shift in narrative focus away from the Valmont-Merteuil-Tourvel triangle to the love affair of Cécile and Danceny (Henry Thomas) shifts the emphasis from power to weakness. The moral background of the novel, which throws into stark relief the cruelties of Valmont and Merteuil, vanishes here. No one is religious, society metes out no punishments, and, most surprisingly, Mme. de Rosemonde (Fabia Drake) is a lascivious bawd who smirks and winks as a pregnant Cécile marries Gercourt. These changes destroy any sort of eroticism in the film, which incidentally made a poor commercial showing.

29. Her speech in the scene is no doubt inspired by a passage in one of the novel's early letters from Merteuil to Valmont in which she says, about the possibility of deserting her lover Belleroche, "He would call me false, and the word 'false' always gives me pleasure; after 'cruel' it is the sweetest in a woman's ear and the least difficult to deserve" (32.5).

30. Peggy Kamuf, *Fictions of Feminine Desire: Disclosures of Heloise* (Lincoln: University of Nebraska Press, 1982), 135–36.

31. The misunderstanding between Valmont and Merteuil seems essential to maintaining their respective positions as sadist and masochist. As Lynn Chancer observes, violation of the masochist's contract is necessary to continue the pleasure of such relationships. There must be a contract because the sadist must feel in control, but there must be violation of it because "If the masochist resists, the sadist can go on taking pleasure in asserting power anew, over and over, thus prolonging and sustaining the dynamic." *Sadomasochism in Everyday Life: The Dynamics of Power and Powerlessness* (New Brunswick: Rutgers University Press, 1992), 50, 65.

32. Nancy K. Miller, "Rereading as a Woman: The Body in Practice" in *The Female Body in Western Culture* (Cambridge: Harvard University Press, 1985), 358–59.

33. Bill Overton, "The Play of Letters: *Les Liaisons dangereuses* on the Stage," *Theatre Research International* 13 (Autumn 1988): 269.
34. E. Ann Kaplan, "Is the Gaze Male?" in *Powers of Desire: The Politics of Sexuality*, ed. Ann Snitow, Christine Stansell, and Sharon Thompson (New York: Monthly Review Press, 1983), 315.
35. Rita Felski, "The Counterdiscourse of the Feminine in Three Texts by Wilde, Huysmans, and Sacher-Masoch," *PMLA* 106.5 (October 1991): 1102–103.
36. Barbara Ehrenreich, Elizabeth Hess, and Gloria Jacobs, *Re-Making Love: The Feminization of Sex* (New York: Anchor-Doubleday, 1986), 123, 124.
37. Walter Benn Michaels, *The Gold Standard and the Logic of Naturalism: American Literature at the Turn of the Century* (Berkeley and Los Angeles: University of California Press, 1987), 125, 133.
38. Naomi Scheman, "Missing Mothers/Desiring Daughters: Framing the Sight of Women," *Critical Inquiry* 15 (Autumn 1988): 70.
39. Christopher Hampton, *Dangerous Liaisons: The Film* (London: Faber and Faber, 1989), 75.
40. See Jane Gallop, *Thinking Through the Body*, for an explanation of the logic—and, in brief, the history—of contemporary feminist rejection of "the perverse" (106–108).
41. Naomi Greene, "Deadly Statues: Eros in the Films of Jean Cocteau" *The French Review* 16 (May 1988): 893. While Greene generally follows Deleuze's theory here, her condemnatory attitude toward both Cocteau and masochists in general seems the opposite of Deleuze's.
42. Adrienne Rich, "I Dream I'm the Death of Orpheus" in *The Norton Anthology of Literature by Women: The Tradition in English*, ed. Sandra M. Gilbert and Susan Gubar (New York: Norton, 1985), 2032.
43. It may be inaccurate to attribute to Bersani the idea that only masochism shatters the unified self, since his famous essay "Is the Rectum a Grave?" (*October* 41.6 [Winter 1987]: 197–222) suggests that all sexual pleasure is "masochistic" because it entails the "loss of control" (217). My use of the term "shatters" in this context comes from his work.

5. Re-viewing the Blood Orgasm

1. In applying Jean Clavreul's "The Perverse Couple" to male masochism, Parveen Adams uses the quoted phrase without questioning why we should accept *as* reality a Freudian explanation of difference—or of the "pathology" of its disavowal. ("Of Female Bondage," in *Between Feminism and Psychoanalysis*, ed. Teresa Brennan [New York: Routledge, 1989], 259, 263.) Adams argues that lesbian sadomasochism is not perverse but subversive. For an overview of feminist discussions of women's sadomasochistic role playing and also a defense of some pornographic representations of female masochism see Linda Williams, *Hard Core: Power, Pleasure and the "Frenzy of the Visible"* ([Berkeley and Los Angeles: University of California Press, 1989], 206–28.) While only a few critics go so far as to stigmatize sexually masochistic men as dangerous to society, even fewer question the popular idea (derived from psychoanalytic theory) that male

masochism is a pathological condition if it is manifested as conscious fantasy or in the performance of sexual rituals.

2. Samuel Johnson, *The Preface to Shakespeare* in *The Restoration and Eighteenth Century*, ed. Martin Price (New York: Oxford University Press, 1973), 565.

3. Woolf writes: "Opinions that one now pastes in a book labelled cock-a-doodle-dum and keeps for reading to select audiences on summer nights once drew tears, I can assure you. Among your grandmothers and great-grandmothers there were many that wept their eyes out." (Virginia Woolf, *A Room of One's Own* [1929; reprint, New York: Harbrace, 1957], 57.) In discussing gender as "the product of various social technologies, such as cinema, and of institutionalized discourses, epistemologies, and critical practices, as well as practices of everyday life," Theresa de Lauretis reminds us that the "medical practice" of psychoanalysis "is much more of a technology of gender than its theory." (Theresa de Lauretis, *Technologies of Gender* [Bloomington: Indiana University Press, 1987], 2, 21.) Still, we might contemplate all the tears that have been shed as a result of this medical-practice-as-gender-technology before discounting the position of those who see nothing compatible with feminism in either the theory or the practice.

4. Gilles Deleuze and Félix Guattari, *Anti-Oedipus: Capitalism and Schizophrenia*, trans. Robert Hurley, Mark Seem, and Helen R. Lane (Minneapolis: University of Minnesota Press, 1983), 270–71.

5. Jane Gallop, *Around 1981: Academic Feminist Literary Theory* (New York: Routledge, 1992), 239.

6. For a feminist reading of male masochism that maintains distinctions between masculinity and femininity, see Kaja Silverman's *Male Subjectivity at the Margins* (New York: Routledge, 1992). Although Silverman finds at least one "variety of masochism . . . in no way incompatible with virility" (10) and believes that "[o]nly the narrowest of borders . . . separates normative male subjectivity from masochism" (363), she insists on the femininity of the male masochist, who is in her view "a feminine yet heterosexual male subject" (212). While I would agree with Silverman that "[s]ince the category of masculinity has traditionally been a very restrictive one, those defying its conditions generally find themselves relegated to the more accommodating category of femininity" (342), I think that because the category of masculinity is differently configured at different times, it is important to look closely at each (cultural con)text in which a male's characteristics are marked as feminine rather than accepting one cultural moment's gendering of behavior or desires as if it were universal.

7. This expression, endlessly played with in the pornography of male masochism, is mentioned in Thaïs Morgan's "A Whip of One's Own: Dominatrix Pornography and the Construction of a Post-modern (Female) Subjectivity" (*The American Journal of Semiotics* 6.4 [1989]: 109–36) in the context of her development of the argument that such pornography's "effect is to dislocate and destroy rather than to relocate and affirm the hypercode of sexual difference," in other words, its "masculinity" and "femininity" write the quote marks around the words (131).

8. Edgar Allan Poe, "Eleonora," *The Complete Tales and Poems of Edgar Allan Poe* (New York: Vintage-Random, 1975), 653.

9. Hilton Kramer, *New York Times*, July 2, 1989, quoted in Richard Gold-

stein's "The Critic and the Commissar: Hilton Kramer's New Criterion," *Village Voice*, July 18, 1989, 41–42.

10. Walter Kendrick, *The Secret Museum: Pornography in Modern Culture* (New York: Viking, 1987), 9–11; Jacques Lacan, "The Signification of the Phallus," in *Ecrits: A Selection*, trans. Alan Sheridan (New York: Norton, 1977), 288.

11. Charles Dickens, *Great Expectations*, ed. Angus Calder (New York: Penguin, 1965), 378. All further citations are included parenthetically in the text.

12. Michel Foucault, *The History of Sexuality: An Introduction*, vol. I, trans. Robert Hurley (New York: Vintage-Random, 1980), 33.

13. Theodor Reik, *Masochism in Sex and Society*, trans. Margaret H. Beigel and Gertrud M. Kurth (New York: Grove, 1962), 386–87. For a typical reading of masochism in *Great Expectations*, see Shuli Barzilai, "Dickens's *Great Expectations*: The Motive for Moral Masochism," *American Imago* 42.1 (Spring 1985): 45–67.

14. Kaja Silverman, *Male Subjectivity at the Margins* (New York: Routledge, 1992), 206.

15. The very premise of literary periodization emphasizes clearly marked differences between socially determined conventions in different eras. The myth of modern sexual freedom that Foucault's *History of Sexuality* addresses was partially founded on totalizing Victorians' textually expressed sexual attitudes into a uniform prudery. I find the original ending of *Great Expectations* not so much consistent with the rest of the narrative as with the modern concept of *a* Victorian position on sex and gender, which has been so searchingly challenged by historians, philosophers, and literary critics in the last twenty years.

16. Susan Sontag, "The Artist as Exemplary Sufferer," in *Against Interpretation* (New York, Delta-Dell, 1966), 48.

17. C. S. Lewis, *The Allegory of Love* (London: Oxford University Press, 1958), 3.

18. D. H. Lawrence, "Surgery for the Novel—Or a Bomb," in *Phoenix*, ed. Edward D. McDonald (New York: Penguin, 1978), 519.

19. R. Howard Bloch, "Chaucer's Maiden's Head, 'The Physician's Tale' and the Poetics of Virginity," *Representations* 28 (Fall 1989): 120–22, 133–134. For another view of the politics of courtly love see Richard Dellamora's discussion of " 'The New Chivalry' and Oxford Politics" (*Masculine Desire: The Sexual Politics of Victorian Aestheticism* [Chapel Hill: University of North Carolina Press, 1990], 147–66). For discussion of the poetry of women troubadours, see Meg Bogin, *The Women Troubadours* (New York: Paddington Press, 1976), Jean Markale, *L'amour courtois, ou, le couple infernal* (Paris: Imago, 1987), and *The Voice of the Trobairitz: Perspectives on the Women Troubadours*, ed. William D. Paden (Philadelphia, University of Pennsylvania Press, 1989).

20. Mario Praz, *The Romantic Agony*, trans. Angus Davidson (Cleveland: Meridian-World, 1956), 191–271.

21. Steven Marcus, *The Other Victorians* (New York: Basic Books, 1974), 252–62. It seems necessary to mention here that James Kincaid challenges Marcus's assessment of the amount of pornography and flagellation literature published by the Victorians, pointing to the lack of evidence other than hearsay

that more than a "small amount of specifically erotic literature was available" (*Child-Loving: The Erotic Child and Victorian Culture* [New York: Routledge, 1992], 170.) However, substantial changes in what was considered erotic between our era and the nineteenth century make this claim difficult to assess. It does seem obvious from Sacher-Masoch's works alone that many more books centering on eroticized beating were published in the nineteenth century than had been previously.

22. The pervasiveness of this motif in "high culture" is illustrated by even a short list of respected texts that dramatize a man's eroticized punishment by a woman acting as a prostitute: Meredith's *The Ordeal of Richard Feverel*, Hardy's *Jude the Obscure*, Lawrence's *Women in Love*, Mann's *Doctor Faustus*, Proust's *Remembrance of Things Past*, Joyce's *Ulysses*, and Pynchon's *Gravity's Rainbow*.

23. Irving Singer, *Courtly and Romantic*, vol. 2 of *The Nature of Love* (Chicago: University of Chicago Press, 1984), 58.

24. D. A. Miller, *The Novel and the Police* (Berkeley: University of California Press, 1988), 192–220.

25. Emily Brontë, *Wuthering Heights*, ed. William M. Sale (New York: Norton, 1972), 97. All further citations are included parenthetically in the text.

26. Sigmund Freud, "The Economic Problem of Masochism," in *The Standard Edition of the Complete Psychological Works*, vol. 19, trans. James Strachey (London: Hogarth, 1953), 162.

27. Ian Gibson, *The English Vice: Beating, Sex, and Shame in Victorian England and After* (London: Duckworth, 1978), 30–32, 48–98, 203. All further citations are included parenthetically in the text. While I agree with Gibson that corporal punishment of children is a form of molestation and should be prohibited by law, I do not agree with his interpretation of masochism.

28. Mary Poovey, *Uneven Developments: The Ideological Work of Gender in Mid-Victorian England* (Chicago: University of Chicago Press, 1988), 9–11.

29. Sigmund Freud, "A Child Is Being Beaten," *The Standard Edition of the Complete Psychological Works of Sigmund Freud*, vol. 17, trans. James Strachey (London: Hogarth, 1953), 195.

30. Sherwood Williams, "The Gay Science: Paradox and Pathology in Wilde and Melville," an unpublished manuscript.

31. Parveen Adams, "Per Os(cillation)," *Camera Obscura* 17 (May 1988): 10, 24–25.

32. Much feminist criticism maintains that women's writing tends to have a unique gender-related revisionary relation to prior texts, especially when they have been privileged. For example, see Adrienne Rich, "When We Dead Awaken: Writing as Re-Vision," in *On Lies, Secrets, and Silence: Selected Prose, 1966–1978* (New York: Norton, 1979), 33–49; Luce Irigaray, *Ce sexe qui n'en est pas un* (Paris: Minuit, 1977); Sandra Gilbert and Susan Gubar, *The Madwoman in the Attic* (New Haven: Yale University Press, 1979); Alicia Ostriker, "The Thieves of Language: Women Poets and Revisionist Mythmaking," *Signs* 8.1 (Autumn 1982): 68–90. While I see such revisionary impulses as less strongly linked to gender than to writers' concepts of their own placement in or against

traditions, I think that this theory gives us a helpful starting point to consider the interplay between feminist modern and postmodern novels and Victorian textual representations of male masochism.

33. Donna Haraway, "A Manifesto for Cyborgs: Science Technology, and Socialist Feminism in the 1980s" in *Feminism/Postmodernism*, ed. Linda Nicholson (New York: Routledge, 1990), 217.

34. Kathy Acker, *Great Expectations* in *Blood and Guts in High School Plus Two* (London: Picador-Pan, 1984), 198–99. All further citations are included parenthetically in the text.

35. Kathy Acker, *Don Quixote* (New York: Grove, 1986), 139–40.

36. David Brande, "Making Yourself a Body Without Organs: The Cartography of Pain in Kathy Acker's *Don Quixote*," *Genre* 24 (Summer 1991): 203.

37. Larry McCaffery, "The Artists of Hell: Kathy Acker and 'Punk' Aesthetics" in *Breaking the Sequence: Women's Experimental Fiction*, ed. Ellen G. Friedman and Miriam Fuchs (Princeton: Princeton University Press, 1989): 219.

38. Pauline Palmer, "From 'Coded Mannequin' to Bird Woman: Angela Carter's Magic Flight," in *Women Reading Women's Writing*, ed. Sue Roe (Brighton: Harvester Press, 1987), 189–90. All further citations are included parenthetically in the text.

39. Andrea Dworkin, *Pornography: Men Possessing Women* (New York: Putnam's Sons, 1981), 84–85; Susanne Kappeler, *The Pornography of Representation* (Minneapolis: University of Minnesota Press, 1986), 133–36, 144, 210. For a thorough and well-balanced placement of Carter's work within the feminist debate over pornography, see Robin Ann Sheets, "Pornography, Fairy Tales, and Feminism: Angela Carter's 'The Bloody Chamber' " *The Journal of the History of Sexuality* 1 (April 1991): 633–57.

40. Angela Carter, *The Sadeian Woman* (New York: Pantheon, 1978), 132. All further citations included parenthetically in the text.

41. Parveen Adams, "Per (Os)cillation," 24–25; also see Gilles Deleuze, *Masochism: An Interpretation of Coldness and Cruelty*, trans. Jean McNeil (New York: Braziller, 1971), especially 50–60.

42. Angela Carter, *The Passion of New Eve* (London: Virago Press, 1982), 75, 101. All further citations are included parenthetically in the text.

43. Susan Rubin Suleiman, "(Re)Writing the Body: The Politics and Poetics of Female Eroticism," in *The Female Body in Western Culture*, ed. Susan Rubin Suleiman (Cambridge: Harvard University Press, 1986), 27; Ricarda Schmidt, "The Journey of the Subject in Angela Carter's Fiction," *Textual Practice* 3 (Spring 1989): 64.

44. Apollinaire, cited by Austryn Wainhouse, Foreword to *Juliette*, Donatien-Alphonse-François de Sade, trans. Wainhouse (New York: Grove Press, 1976), ix.

45. Tania Modleski, "The Incredible Shrinking He(r)man: Male Regression, the Male Body and Film" *Differences* 2 (Summer 1990): 67.

46. Angela Carter, *Nights at the Circus* (New York: Viking-Penguin, 1985), 12. All further citations are included parenthetically in the text.

47. See Bram Dijkstra, *Idols of Perversity: Fantasies of Feminine Evil in Fin-de-Siècle Culture* (New York: Oxford University Press, 1986). For another view

of the evil woman within Victorian iconography see Susan P. Casteras, "Malleus Malifacarum or *The Witches' Hammer:* Victorian Visions of Female Sages and Sorceresses" in *Victorian Sages and Cultural Discourse: Renegotiating Gender and Power*, ed. Thaïs Morgan (New Brunswick: Rutgers University Press, 1990).

48. For another view, informed by feminist film theories about the gaze, of how *Nights at the Circus* resists "the claustrophobic enclosure of Woman within narratives of male desire and practices a deconstruction of the very terms on which that enclosure depends: masculinity and femininity," see Sally Robinson, *Engendering the Subject: Gender and Self-Representation in Contemporary Women's Fiction* ([Albany: SUNY Press, 1991], 117–33).

49. Joanne Gass, "Panopticism in *Nights at the Circus*," paper delivered at the 18th Annual Twentieth-century Literature Conference, University of Louisville, Kentucky, 24 February 1990.

Conclusion

1. See Julia Kristeva, "Romeo and Juliet: Love-Hatred in the Couple," in *Tales of Love*, trans. Leon S. Roudiez (New York: Columbia University Press, 1987), 209–33, for a particularly apropos reading of *Romeo and Juliet* as each other's "unconscious" enemies.

2. Jeanette Winterson, *Oranges Are Not the Only Fruit* (New York: Atlantic Monthly Press, 1987), 170.

3. Coppélia Kahn, *Man's Estate: Masculine Identity in Shakespeare* (Berkeley and Los Angeles: University of California Press, 1981), 93, 98, 89.

4. Which is why, despite my many disagreements with Kaja Silverman's psychoanalytically based theories, I agree with her that exploring "male subjectivity at the margins" is of the utmost importance.

5. See Patrocinio P. Schweickart, "Reading Ourselves: Toward a Feminist Theory of Reading" in *Gender and Reading: Essays on Readers, Texts, and Contexts*, ed. Elizabeth A. Flynn and Patrocinio P. Schweickart (Baltimore: Johns Hopkins University Press, 1986), for a persuasive discussion of the ways a dialogic approach to literature can work better for feminist critics than a deconstructive one by giving us an understanding of our attraction to certain male-centered texts, not only negatively as what Judith Fetterley calls "immasculation," but positively as an engagement with their stories of opposition to the limitations on human experience imposed by a patriarchal culture. While Schweickart seems right to argue that some feminist enjoyment in reading such texts comes from overlooking the protagonist's gender, I would like to emphasize that for many feminist readers another part of the pleasure comes from recognizing the text's identification of a male character—and a male author—with revulsion toward patriarchy.

BIBLIOGRAPHY

Acker, Kathy. *Don Quixote*. New York: Grove, 1986.
———. *Great Expectations*. *Blood and Guts in High School Plus Two*. London: Picador-Pan, 1984.
Adams, Parveen. "Of Female Bondage." In *Between Feminism and Psychoanalysis*. Ed. Teresa Brennan. New York: Routledge, 1989.
———. "Per Os(cillation)." *Camera Obscura* 17 (May 1988): 7–30.
Apollinaire, Guillaume. "Preface." In *Juliette*. Donatien-Alphonse-François de Sade. Paris: Pauvert, 1949. Cited in Austryn Wainhouse. "Foreword." *Juliette*. Trans. Wainhouse. New York: Grove Press, 1976. vii-x.
Ardis, Ann. *New Women, New Novels*. New Brunswick: Rutgers University Press, 1990.
Austen, Jane. *Pride and Prejudice*. 1813. Reprint. New York: Norton, 1966.
Babcock, Barbara. *The Reversible World: Symbolic Inversion in Art and Society*. Ithaca: Cornell University Press, 1978.
Barale, Michèle. *Daughters and Lovers: The Life and Works of Mary Webb*. Middleton: Wesleyan University Press, 1986.
Barker, Francis. *The Tremulous Private Body: Essays on Subjection*. London: Metheun, 1984.
Barthes, Roland. *A Lover's Discourse: Fragments*. Trans. Richard Howard. New York: Hill and Wang, 1978.
———. *Sade/Fourier/Loyola*. Trans. Richard Miller. New York: Hill and Wang, 1976.
Barzilai, Shuli. "Dickens's *Great Expectations:* The Motive for Moral Masochism." *American Imago* 42.1 (Spring 1985): 45–67.
Bataille, Georges. *Eroticism: Death and Sensuality*. 1957. Reprint. San Francisco: City Lights Books, 1986.
Bauer, Dale. *Feminist Dialogics*. Albany, N.Y.: SUNY University Press, 1988.
Benjamin, Jessica. *The Bonds of Love: Psychoanalysis, Feminism, and the Problem of Domination*. New York: Pantheon, 1988.
Bergler, Edmund. *Curable and Incurable Neurotics: Problems of Incurable Neurotics: Problems of "Neurotic" versus "Malignant" Masochism*. New York: Liveright, 1961.
Bersani, Leo. "Against *Ulysses*." *Raritan* 8.2 (Fall 1988): 1–32.

———. *Baudelaire and Freud.* Berkeley and Los Angeles: University of California Press, 1977.

———. *The Freudian Body.* New York: Columbia, 1986.

———. "Is the Rectum a Grave?" *October* 43 (Winter 1987): 197–222.

Bersani, Leo, and Ulysse Dutoit. *The Forms of Violence: Narrative in Assyrian Art and Modern Culture.* New York: Schocken, 1985.

Bloch, R. Howard. "Chaucer's Maiden's Head, 'The Physician's Tale' and the Poetics of Virginity." *Representations* 28 (Fall 1989): 113–34.

Bogue, Ronald. *Deleuze and Guattari.* New York: Routledge, 1989.

Bondanella, Peter. *Italian Cinema from Neorealism to the Present.* New York: Ungar, 1983.

Brande, David. "Making Yourself a Body without Organs: The Cartography of Pain in Kathy Acker's *Don Quixote.*" *Genre* 24 (Summer 1991): 191–209.

Brontë, Emily. *Wuthering Heights.* 1847. Reprint. New York: Norton, 1972.

Brown, Richard. *James Joyce and Sexuality.* Cambridge: Cambridge University Press, 1985.

Bruckner, Pascal. *The Tears of the White Man: Compassion as Contempt.* Trans. William R. Beer. New York: MacMillan, 1986.

Butler, Judith. *Gender Trouble.* New York: Routledge, 1990.

Califia, Pat. "Feminism and Sadomasochism." *Co-Evolutionary Quarterly* 33 (Spring 1982): 33–40.

Carter, Angela. "Black Venus." *Saints and Strangers,* 109–26. New York: Penguin, 1987.

———. *Nights at the Circus.* New York: Viking Penguin, 1985.

———. *The Passion of New Eve.* London: Virago Press, 1982.

———. *The Sadeian Woman: And the Ideology of Pornography.* New York: Pantheon, 1978.

Caserio, Robert L. "Mobility and Masochism: Christine Brooke-Rose and J. G. Ballard." *Novel* 21 (Winter/Spring 1988): 291–309.

Casteras, Susan P. "*Malleus Malifacarum* or *The Witches' Hammer:* Victorian Visions of Female Sages and Sorceresses." In *Victorian Sages and Cultural Discourse: Renegotiating Gender and Power,* ed. Thaïs Morgan, 142–70. New Brunswick: Rutgers University Press, 1990.

Chancer, Lynn S. *Sadomasochism in Everyday Life: The Dynamics of Power and Powerlessness.* New Brunswick: Rutgers University Press, 1992.

Chasseguet-Smirgel, Janine. *Creativity and Perversion.* New York: Norton, 1984.

Cixous, Hélène. "The Laugh of the Medusa." 1975. Trans. Keith Cohen and Paula Cohen. In *Feminisms: An Anthology of Literary Theory and Criticism*, ed. Robyn R. Warhol and Diane Price Herndl, 334–49. New Brunswick: Rutgers University Press, 1991.

Clavreul, Jean. "The Perverse Couple." *Returning to Freud: Clinical Psychoanalysis in the School of Lacan*. Trans. Stuart Schneiderman, 215–33. New Haven: Yale University Press, 1980.

Clover, Carol J. *Men, Women, and Chainsaws: Gender in the Modern Horror Film*. Princeton: Princeton University Press, 1992.

Cooper, Arnold M. "Masochism as a Character Trait." Keynote Address at the Masochism Symposium held by the Psychiatric Services of Children's Hospital of San Francisco. San Francisco, 25 October 1986.

Corber, Robert J. "Representing the 'Unspeakable': William Godwin and the Politics of Homophobia." *Journal of the History of Sexuality* 1.1 (July 1990): 85–101.

Creed, Barbara. "From Here to Modernity: Feminism and Postmodernism." *Screen* 28.2 (Summer 1987): 47–67.

Creet, Julia. "Daughter of the Movement: The Psychodynamics of Lesbian S/M Fantasy." *Differences* 3.2 (Summer 1991): 135–59.

Dangerous Liaisons. Dir. Stephen Frears. With Glenn Close, John Malkovich, Michelle Pfeiffer, and Keanu Reeves. Los Angeles: Warner Brothers, 1989.

Dante Alighieri. *The Inferno*. Trans. John Ciardi. New York: Mentor-NAL, 1954.

Davidson, Donald. "The Traditional Basis of Thomas Hardy's Fiction." *Hardy: A Collection of Critical Essays*, ed. Albert J. Guerard, 10–23. Englewood Cliffs: Prentice-Hall, 1963.

Defoe, Daniel. *Moll Flanders*. 1722. Reprint. New York: Penguin, 1989.

De Laclos, Choderlos. *Les liaisons dangereuses*. 1782. Reprint. Paris: Flammarion, 1981.

———. *Les liaisons dangereuses*. Trans. Richard Aldington. New York: Signet-New American Library, 1981.

De Lauretis, Theresa. "Cavani's *Night Porter*: A Woman's Film?" *Film Quarterly* 30.2 (Winter 1976): 35–38.

———. *Technologies of Gender*. Bloomington: Indiana University Press, 1987.

Delavenay, Emile. "D. H. Lawrence and Sacher-Masoch." *The D. H. Lawrence Review* 6.2 (Summer 1973): 119–48.

Deleuze, Gilles. *Masochism: An Interpretation of Coldness and Cruelty*. Trans. Jean McNeil. New York: Georges Braziller, 1971.

Deleuze, Gilles, and Félix Guattari. *Anti-Oedipus: Capitalism and Schizophrenia*. Trans. Robert Hurley, Mark Seem, and Helen R. Lane. Minneapolis: University of Minnesota Press, 1983.

———. *A Thousand Plateaus: Capitalism and Schizophrenia*. Trans. Brian Massumi. London: Athlone, 1988.

Dellamora, Richard. *Masculine Desire: The Sexual Politics of Victorian Aestheticism*. Chapel Hill: University of North Carolina Press, 1990.

Derrida, Jacques. *Glas*. Paris: Galilée, 1974

Dickens, Charles. *David Copperfield*. 1869. Reprint. New York: Oxford, 1981.

———. *Great Expectations*. 1861. Reprint. New York: Penguin, 1965.

Dijkstra, Bram. *Idols of Perversity: Fantasies of Feminine Evil in Fin-de-Siècle Culture*. New York: Oxford University Press, 1986.

Doherty, Gerald. "The Greatest Show on Earth: D. H. Lawrence's *St. Mawr* and Antonin Artaud's Theatre of Cruelty." *The D. H. Lawrence Review* 22.1 (Spring 1990): 5–22.

Dollimore, Jonathan. "The Cultural Politics of Perversion: Augustine, Shakespeare, Freud, Foucault." *Genders* 8 (Summer 1990): 1–16.

Dubois, Ellen Carol. "Introduction." In *Feminist Theorists: Three Centuries of Key Women Thinkers*, ed. Dale Spender, ix–xiii. New York: Pantheon, 1983.

Durgnat, Raymond. "Skin Games." *Film Comment* 17.6 (Nov./Dec. 1981): 28–32.

Dworkin, Andrea. *Pornography: Men Possessing Women*. New York: Putnam's, 1981.

Ehrenreich, Barbara, Elizabeth Hess, and Gloria Jacobs. *Re-Making Love: The Feminization of Sex*. New York: Anchor-Doubleday, 1986.

Ellis, Henry Havelock. *Studies in the Psychology of Sex*. Vol. 1. 1911. Reprint. New York: Random, 1936.

Ellmann, Richard. *James Joyce*. New York: Oxford University Press, 1982.

———. *Ulysses on the Liffey*. New York: Oxford University Press, 1972.

Faderman, Lillian. "The Return of Butch and Femme: A Phenomenon in Lesbian Sexuality of the 1980s and 1990s." *Journal of the History of Sexuality* 2.4 (April 1992): 578–96.

Fanon, Frantz. *Black Skin, White Masks*. Trans. Charles Lam Markham. New York: Grove, 1965.

Felski, Rita. "The Counterdiscourse of the Feminine in Three Texts by Wilde, Huysmans, and Sacher-Masoch" *PMLA* 106 (October 1991): 1094–105.

Foucault, Michel. "Anti-Retro: Entretien avec Michel Foucault," by Pascal Bomitzer *Cahiers du Cinéma* No. 251–52 (July-August 1974): 5–36.

———. *The History of Sexuality: An Introduction*. Vol. 1. Trans. Robert Hurley. New York: Vintage-Random, 1980.

————. *The Use of Pleasure*. Vol. 2 of *The History of Sexuality*. Trans. Robert Hurley. New York: Vintage, 1986.

Freud, Sigmund. *Beyond the Pleasure Principle*. 1920. Reprint, trans. and ed. James Strachey. New York: Norton, 1961.

————. *Civilization and Its Discontents*. 1930. Reprint, trans. and ed. James Strachey. New York: Norton, 1961.

————. *The Standard Edition of the Complete Psychological Works of Sigmund Freud*, trans. James Strachey. London: Hogarth, 1953.

————. *Three Essays on the Theory of Sexuality*. 1905. Reprint, trans. James Strachey. New York: Basic Books, 1975.

Friedman, R. M. "Exorcising the Past: Jewish Figures in Contemporary Films." *Journal of Contemporary History* 19 (July 1984): 511–27.

Fuss, Diana. *Essentially Speaking: Feminism, Nature, and Difference.* New York: Routledge, 1989.

Gallagher, Catherine, Joel Fineman, and Neil Hertz. "More About 'Medusa's Head.' " *Representations* 4 (Fall 1983): 55–72.

Gallop, Jane. *Around 1981: Academic Feminist Literary Theory*. New York: Routledge, 1992.

————. *Thinking Through the Body*. New York: Columbia University Press, 1988.

Gass, Joanne. "Panopticism in *Nights at the Circus*." Paper presented at the Twentieth-century Literature Conference, University of Louisville, Kentucky, 24 February 1990.

Genette, Gérard. *Palimpsestes: La littérature au second degré*. Paris, Éditions du Seuil, 1982.

Gibson, Ian. *The English Vice: Beating, Sex, and Shame in Victorian England and After*. London: Duckworth, 1978.

Gilbert, Sandra M. "Potent Griselda: 'The Ladybird' and the Great Mother." In *D. H. Lawrence: A Centenary Consideration*, ed. Peter Balbert and Philip L. Marcus, 130–61. Ithaca: Cornell University Press, 1985.

Gilbert, Sandra M., and Susan Gubar. *The Madwoman in the Attic: The Woman Writer and the Nineteenth-Century Literary Imagination*. New Haven: Yale University Press, 1979.

————. *Sexchanges*. Vol. 2 of *No Man's Land: The Place of the Woman Writer in the Twentieth Century*. New Haven: Yale University Press, 1989.

Gilbert, Stuart. *James Joyce's Ulysses: A Study*. London: Faber, 1952.

Gilman, Charlotte Perkins. *Herland*. 1915. Reprint. New York: Pantheon, 1979.

Girard, René. *Deceit, Desire, and the Novel*. Baltimore: Johns Hopkins University Press, 1965.

―――. *Violence and the Sacred*. Trans. Patrick Gregory. Baltimore: Johns Hopkins University Press, 1977.

Greene, Naomi. "Deadly Statues: Eros in the Films of Jean Cocteau." *The French Review* 61.6 (May 1988): 890–98.

Gubar, Susan. "Representing Pornography: Feminism, Criticism, and Depictions of Female Violation." *Critical Inquiry* 13.4 (Summer 1987): 712–41.

Hampton, Christopher. *Dangerous Liaisons: The Film*. London: Faber and Faber, 1989.

Haraway, Donna. "A Manifesto for Cyborgs: Science Technology, and Socialist Feminism in the 1980s." In *Feminism/Postmodernism*, ed. Linda Nicholson, 190–233. New York: Routledge, 1990.

Hardy, Thomas. *Tess of the d'Urbervilles*. 1891. Reprint. New York: Penguin, 1978.

Hayman, David. *Ulysses: The Mechanics of Meaning*. Englewood Cliffs, N.J.: Prentice-Hall, 1970.

Hertz, Neil. "Medusa's Head: Male Hysteria Under Political Pressure." *Representations* 4 (Fall 1983): 27–54.

Herzog, Kristin. *Women, Ethnics, and Exotics*. Knoxville: University of Tennessee Press, 1983.

Hyde, Virginia. "Architectural Monuments: Centers of Worship in *Women in Love*." *Mosaic* 17.4 (Fall 1984): 73–92.

Irigaray, Luce. *Ce sexe qui n'en est pas un*. Paris: Minuit, 1977.

Jameson, Fredric. "Nostalgia for the Present." *The South Atlantic Quarterly* 88 (Spring 1989): 517–37.

Jardine, Alice. *Gynesis: Configurations of Woman and Modernity*. Ithaca: Cornell University Press, 1985.

Johnson, Barbara. *A World of Difference*. Baltimore: Johns Hopkins University Press, 1984.

Johnson, Samuel. *The Preface to Shakespeare*. 1765. In *The Restoration and the Eighteenth Century*, ed. Martin Price. New York: Oxford University Press, 1973.

Joyce, James. *Ulysses*. 1914. Reprint. New York: Random, 1961.

Kahn, Coppélia. *Man's Estate: Masculine Identity in Shakespeare*. Berkeley and Los Angeles: University of California Press, 1981.

Kamuf, Peggy. *Fictions of Feminine Desire: Disclosures of Heloise*. Lincoln: University of Nebraska Press, 1982.

Kaplan, E. Ann. "Is the Gaze Male?" In *Powers of Desire: The Politics of Sexuality*, ed. Ann Snitow, Christine Stansell, and Sharon Thompson, 309–327. New York: Monthly Review Press, 1983.

Kappeler, Susanne. *The Pornography of Representation*. Minneapolis: University of Minnesota Press, 1986.

Kelly, Joan. *Women, History, and Theory.* Chicago: University of Chicago Press, 1984.

Kendrick, Walter. *The Secret Museum: Pornography in Modern Culture.* New York: Viking, 1987.

Kenner, Hugh. *Ulysses.* London: George Allen Unwin, 1980.

Kincaid, James. *Child-Loving: The Erotic Child and Victorian Culture.* New York: Routledge, 1992.

Krafft-Ebing, Richard von. *Psychopathia Sexualis: A Medico-Forensic Study.* 1886. Reprint, trans. Harry Wedeck. New York: Putnam's Sons, 1965.

Kramer, Hilton. *New York Times,* 2 July 1989. Quoted in Richard Goldstein, "The Critic and the Commissar: Hilton Kramer's New Criterion." *Village Voice,* 18 July 1989: 41–42.

Kristeva, Julia. *Tales of Love.* Trans. Leon S. Roudiez. New York: Columbia University Press, 1987.

Lacan, Jacques. "The Signification of the Phallus." *Ecrits: A Selection.* Trans. Alan Sheridan, 281–91. New York: Norton, 1977.

——. "The Meaning of the Phallus." 1958. In *Feminine Sexuality: Jacques Lacan and the École Freudienne,* trans. Jacqueline Rose. Ed. Juliet Mitchell and Jacqueline Rose, 74–85. New York: Norton, 1982.

Langland, Elizabeth. "Becoming a Man in *Jude the Obscure.*" In *The Sense of Sex: Feminist Perspectives on Hardy,* ed. Margaret Higonnet, 32–48. Urbana: University of Illinois Press, 1993.

——. "Nobody's Angels: Domestic Ideology and Middle-Class Women in the Victorian Novel." *PMLA* 107. 2 (March 1992): 290–304.

Lawrence, D. H. *Women in Love.* 1920. Reprint, ed. David Farmer, Lindeth Vasey, and John Worthen. Cambridge: Cambridge University Press, 1987.

Lawrence, D. H. *Sons and Lovers: Text, Background and Criticism.* Ed. Julian Moynahan. New York: Viking, 1968.

——. "Surgery for the Novel—Or a Bomb." *Phoenix.* Ed. Edward D. McDonald, 517–20. New York: Penguin, 1978.

Lewis, C. S. *The Allegory of Love.* London: Oxford University Press, 1958.

McCaffery, Larry. "The Artists of Hell: Kathy Acker and 'Punk' Aesthetics." In *Breaking the Sequence: Women's Experimental Fiction,* ed. Ellen G. Friedman and Miriam Fuchs. Princeton: Princeton University Press, 1989. 215–30.

McClure, John A. "Late Imperial Romance." *Raritan* 10.4 (Spring 1991): 111–30.

Marcus, Steven. *The Other Victorians.* New York: Basic Books, 1974.

Marotti, Arthur. " 'Love Is Not Love': Elizabethan Sonnet Sequences and the Social Order." *ELH* 49.2 (Summer 1982): 396–428.

Massé, Michelle A. *In the Name of Love: Women Masochism, and the Gothic.* Ithaca: Cornell University Press, 1992.

Meibomius, John Henry. *On the Use of Flogging in Venereal Affairs.* Chester, Pennsylvania: Import Publishing, 1961.

Meredith, George. *The Ordeal of Richard Feverel.* 1859. Reprint. New York: Modern Library, 1950.

Michaels, Walter Benn. *The Gold Standard and the Logic of Naturalism: American Literature at the Turn of the Century.* Berkeley and Los Angeles: University of California Press, 1987.

Michie, Helena. " 'There Is No Friend Like a Sister': Sisterhood as Sexual Difference." *ELH* 56.2 (Summer 1989): 199–212.

Miller, D. A. *The Novel and the Police.* Berkeley and Los Angeles: University of California Press, 1988.

Miller, Nancy K. "Rereading as a Woman: The Body in Practice." In *The Female Body in Western Culture,* ed. Susan Rubin Suleiman, 354–62. Cambridge: Harvard University Press, 1985.

Modleski, Tania. "The Incredible Shrinking He(r)man: Male Regression, the Male Body and Film." *Differences* 2:2 (Summer 1990): 55–75.

Moore, Harry T. *The Priest of Love: A Life of D. H. Lawrence.* Harmondsworth: Penguin, 1974.

Moraga, Cherríe. "La Güera." In *This Bridge Called My Back: Writings of Radical Women of Color,* ed. Gloria Anzaldua and Cherríe Moraga, 27–34. New York: Kitchen Table, Women of Color Press, 1982.

Morgan, Thaïs E. "A Whip of One's Own: Dominatrix Pornography and the Construction of a Post-Modern (Female) Subjectivity." *The American Journal of Semiotics.* 6.4 (1989): 109–36.

Mulvey, Laura. "Visual Pleasure and Narrative Cinema." *Screen* 16.3 (Autumn 1975): 6–18.

Murdoch, Iris. *The Sacred and Profane Love Machine.* London: Penguin, 1974.

———. *A Severed Head.* 1961. Reprint. New York: Viking-Compass, 1963.

Newfield, Christopher. "The Politics of Male Suffering: Masochism and Hegemony in the American Renaissance." *Differences* 1.3 (Fall 1989): 55–87.

Newton, Judith Lowder. *Women, Power, and Subversion: Social Strategies in British Fiction 1778–1860.* Athens: University of Georgia Press, 1981.

The Night Porter. Dir. Liliana Cavani. With Dirk Bogarde and Charlotte Rampling. Los Angeles: Embassy, 1973.

Orgel, Stephen. "Nobody's Perfect: Or Why Did the English Stage Take Boys for Women?" *The South Atlantic Quarterly* 88 (Winter 1989): 7–29.

Orpheus. Dir. Jean Cocteau. With Jean Marais and Maria Casares. Los Angeles: Orion, 1949.

Ostriker, Alicia. "The Thieves of Language: Women Poets and Revisionist Mythmaking," *Signs* 8.1 (Autumn 1982): 314–38.

Overton, Bill. "The Play of Letters: *Les Liaisons dangereuses* on the Stage." *Theatre Research International* 13.3 (Autumn 1988): 263–74.

Palmer, Pauline. "From 'Coded Mannequin' to Bird Woman: Angela Carter's Magic Flight." In *Women Reading Women's Writing*, ed. Sue Roe, 179–208. Brighton: Harvester Press, 1987.

Pietropaolo, Laura. "Sexuality as Exorcism in Liliana Cavani's *Night Porter.* In *Donna: Women in Italian Culture*, ed. Ada Testaferri, 71–79. University of Toronto Italian Series 7. Toronto: Dovehouse Editions, 1989.

Poe, Edgar Allan. "Eleonora." *The Complete Tales and Poems of Edgar Allan Poe.* New York: Vintage-Random, 1975.

Poovey, Mary. *Uneven Developments: The Ideological Work of Gender in Mid-Victorian England.* Chicago: University of Chicago Press, 1988.

Praz, Mario. *The Romantic Agony.* Trans. Angus Davidson. Cleveland: Meridian-World, 1956.

Reik, Theodore. *Masochism in Sex and Society.* 1941. Reprint, trans. Margaret H. Beigel and Gertrud M. Kurth. New York: Grove, 1962.

Restuccia, Frances L. *Joyce and the Law of the Father.* New Haven: Yale University Press, 1989.

Rich, Adrienne. "I Dream I'm the Death of Orpheus." *The Norton Anthology of Literature by Women: The Tradition in English.* Ed. Sandra M. Gilbert and Susan Gubar, 2032. New York: Norton, 1985.

———. "When We Dead Awaken: Writing as Re-Vision." *On Lies, Secrets, and Silence: Selected Prose, 1966–1978.* New York: Norton, 1979.

Rich, B. Ruby. "Feminism and Sexuality in the 1980s." *Feminist Studies* 12.3 (Fall 1986): 525–561.

Robinson, Lillian S. "Treason Our Text: Feminist Challenges to the Literary Canon." In *The New Feminist Criticism*, ed. Elaine Showalter, 105–21. New York: Pantheon, 1985.

Robinson, Paul. *The Modernization of Sex.* New York: Harper Colophon, 1977.

Robinson, Sally. *Engendering the Subject: Gender and Self-Representation in Contemporary Women's Fiction.* Albany, N.Y.: SUNY Press, 1991.

Rosaldo, Renato. "Imperialist Nostalgia." *Representations* 26 (Spring 1989): 107–22.

Rubin, Gayle. "Thinking Sex: Notes for a Radical Theory of the Politics of Sexuality." In *Pleasure and Danger: Exploring Female Sexuality*, ed. Carole S. Vance, 267–319. Boston: Routledge, 1984.

Russell, Diana. "Sadomasochism: A Contra-Feminist Activity." In *Against Sadomasochism: A Radical Feminist Analysis*, ed. Robin Ruth Linden, Darlene R. Pagano, Diana E. H. Russell, and Susan Leigh Star, 176–183. East Palo Alto, Calif.: Frog in the Well, 1982.

Sacher-Masoch, Leopold von. *Venus in Furs*. Trans. Aude Willm. In *Masochism: An Interpretation of Coldness and Cruelty*. New York: Braziller, 1971.

Samois. *Coming to Power: Writings and Graphics on Lesbian S/M*. Boston: Alyson Publications, 1982.

Sánchez-Eppler, Karen. "Bodily Bonds: The Intersecting Rhetorics of Feminism and Abolition." *Representations* 24 (Fall 1988): 28–59.

Scarry, Elaine. *The Body in Pain: The Making and Unmaking of the World*. New York: Oxford University Press, 1985.

Scheman, Naomi. "Missing Mothers/Desiring Daughters: Framing the Sight of Women." *Critical Inquiry* 15.1 (Autumn 1988): 62–89.

Schleiner, Winfried. "*Medicus prudens* or *medicus Christianus*: Perspectives on Medical Ethics in the Renaissance." Unpublished manuscript.

Schmidt, Ricarda. "The Journey of the Subject in Angela Carter's Fiction." *Textual Practice* 3.1 (Spring 1989): 56–75.

Schweickart, Patrocinio P. "Reading Ourselves: Toward a Feminist Theory of Reading." In *Gender and Reading: Essays on Readers, Texts, and Contexts*, ed. Elizabeth A. Flynn and Patrocinio P. Schweickart, 17–44. Baltimore: Johns Hopkins University Press, 1986.

Scott, Gini Graham. *Erotic Power: An Exploration of Dominance and Submission*. Secaucus, N.J.: Citadel, 1983.

Sedgwick, Eve Kosofsky. *Between Men: English Literature and Male Homosocial Desire*. New York: Columbia University Press, 1985.

———. *Epistemology of the Closet*. Berkeley and Los Angeles: University of California Press, 1990.

Senn, Fritz. *Joyce's Dislocutions: Essays on Reading as Translation*. Ed. John Paul Riquelme. Baltimore: Johns Hopkins University Press, 1984.

Shakespeare, William. *A Midsummer Night's Dream*. New York: Signet, 1963.

———. *Romeo and Juliet*. New York: Signet, 1964.

Shattuc, Jane. "Postmodern Misogyny in *Blue Velvet*." *Genders* 13 (Spring 1992): 73–89.

Sheets, Robin Ann. "Pornography, Fairy Tales, and Feminism: Angela Carter's 'The Bloody Chamber.'" *The Journal of the History of Sexuality* 1.4 (April 1991): 633–57.

Showalter, Elaine. "Toward a Feminist Poetics." In *Women's Writing and Writing About Women*, ed. Mary Jacobus, 22–41. New York: Barnes and Noble, 1979.

Siegel, Carol. *Lawrence Among the Women: Wavering Boundaries in Women's Literary Traditions.* Charlottesville: University Press of Virginia, 1991.

Silverman, Kaja. "Fassbinder and Lacan: A Reconsideration of Gaze, Look, and Image," *Camera Obscura* 19 (January 1989): 54–85.

———. "*Histoire d'O:* The Construction of a Female Subject." In *Pleasure and Danger: Exploring Female Sexuality*, ed. Carole S. Vance, 320–49. Boston: Routledge, 1984.

———. "History, Figuration, and Female Subjectivity in *Tess of the d'Urbervilles.*" *Novel* 18 (1984): 5–28.

———. *Male Subjectivity at the Margins.* New York: Routledge, 1992.

———. "Masochism and Male Subjectivity." *Camera Obscura* 17 (May 1988): 31–68.

———. "Masochism and Subjectivity." *Framework* 12 (1980): 1–9.

———. "White Skin, Brown Masks: The Double Mimesis, or With Lawrence in Arabia." *Differences* 1.3 (Fall 1989): 3–54.

Simpson, Donald. "Literary Critics and the Return to History." *Critical Inquiry* 14.4 (Summer 1988): 721–47.

Singer, Irving. *Courtly and Romantic.* Vol. 2 of *The Nature of Love.* Chicago: University of Chicago Press, 1984.

Sinzelle, Claude. "Skinning the Fox: A Masochist's Delight." In *D. H. Lawrence in the Modern World*, ed. Peter Preston and Peter Hoare, 161–79. Cambridge: Cambridge University Press, 1989.

Something Wild. Dir. Jonathan Demme. With Jeff Daniels, Melanie Griffith, and Ray Liotta. Los Angeles: Orion, 1989.

Sontag, Susan. "The Artist as Exemplary Sufferer." 1962. Reprint. *Against Interpretation.* New York, Delta-Dell, 1966.

———. "Fascinating Fascism." 1974. Reprint. *A Susan Sontag Reader.* New York: Vintage-Random, 1983.

Spengler, Andreas. "Manifest Sadomasochism of Males: Results of an Empirical Study." In *S and M: Studies in Sadomasochism*, ed. Thomas Weinberg and G. W. Levi Kamel, 57–72. New York: Prometheus, 1983.

Spivak, Gayatri Chakravorti. "Imperialism and Sexual Difference." In *Contemporary Literary Criticism: Literary and Cultural Studies*, ed. Robert Con Davis and Ronald Schleiffer, 517–26. White Plains, N.Y.: Longman, 1989.

Stoller, Robert J. *Pain and Pleasure: A Psychoanalyst Explores the World of S&M.* New York: Plenum, 1991.

Stoltenberg, John. "Sadomasochism: Eroticized Violence, Eroticized

Powerlessness." In *Against Sadomasochism: A Radical Feminist Analysis*, ed. Robin Ruth Linden, Darlene R. Pagano, Diana E. H. Russell, and Susan Leigh Star, 124–30. East Palo Alto, Calif.: Frog in the Well, 1982.

Stone, Mirto Golo. "The Feminist Critic and Salomé: On Cavani's *The Night Porter*." *Romance Languages Annual* 1989 (1990): 41–44.

Stowe, Harriet Beecher. *Uncle Tom's Cabin*. 1852. Reprint. New York: Penguin, 1981.

Studlar, Gaylyn. *In the Realm of Pleasure: Von Sternberg, Dietrich, and the Masochistic Aesthetic*. Urbana: University of Illinois Press, 1988.

Suleiman, Susan Rubin. "(Re)Writing the Body: The Politics and Poetics of Female Eroticism." In *The Female Body in Western Culture*, ed. Susan Rubin Suleiman, 16–24. Cambridge: Harvard University Press, 1986.

Sultan, Stanley. *The Argument of Ulysses*. Columbus: Ohio State University Press, 1964.

Tindall, William York. *A Reader's Guide to James Joyce*. New York: Farrar, Straus Giroux, 1959.

Trinh T. Minh-ha. *Woman, Native, Other: Writing Postcoloniality and Feminism*. Bloomington: Indiana University Press, 1989.

Turim, Maureen C. Review of *In the Realm of Pleasure*, by Gaylyn Studlar. *Journal of the History of Sexuality* 1.4 (April 1991): 713–17.

Valmont. Dir. Milos Forman. With Colin Firth, Annette Bening, and Meg Tilly. Los Angeles: Orion, 1989.

Valverde, Mariana. "Beyond Gender Dangers and Private Pleasures: Theory and Ethics in the Sex Debates." *Feminist Studies* 15 (Summer 1989): 237–54.

———. *Sex, Power, and Pleasure*. Baltimore: New Society, 1987.

Walkowitz, Judith. *City of Dreadful Delight: Narratives of Sexual Danger in Late-Victorian London*. Chicago: University of Chicago Press, 1992.

Webb, Mary. *Gone to Earth*. 1917. Reprint. New York: Dial-Virago, 1979.

———. *Seven for a Secret*. New York: Dial-Virago, 1984.

Williams, Linda. *Hard Core: Power, Pleasure and the "Frenzy of the Visible"*. Berkeley and Los Angeles: University of California Press, 1989.

———. "Power, Pleasure, and Perversion: Sadomasochistic Film Pornography." *Representations* 27 (Summer 1989): 37–65.

———. "Reading and Submission: Feminine Masochism and Feminist Criticism." *New Formations* 7 (Spring 1989): 9–11.

Williams, Sherwood. "The Gay Science: Paradox and Pathology in Wilde and Melville." Unpublished manuscript.

Winsor, Dorothy A. "Iris Murdoch's Conflicting Ethical Demands:

Separation Versus Passivity in *The Sacred and Profane Love Machine.*" *Modern Language Quarterly* 44 (December 1983): 394–409.

Winterson, Jeanette. *Oranges Are Not the Only Fruit.* New York: Atlantic Monthly Press, 1987.

Wittig, Monique. "The Mark of Gender." *Feminist Studies* 5.2 (Fall 1985): 63–73.

Woolf, Virginia. *A Room of One's Own.* 1929. Reprint. New York: Harbrace, 1957.

INDEX

CAROL SIEGEL is Associate Professor of English at
Washington State University, Vancouver. She is the author
of *Lawrence Among the Women: Wavering Boundaries in
Women's Literary Traditions* and various articles on
Modernist authors, gender theory, and film.